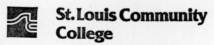

Paul Gauguin

Life and Work

Michel Hoog

Paul Gauguin
Life and Work

RIZZOLI
NEW YORK

Frontispiece *Crouching Tahitian Girl. c.* 1891-2. Charcoal and pastel on paper, 55.3 × 47.8 cm. Art Institute of Chicago (Gift of Tiffany and Mrs Margaret Blake)

Translated from the French by Constance Devanthéry-Lewis

French-language edition, *Paul Gauguin—Vie et œuvre*
Copyright © 1987 by Office du Livre S.A.
Fribourg, Switzerland

English translation published in 1987 in the United States of America by:
Rizzoli International Publications, Inc.
597 Fifth Avenue/New York 10017

Library of Congress Cataloging-in-Publication Data
Hoog, Michel.
  Paul Gauguin, life and work.
  Translation of: Paul Gauguin, vie et œuvre.
  Bibliography: p.
  Includes index.
  1. Gauguin, Paul, 1848-1903. 2. Artists—France—Biography.
  I. Title
N6853.G34H6613 1987   759.4 [B]   87-45389
ISBN 0-8478-0843-2

Printed and bound in Japan

Contents

Preface

Does a new book about Gauguin require justification? Is it not enough to wish to spend some time in the company of his works?

It is true that Gauguin as a man was both attractive for his determination and repellent for his excesses. He was not alone among his contemporaries in challenging time-honoured values: Flaubert abhorred 'stupidity'; Mallarmé rejected formal conventions; and Rimbaud and Claudel deplored rationalism, fleeing Europe. The Western world was already familiar with exoticism, but Gauguin was not content to experience it through lectures and pleasure trips; for better or for worse, he lived it, and nourished his art with it. By sacrificing both his own existence and that of his family to an unyielding artistic calling, he rejoined such romantic heroes as Van Gogh and Nietzsche in their lonely despair; Maupassant and Toulouse-Lautrec in their physical debility.

Ever lucid, Gauguin rejected academicism, considered Impressionism outmoded—because he himself went beyond it—and sought to revive a classical approach to composition using new themes. At that very moment, Cézanne, Degas, Seurat and Hodler were driven by the same preoccupation. For many years, historians have pointed out Gauguin's debt to Egyptian, Indian, Javanese and Japanese art; few have linked the monumental grandeur of his art to such great builders of Western art as Giotto, Raphael,

Poussin and Delacroix. Though he often affected ignorance, Gauguin was well versed both in literature and in art; the biographer who referred to his 'mediocre education and limited knowledge' was ill informed.

In his intellectual convictions, as well as in his aesthetic choices, Gauguin threw over the dominating ideology in order to innovate, and to allow others to do so. When considering his case, must we choose between an interpretation of art history which centres on collective phenomena, or one which emphasizes individual achievements? The turn of the century, so rich in individual innovators, appears to reinforce the 'concept of the artistic personality, [which asserts that] a great artist is the direct source of the style of his epoch'.[1]

Whatever Gauguin's antecedents may have been, his art constituted a breakthrough—a personal creation of an intensity seldom paralleled. But to place him in the context of his historical period is not to minimize his importance as an individual. Without him, and a few other 'ice-breakers'—to borrow Emil Nolde's expression—the burgeoning twentieth century might never have known such an explosion of artistic creativity. The challenge of a new book on Gauguin is to explore the influences of the past that fed his innovative talent and led him to become a master of Modern Art.

Chapter I   An Eventful Youth

Paul Gauguin was born on 7 June 1848, in the heart of Paris, Rue Notre-Dame de Lorette. Next door to his birthplace was the studio of Eugène Delacroix. Gauguin's father, Clovis Gauguin, was a journalist for *Le National*, a daily newspaper of liberal leanings which, after endorsing the July Monarchy, went over to the opposition and hailed the fall of Louis-Philippe in February 1848 as a victory. Clovis Gauguin appears not to have taken a stand during the violent events of May-June 1848 which brought moderate Republicans and Socialists to arms. It was a decisive moment—one that would result in enduring changes in the country's political alignments. The middle class took the side of law and order, rallying behind General Cavaignac when he moved to put down the workers' riots of 23-26 June. According to Jean-François Kahn, this was the moment of Victor Hugo's political conversion: until then a firm royalist, he now passed just as resolutely over to what might be called the leftist opposition party, while a good portion of public opinion soon sided with the President-Prince. Clovis Gauguin, too, fell in with the opposition and went into volontary exile with his family, without waiting for the coup d'état that his son later held he sensed was imminent.

We know very little of Gauguin's paternal ancestors, except that they came from Orleans. But his mother's background was more colourful, and thanks to the work of Henri Perruchot we can look back upon three generations of unique personalities.

During the French Revolution, a young French emigrée, Thérèse Laisnay, was living in Spain with a Spanish Dragoons colonel, Don Mariano Tristan y Moscoso, a man of noble family with Peruvian ties. Mariano's brother, Pio, lived in Peru, where his social and political influence were considerable; for a time during Spanish rule he had even been appointed viceroy. Like many other emigrés, the colonel and Thérèse returned to France after the Treaty of Amiens in 1802. In that year they settled in Vaugirard, which was little more than a suburb of Paris at the time. There the wealthy Don Mariano bought a large estate called the Petit Château. Twenty-four years later Paul Gauguin lived in Vaugirard, too, but by then the effects of urbanization had made it a district of Paris.

Mariano and Thérèse had two children. One of them, Flora, was born in 1803. In 1807 Don Mariano died suddenly without having formalized his marital situation. This irregular state of affairs affected significantly the future of their great-grandson, Paul Gauguin. Thérèse struggled hard to get the estate; however, the uprising of the Spanish population against Napoleon (made famous by Goya's *Dos de Mayo*) resulted in the sequestration of the wealth of Spanish nationals living in France. As a result, the family had an increasingly difficult time getting by financially. Thérèse undertook proceedings to be recognized as Don Mariano's legitimate spouse, and thereby become his legal heiress on behalf of her young children. She appealed to her children's uncle in Lima. Thanks to her daughter Flora's accounts, we can appreciate the somewhat fanciful temperament of Gauguin's great-grandmother, a forceful

2 *Still-Life with Fish.* *c.* 1878. Oil on canvas, 46 × 55 cm. Konstmuseet, Göteborg

3 *Interior, Rue Carcel.* 1881. Oil on canvas, 130 × 162 cm. Nasjonalgalleriet, Oslo

woman spurred on by the dream of a prestigious ancestry that shone in stark contrast to her daily lot. That same dream was also to inspire her daughter, Flora, her granddaughter, Aline, and her great-grandson, Paul.

Flora showed herself to be made of exceptionally strong fibre, too. The financial discomfort that marked her youth was made all the more unbearable by the reminder of a rich American uncle, further mystified by accounts of his royal Incan ancestry. Flora was a handsome girl, with a wilful and authoritarian personality. At eighteen she began an apprenticeship in the studio of a Parisian lithographer, André-François Chazal, who soon fell in love with his pretty apprentice. Despite family opposition, they were married in 1821, and Flora thus entered a family of artists: Paul Gauguin's grandfather, uncle and cousins on Chazal's side were all painters. Indeed, when he chose a career as an artist in 1883, Gauguin was carrying on a family tradition.

The Chazal marriage deteriorated quickly. By the time their second child, Aline, was born in 1825, Flora had already left home, fleeing an unfaithful husband whose mediocrity could hardly measure up to the aspirations of such an ambitious and spirited woman. She decided to sail for Peru, where she attempted in vain to obtain her share of her father's fortune from her uncle Don Pio, a desire her own daughter was to pursue fifteen years later. Flora then returned to France, and in 1835 she published the story of her life under the revealing title *Pérégrinations d'une Paria*. During her absence, her husband had tried to get custody of Aline. Exasperated by the publication of his wife's book, in which she exposed their marital problems for all the world to see, he attempted to assassinate her. The Chazals thus achieved celebrity, if only of the gritty sort that comes with such widely publicized incidents. Chazal was sentenced to twenty years hard labour. As for Flora, she embarked on a career that would earn her further renown. Reassuming her maiden name, she became a journalist, writer, Saint-Simonian and militant feminist. In 1840, after a trip to England, she published *Promenades dans Londres*. In 1843 she wrote *L'Union ouvrière*, in which she advocated the creation of trade unions. In an attempt to put her theories into practice, she set out in 1844 on a propaganda tour through the French provinces, which met with only lukewarm response. Flora Tristan died of exhaustion in Bordeaux. Ironically, of the many works that discuss this important figure in the history of French Socialism, few mention her relationship to Gauguin. Her grandson later took after her by sacrificing his life for his convictions. In 1846 Flora's daughter Aline, under the wing of George Sand, married a young journalist named Clovis Gauguin.

One way of looking at history is to seek out causes and explanations for every event. Given this approach, we might be tempted to reconstruct Gauguin's complex personality and justify many episodes in his colourful life by attributing them to heredity. Thus, his father's decisions, his mother's independent spirit and assertiveness, his grandmother Flora's crusading temperament, his grandfather Chazal's artistic talent and, in the background, the fabulous ancestry of Inca kings, could all be seen as bearing on the painter's destiny. But espousing such an approach would be to risk making arbitrary judgments and, ultimately, to understand nothing. What if Gauguin had inherited from Chazal only his mediocrity and his criminal tendencies? Or from Flora Tristan only her feverish taste for political militancy? To reconstruct rigidly Gauguin's personality according to those of his ancestors is to fall prey to a sterile and falsely 'scientific' method.

Still, there is one point on which Gauguin's past does seem to have greatly influenced his decisions. His many voyages formed a pattern, each one somehow picking up on the last. The childhood trip to South America was in fact ordained by his mother, and a throw-back to his grandmother's earlier voyage. He later went back to South America as a sailor, stopping in Panama and Oceania, sites he returned to again as a painter.

Clovis Gauguin, his wife and their two children set

sail for South America. They were both fleeing the regime of the President-Prince, and striving—as Flora Tristan had done fifteen years earlier—to recover that famous American fortune. They set sail on a small boat, whose captain soon revealed himself a brute with his passengers, and perhaps too forthcoming with the comely Aline. The voyage proved disastrous. On 30 October Clovis died of a heart attack in a Patagonian port by the sinister name of Port-Famine and was buried there.

Such is the account offered by Gauguin's biographers, although the details of these episodes, and their interpretation, are in fact based on a single and rather tardy source: Gauguin's own *Avant et après*, which was written fifty years later. His mother's accounts, of this voyage as well as of many other episodes, thus formed the basis for a family saga which Gauguin transcribed from memory. When reading his account, we must bear in mind the effects on a young boy's imagination of a departure from a native land where his father could no longer express his opinions and thereby earn his living as a journalist, and a long and dramatic voyage capped by a warm welcome in a sunny country, though without his father. Don Pio, a charming man, quickly won over his French relations. His wealth and social standing had increased since Flora's passage; his eldest daughter had married a politician named José-Rufino Echenique who became President of the Republic of Peru in 1851, shortly after Aline and her children arrived there.

Henri Perruchot has aptly expressed how Gauguin may have been marked by his Peruvian childhood: 'A vast and luxurious residence, where grand receptions were given and the most eminent figures of the Peruvian government mingled: such was the milieu in which little Paul lived until the age of six and a half. Were it not for Louis-Napoleon Bonaparte, his everyday world would have been that of a French child of modest background, growing up beneath the skies of the forty-ninth parallel of the northern hemisphere. The facts were entirely different: he grew up as a little Peruvian, surrounded by princely opulence in the midst of the exotic, hot and violently colourful universe of the twelfth parallel of the southern hemisphere. Until the age of six and a half, the language he learned was not French, but Spanish; the trees he knew were not the oak and the poplar, but the palm, the magnolia and the jacaranda; the animals he first observed were swan-necked llamas, herds of which invaded the market-places of Lima, and urubus, those red-footed, blue-necked vultures that perched on the terraced roofs; he did not know what rain was, as it virtually never rains in Lima; but earthquakes were familiar to him, for the earth trembled in Peru nearly every month'.[1]

Civil unrest was breaking out in Peru, and in 1855, General Castilla overturned the government. Aline Gauguin deemed it best to return to France, especially as her father-in-law, Guillaume Gauguin, who lived in Orleans, was pressing her to do so. His correspondence announced that he was leaving half his fortune to Aline's children; the other half was destined for his son Isidore. In fact, Guillaume had already died when Aline arrived in Orleans with her children Marie and Paul, who were greeted there by their uncle Isidore. In the following year, 1856, Don Pio y Tristan died in Peru. His will accorded Aline a comfortable pension, amounting to 25,000 francs, but his Peruvian survivors contested this generosity. José-Rufino Echenique, now exiled President of Peru and Aline's cousin by marriage, came to France to propose a compromise settlement. This she refused, once more affirming her assertive character. Her Gauguin inheritance was modest, and Aline was obliged to work to support herself and her children. The contrast between his lush Peruvian childhood and his difficult adolescence must have seemed ever more striking to the young Gauguin.

Gauguin's schooling was divided between boarding schools in Orleans—notably la Chapelle Saint-Mesmin—and in Paris. He appears to have been an average student; and we should not read too much into his own retrospective commentary on his school years, though it probably provides some general insight into the nature of nineteenth-century

4 *Mette Gauguin in Evening Dress*. 1884. Oil on canvas, 65 × 54 cm. Nasjonalgalleriet, Oslo

5 *Vase of Flowers*. 1881. Oil on canvas, 19 × 27 cm. Musée des Beaux-Arts, Rennes

boarding schools. Gauguin completed the sort of classical education typically offered by institutions like the Petit Séminaire d'Orléans, a type of 'seminary' that was in no way reserved for young men destined for the priesthood. It would seem that, though he was not a brilliant student like Cézanne or Rimbaud, he did receive a literary education which he followed up after 1870 with further studies. He could thus in no way be considered a 'savage genius': when he decided to break away from the Western intellectual tradition, it was not a case of the philistine rejecting a culture of which he knew little, but rather of a lucid intellectual who had sized up that culture and perceived both its limits and its resistance to change (cf. p. 143).

During his school years Gauguin probably took drawing lessons and received a general introduction to the visual arts. On 21 December 1853 a ministerial ruling established that drawing be included in the curriculum of secondary schools, which, in fact, formalized an already existing programme. Medieval art was studied in boys' schools—not without intention—and in Gauguin's time Charles Montalembert's *Mélanges d'Art* was circulated among the prized books at la Chapelle Saint-Mesmin. It was also a period in which manuals abounded, some of which described methods that were not so old-fashioned as we might think.

Much of Gauguin's education can be attributed to Aline, a more educated woman than most bourgeois mothers of her time. In his adult life, the artist referred to the examples of Pre-Colombian pottery and silver pieces his mother had brought back from Peru. As for the Chazal family, although Gauguin's murderously inclined grandfather was not often mentioned in family conversations, there remained a strong tradition of talented men who had earned an honourable living by exercising artistic activities. The witness at Aline and Clovis's wedding was a painter. Gauguin's background was thus more cultivated and open than that of Monet, Renoir or Cézanne. We should keep in mind this rather atypical context, as well as the social status which Aline claimed for

herself—not to mention financial considerations—in order to fully appreciate her decision to name Gustave Arosa as her children's guardian.

The relations between the Gauguin and Arosa families went far back. Their association may have been enhanced by their common Franco-Spanish backgrounds. Gustave Arosa (1818-83) and his brother Achille, sons of a Spanish father and a French mother, were notable collectors. As partners in a brokerage firm with healthy operations at the Bourse, they disposed of financial resources that allowed them to purchase extensively. A sale that took place for unknown reasons during Gustave's lifetime, in 1878, has left us evidence of the contents of the collection at that date. It included fine examples by Delacroix, Corot, Courbet, Jongkind and the Barbizon School, as well as three Pissarros. In keeping with the customs of the day, the Arosas also bought pottery and objets d'art.

At the risk of, once again, shedding doubt on the most commonly accepted ideas about Gauguin, we would like to propose a few qualifications with regard to the Arosa brothers' influence on the young man. When Gauguin's biographers learned of the spiritual and legal connection that existed between the future painter and a well-known collector, they attributed everything to that relationship; Gustave Arosa became not only Gauguin's surrogate father, but the instigator and guiding light of his artistic calling. This seems a simplistic approach. We should bear in mind that—whether because or in spite of his guardian's influence—Gauguin twice chose careers that were in direct opposition to that of an artist: in 1865 he opted for the navy; in 1871 for the Bourse. It is likely, however, that Gauguin's taste for collecting followed Arosa's example. As far as his leanings toward avant-garde painting are concerned, they could scarcely be linked to Arosa's collection. Collecting Delacroix and Corot in 1865 did not require any particular boldness, though Arosa did buy Courbet and Daumier as well. When he bought his three Pissarros is not known. At any rate, though it is clear that young Gauguin's artistic curiosity was nurtured by Arosa, his knowledge was clearly the result of a natural predisposition to learn, combined with a strong dose of determination. Gauguin had read widely, visited Salons and exhibitions, and reflected on his own artistic background. We are faced here with the whole question of the role of heredity, education and chance in artistic creation—a question that cannot be resolved by systematically applying the vague concept of influence.

In 1865 Gauguin made his first personal decision of import: to become a sailor. Was he spurred on by a simple thirst for adventure, a desire to flee far from Paris, a search for traces of his father or a dream of recovering the lost paradise of his Peruvian childhood? Whatever his reasons for choosing this dangerous and uncomfortable profession, his resolve was as steadfast as the conditions were unfavourable. Because of his age and poor school record in mathematics he could not enter the Naval Academy, and he was not eligible for the status of registered sailor. He decided to enter the profession by the back door— just as Edouard Manet had done seventeen years earlier—by signing on as seaman on a merchant vessel. He may even have fixed South America as the destination of his first expedition, in memory of his childhood voyages. He set out on 7 December 1865. In all likelihood his intelligence, enterprising spirit and common sense stood him well, for after several voyages he was promoted to second lieutenant. From October 1866 to December 1867 he completed a world tour, stopping for the first time in Panama and Oceania, after skirting the coast of South America. Some twenty years later, when he decided to move to Oceania, he was in fact making a return trip to a land already discovered in his youth.

In 1868 Gauguin began his military service. He joined the navy, thus reaffirming his first career choice, and was assigned to the *Jérôme-Napoléon*, a vessel used for the scientific and travel excursions of the Emperor's cousin, Prince Jerome-Napoleon, better known as Plon-Plon. In time, however, owing to his temperamental character, or perhaps to a general apathy, of which we shall observe other examples

later, Gauguin came to abandon the idea of a career as a seaman. Still, his love of the sea cannot be attributed solely to a desire to flee Paris, for it withstood the dangers, difficulties and discomforts characteristic of long ocean voyages at that time. The precise details of his travels do not interest us here. Suffice it to say that, at an early age, Gauguin had already seen many more countries than the majority of his contemporaries—in particular the painters he would soon be frequenting, who were infinitely more familiar with the interiors of Parisian cafés than with landing stages. Indeed, with the exception of Pissarro, who was born in the West Indies, French artists of the mid-nineteenth century scarcely travelled beyond Western Europe and North Africa. Neither personal taste nor circumstance favoured distant or prolonged foreign sojourns (Degas's visit to New Orleans being a notable and rare exception to that rule). Cézanne, who cared little for the comfort of his lodgings, and changed them often, limited his movements to within France, and chiefly between the Ile-de-France and the area around Aix, though he once travelled to the Alps. But the idea of visiting museums in Belgium, like Delacroix, or the coast of Brittany, like Monet and Gauguin, did not even occur to him.

The *Jérôme-Napoléon* was cruising off the coast of Norway when news came of France's declaration of war against Prussia. At the time, Prince Jerome was completing a 'scientific' expedition, in the company of Ernest Renan. It is amusing to imagine Renan and Gauguin on the same boat, the young marine mingling above his station with the pontificating scholar who was sarcastically portrayed by Maurice Barrès in *Huit jours chez M. Renan* (1888). When word came of the beginning of hostilities, the boat reported to Boulogne to embark on war operations. With the fall of the Empire on 4 September 1870, it was renamed the *Desaix*; and after sinking several Prussian boats, it sailed into the Mediterranean and put in at Algiers. Gauguin was discharged in Toulon on 23 April 1871, after seven years of nearly uninterrupted sailing. This marked the end of the first part of his life, only half of

6   *Garden in the Snow*. 1879. Oil on canvas, 60 × 81 cm. Fine Arts Museum, Budapest

7   *Nude*. 1880. Oil on canvas, 115 × 80 cm. Ny Carlsberg Glyptotek, Copenhagen

which took place on French soil. He had already seen nearly all the countries to which, as a painter, he would later return. Indeed, all his travels after 1886 were to lands already known or glimpsed, rather than to ones hitherto unknown.

Gauguin's mother had died during his absence, in 1867, at the age of forty-one, and her house at Saint-Cloud was destroyed during the Siege of Paris. With the death of Aline Gauguin, Gustave Arosa assumed fully his role as her children's guardian. Well-connected in the stock-broking world, Arosa found a job for his ward with Paul Bertin, a brokerage firm with offices at 1 Rue Laffitte. Gauguin and his sister took lodgings not far from there, at 15 Rue La Bruyère. A period of the artist's life thus began which contrasted sharply with the years of wandering that preceded it and with the destiny of the accursed artist that was to follow. For more than a decade Gauguin pursued a successful middle-class existence: a sedentary life, bourgeois marriage, professional success and experience as an amateur painter. The artist's biographers have recovered numerous traces of his life during this period, particularly his letters. The information contained therein is largely uninteresting, except to the extent that it sheds light on Gauguin's later decisions. Nevertheless, it should not be forgotten that to live such an orderly existence during ten long years also constituted a choice.

At the stock market, Gauguin revealed himself to be a skilful broker, selling stocks, advising clients and speculating on his own behalf. It is true that, with the return of peacetime, the Paris Bourse enjoyed a euphoric period, and trading was active. Not everyone was as successful as Gauguin in a profession that required intelligence, sound judgment and the ability to make quick decisions. This success in no way foretold the Gauguin of later years, lacking foresight in his financial dealings, dreaming about fanciful projects and living in extreme poverty. In 1893, in his *Cahier pour Aline*, he wrote: 'The Bourse, and all forms of speculation, should be eliminated...' (Presumably he meant for the sake of morality.) However, he did make a living from the Bourse, and from speculation, and a good one at that. He spent heavily, and acquired many works of art, particularly Impressionist paintings.

John Rewald remarked judiciously: 'His instinct dictated choices which, for his time, were unique. If his own brush had not brought him fame, Gauguin's name would still have been linked to the history of Impressionism, like the collectors Victor Chocquet and Dr Gachet of Auvers. Who else, in 1880, could already boast of owning works of masters such as those Gauguin had hanging on his walls—masters that included Manet, Renoir, Monet, Cézanne, Pissarro, Sisley, Guillaumin, Jongkind, and Daumier...?'[2]

In an elegant boarding house in the Avenue d'Eylau—now Avenue Victor-Hugo—Gauguin met a Danish girl named Mette Gad. She was a tall, handsome girl, educated and intelligent. Though of good family, she was without private means, and had come to Paris to continue her education in the capacity of travelling companion to Marie Heegaard, the daughter of a rich industrialist. In 1873 the young couple married; a year later, Mette's sister married Fritz Thaulow, a Dutch painter. [4]

Gauguin now had all the fittings of a well-to-do young bourgeois, conducive to a comfortable existence; none the less, a challenge to this way of life hovered about him. His contacts with artists like Thaulow and Jean-Paul Aubé were numerous. In addition, Bertin's was in a district of the city known for its many art dealers. At the firm, in 1874, he made the acquaintance of a young painter, Emile Schuffenecker. And of course, though their influence has probably been overestimated, the Arosa brothers did contribute to Gauguin's artistic awakening.

We know little of Gauguin's career as a Sunday painter. The number of extant works from that period is small, and in many cases their dates have not been established with certainty. In addition, they do not constitute a stylistic ensemble. We know that Gauguin visited a private studio, the Académie Colarossi, but how assiduously is unclear. Though he was loquacious on the subject of his childhood, he [2, 6]

8 *Bathsheba* by Rembrandt Harmenszoon Van Rijn. 1654. Oil on canvas, 142 × 142 cm. Musée du Louvre, Paris

had little to say about the decade between 1870 and 1880. It is probably safe to assume that his visits to museums and Salons, the first Impressionist exhibitions, and the study of manuals and photograph albums provided his keen mind with sufficient information on the history of and current trends in painting. Intuition and reflection on the work of others replaced an academic training. His artistic education—like that of his contemporaries—was also greatly enhanced by the wide distribution of photographs of art works, and of reproductions which appeared in illustrated magazines. In fact, the Arosa brothers had perfected a new process called *phototypie* which lent itself particularly well to the reproduction of paintings. Gauguin collected

reproductions of art works. He later took with him to Oceania numerous photographs of works executed by Arosa, as well as plates from the catalogue of the Arosa sale. In this case sentimental value added to documentary interest.

For many years, Gauguin's abandoning of his profession in 1883 was commonly presented as an impulsive act, a sudden decision brought on by the irrepressible need to respond to the artist's calling. His early biographers, including Victor Ségalen, Jean de Rotonchamp and André Fontainas, disseminated this theory and firmly supported it. Gauguin himself claimed that he could give himself over entirely to painting. Such a presentation conjures up the image of the Romantic artist, sacrificing his comfort and the

financial security of his family for his art. Literary images on the theme abound. The destitute lives of many artists were part of cultural lore; and the bohemian artist was not expected to live according to the standards of bourgeois society. His unconventional behaviour was viewed with leniency; and this attitude eased the stigma which normally accrues to men who desert their wives and children. Rather than being harshly judged for such conduct, Gauguin was absolved to the extent that his actions corresponded with a more noble, prestigious and irresistible calling. His decision to break away from it all happened to coincide with a crisis on the Parisian market. Was Gauguin actually dismissed, or was he strongly encouraged to leave? Did he himself sense that the era of easy speculation was ending? He had accumulated considerable savings and a collection of paintings; perhaps he hoped to get by on these means until he succeeded in selling his own work. In any case, this deterioration of the financial situation could only have accelerated or given impetus to a decision that was ripening. Gauguin had already been exhibiting with his Impressionist friends for five years, and by then they had adopted him as one of their own. Did he support Pissarro when the latter criticized Armand Guillaumin for accepting a regular job that none the less left him time to paint? The courageous examples of Claude Monet and of Pissarro himself, struggling against poverty for more than ten years, as well as Joris-Karl Huysmans's favourable review of his *Nude* in 1880 may well have influenced his decision.

Huysmans's review was the first significant one Gauguin received; it was long, detailed and generously laudatory. Gauguin obviously remembered it for a long time, for he mentioned it in a letter to Daniel de Monfreid in 1893. Huysmans, who, like Gauguin, was born in 1848, was already demonstrating the taste for visual observation and interest in art—unusual among writers of the time—that so strongly marked his later work. He hailed 'a work that reveals the incontestable temperament of the modern painter... I do not hesitate to declare that, among the contemporary painters who have done nudes, none has achieved such a forceful note of reality, and in this I am not excepting Courbet...' A long and enthusiastic description of the nude followed, in which Huysmans exercised his inexhaustible vocabulary. Despite one allusion to Rembrandt, Huysmans did not compare Gauguin's work to *Bathsheba*, which had entered the Louvre as recently as 1869. The review concluded; 'I repeat, then, that Gauguin is the first [artist] in years to attempt to present a woman of our time and, despite the heaviness of that shadow that descends from his model's face onto her throat, the painting is a complete success, a bold and authentic canvas.'[3] Such compliments could only confirm Gauguin in his resolve. Huysmans may even have planted in the artist's imagination the seed of an idea that would come to fruition only much later: 'The Venus de Milo is neither more interesting nor more beautiful now than those ancient New World statues, with their gaily-coloured tattoos and feathered headdresses.'[4] Beginning in 1881, Gauguin played an active role in organizing the Impressionists' group shows: his artistic career was unquestionably under way.

9 *Poplars*. 1883. Oil on canvas, 73 × 54 cm. Ny Carlsberg Glyptotek, Copenhagen

Chapter II   'Run, run away'

When Gauguin resolved to leave Paris after fifteen years of city living, his decision was not wholly based on personal considerations. Since his youth, major upheavals had changed the face of the city, beginning with Baron Georges Haussmann's vast programme of architectural reconstruction, and continuing through the early years of the Third Republic. The building up of the city instilled in its inhabitants a need for renewed contact with the countryside, one expression of which was Impressionist painting. This social phenomenon was not limited to Paris; cities all over Western Europe were experiencing explosive growth in varying degrees, and the resulting sprawling suburbs were hotly denounced by writers, sociologists and politicians alike. Claudel spoke of the 'teeming hydra, the City, spewer of smoke' (*La Ville*, 1890). Realism and its counterpart, Naturalism, constituted the dominant literary movements throughout Europe, and a constant leitmotif was the urban scene, with its stark contrasts of wealth and poverty, gruelling work and superficial diversions. But most contemporary authors, whether consciously or not, injected their work with a positivist and rationalist ideology. The overriding characteristic of this literature was a near-mystical belief in progress. It is true that the scientific and technological advances of the era were spectacular—the Eiffel Tower springs to mind—and such progress touched every area of human endeavour, including artistic and intellectual pursuits. An artist like Seurat was strongly imbued with this mentality, which held, among other things, that poverty and unsatisfactory living and working conditions could be remedied by technical progress and education. This was the era of evening classes, public libraries, and the publication of books for the general public on virtually every subject, including art history. It was generally believed that scientific progress and the dissemination of knowledge would inevitably bring about moral progress as well, and this new, secular 'religion' was accompanied by a rejection of traditional morality and religious beliefs. Victor Hugo, with his flair for finding the right turn of phrase, summarized this ideology thus: 'To open a school is to close a prison.'

Realism, rationalism, materialism and the cult of progress gradually filtered down from the level of philosophers, theoreticians and political thinkers to pervade the general culture. Late in the nineteenth century, as a reaction to this ideology, and to the pressure of a dull—in many cases even miserable—everyday existence, the Symbolist movement was born. Its concerns were the antithesis of those of the ambient milieu: an escape into an interior sphere, an exploration of dreams, the imagination and the subconscious, and a search for sophistication in formal expression. But Symbolism as a movement was too diffuse to be grouped under one heading.

Among the most notable figures associated with this critical spirit were Gustave Moreau (1826-98), Henri Fantin-Latour (1836-1904), Odilon Redon (1840-1916), Stéphane Mallarmé (1842-1898) and Joris-Karl Huysmans (1848-1907). During the 1870s, Redon conducted a sort of auto-psychotherapy with

10 *The Market Garden at Vaugirard*. 1879. Oil on canvas,
66 × 100.3 cm. Smith College Museum of Art, Northampton, Massachusetts

11   *Garden in the Rue Carcel*. *c*. 1882. Oil on canvas, 87 × 114 cm.
Ny Carlsberg Glyptotek, Copenhagen

his famous series of *noirs*; his form of self-expression did not require a literary medium. Between 1888 and 1890 Maurice Barrès wrote *Trois stations de psychothérapie*, in which all three character studies were of visual artists: Leonardo da Vinci, Maurice Quentin de-la-Tour and Marie Bashkirtseff. Huysmans, in a striking break with Naturalism, published *A rebours* in 1884 and *En rade* in 1888—works that signalled the onset of an aesthetic and spiritual conversion. It was not coincidental that this period was also marked by the early works of Henri Bergson and of Sigmund Freud, who, in fact, visited Paris at the time. Fantin-Latour, who was described by Marcel Proust as suffering from 'the bourgeois, settled way of life', was another who felt the need to break away from the mould; his personal escape route was through images imbued with heroism, sensuality and the fantastic.

The travel theme, ever popular with poets, now took on a new intensity: 'Run, run away' sighed Mallarmé, without ever budging from the Rue de Rome. Charles Cros (1842-88), the unclassifiable scholar and inventor who was very much at the centre of Paris's fringe literary milieu, dreamed in his poems of 'faraway lands':

> Au plus grand nombre je déplais
> Car je semble tombé des nues
> Rêvant de terres inconnues
> D'où j'exile les gens trop laids.
>
> *(Le coffret de santal)*

(I am reviled by most people/ For I seem completely amazed/ Dreaming of distant lands/ From which I exile the ugly.)

Jean Cassou has aptly described this generation of artists: 'This whole *fin de siècle* period was an era of head clerks—mundane, bourgeois head clerks. And the dreams that inspired the period were head clerks' dreams... At this, the final moment of the nineteenth century... we must keep in mind the abyssal, absurd rift—the total heterogeneousness—that separated the monotonous days of all those head clerks and the

dreams they engendered and projected: beautiful, fabulous dreams, adorned with colourful, cheap finery, glittering with Oriental stones and peppered with satanical magic, peopled with ambiguous bodies and enigmatic symbols, quivering with rare voluptuousness, cruel sophistication, divine metamorphoses. The sarcastic voice of Rimbaud taunted them with "And what of my office?..." ' [1]

Rimbaud was an example of an individual revolt followed by an escape to 'the incredible Floridas'. Unlike Gauguin, however, his work was most original when he was confined to the 'hell' of Charleville, Paris and Brussels; he became mute as soon as he left the West. Gauguin, on the other hand, required that exoticism—though, as we have seen, he too led a conventional businessman's existence, apparently without suffering for it.

Others sought refuge from the harshness of reality in a more lyrical, mythical past. Interest in the Middle Ages was not a novelty, but what might be called a sort of 'troubadour symbolism' held sway in the 1880s, reinforced by the rage for Wagner. Edouard Dujardin, the founder of the *Revue wagnérienne*, was one of the first to show interest in Redon, and, in 1888, to notice *cloisonnisme*, although he mentioned only Louis Anquetin in conjunction with the movement. Apart from one picture of *Joan of Arc* (1889), Gauguin appears not to have been drawn into this cult of the past.

At the moment when Gauguin began frequenting the literary scene, intellectual life was particularly intense in Paris. Poems signed by unknowns abounded, and any classification of such a burgeoning is inevitably somewhat arbitrary. The essential thing to keep in mind is the richness and diversity of a milieu in which aesthetic, philosophical and political arguments blended together in a general climate of polemic. Each coterie was marked as much by enthusiastic adherence as by intolerant exclusion; groups formed, founded a journal, then disbanded. With the exception of Mallarmé, the venerated master who welcomed young artists, Gauguin included, to his famous Tuesday gatherings in the

Rue de Rome, the names of the most popular writers of the day have, though, now fallen into semi-oblivion. Few, besides literary historians, have ever heard, for example, of René Ghil, Gustave Kahn, Adolphe Retté, Ephraim Mikhael or Francis Viélé-Griffin. Hardly anyone remembers a work such as *Les Déliquescences d'Adoré Floupette*, a charming pastiche in which Gabriel Vicaire and Henri Beauclair poke fun at the idiosyncrasies of the Symbolist poets. And even the early works of subsequently famous writers such as Maurice Maeterlinck, Francis Jammes or Henri de Régnier would not have sufficed to reserve their authors a place in the annals of litera-ture. But this soil did ultimately prove fertile, for several of the twentieth century's major writers who frequented this *fin de siècle* milieu were certainly marked by it. A notable example is André Gide—who may have passed Gauguin on the road to Pont-Aven—though his cautiousness and uncertainty prevented him from subscribing to any movement for a sustained length of time. Paul Claudel's power-ful lyricism was already near maturity in a work such as *Tête d'or*, written in 1889 when he was only twenty-one years old. Claudel later converted, and, like Gauguin, fled from Western civilization. Paul Valéry also began his career with a few refined texts published in confidential journals. As for Marcel Proust, his dandyism and eclectic curiosity long over-shadowed his stature as a writer of fiction. Neverthe-less, shortly after establishing himself with *A la recherche du temps perdu*, he discovered the Sym-bolist milieu and was influenced by it. [2]

Gauguin found himself quite naturally involved with the Symbolist movement in Paris, whose incep-tion was officially proclaimed in a manifesto by Jean Moréas published in *Le Figaro* in 1886. Member writers, many of whom had tried their hand at art criticism, were tempted to seek counterparts in the visual arts; it was at this point that Gustave Moreau, Redon, Fantin-Latour, Puvis de Chavannes and Eugène Carrière—to mention only the French—were brought into the fold. Albert Aurier, and then Charles Morice, recognized a kindred spirit in Gauguin's *Vision after the Sermon* and told him of the group's interest and admiration. Gauguin was initially favourable to the idea of allying himself with the group, probably because he was pleased to see his name mentioned in the press, but he soon proved reticent. Maurice Denis gave this account: 'Aurier brought Gauguin to the Café François Premier. There, he presented the painter to the admiration of Stuart Merril and a multitude of other young people. [There was] great excitement around Gauguin... He was very surprised that in his absence people had become so taken with him.' [3] Denis did not say whether Gauguin came to the café frequently. He probably did not regularly attend reunions at the Café Voltaire but would more likely have seconded Verlaine's tongue-in-cheek play on words: 'They get on my nerves, those Cymbalists.' In fact, Gauguin was probably never really friends with a writer, except briefly with Charles Morice. When, in 1891, he wanted his auction publicized by an article, he wondered whom to ask. Mallarmé suggested Octave Mirbeau, who was not exactly a confirmed Sym-bolist. Mirbeau did write a piece and, though he used Symbolist language, it was very general. In short, while Gauguin affirmed his adherence to a general ideological trend, he never pledged allegiance to any particular literary circle.

He did, however, align himself with those who championed artists' rights and repudiated conform-ity, amateurism and dilettantism. Even when, begin-ning in 1895, the Symbolist movement was called into question, he continued to approve of the avant-garde's condemnation of Realism and Naturalism. Zola, whose creative genius was widely ac-knowledged, had none the less become the symbol of Realism and served as an alibi for a multitude of works by mediocre writers of fiction and drama; their proliferation provoked bitterness and some-times vehement criticism by those who were not satisfied with descriptions of everyday triviality. Léon Bloy, while granting Zola's powers as a novelist, could not speak harshly enough of his choice of subject-matter.

29

12 *Rue Carcel in the Snow*. *c*. 1882. Oil on canvas, 60 × 50 cm. Ny Carlsberg Glyptotek, Copenhagen

13 *Osny, Climbing Path*. 1883. Oil on canvas, 76 × 101 cm. Ny Carlsberg Glyptotek, Copenhagen

Claudel, whose judgments were somewhat lacking in nuance, went so far as to call Zola's novels bad books. Zola was not a favourite of Gauguin's who contended that 'with him, came trivial naturalism and pornography'[4]; in a letter to Mette dated June 1886, he condemned *L'Œuvre* as Zola's 'worst book from every point of view'. This may well have been because, like many of his contemporaries, Gauguin had recognized in the character of Lantier, the failed painter, a caricature of Cézanne, Zola's childhood friend. During the Dreyfus affair, the majority of Symbolist writers were Dreyfusards and approved of Zola's attitude, but this did not signify either a personal or an artistic reconciliation.

In fiction, the myth of the 'noble savage', as promulgated by Rousseau, was now replaced by the theme of the explorer encountering the native—who was sometimes portrayed as hostile, sometimes simple, but possessing a form of empirical, even magical, knowledge that made up for his ignorance of the 'beneficial effects of civilization'. Mayne Reid's and Jules Verne's characters depicted the prototypical white man setting off to explore real or imaginary far-off lands. Verne's work, like that of Robert Louis Stevenson—who preceded Gauguin in Oceania by only a short time—did not signify a true refusal of civilization and its technology. For them—as for Gauguin—a change of scenery was a necessary condition for aesthetic creation. J.Y. Tadié wrote: 'Stevenson... was also a chronically ill person, and, paradoxically, Jules Verne and Conrad—who was also a depressive—were also chronically ill after their accidents. Their imaginations, or perhaps the act of writing, provided compensation. Stevenson was above all an artist.'[5] This assertion applies to Gauguin as well; for him, as for Mallarmé, formal perfection was as much a moral requirement as an aesthetic one.

While many readers of Jules Verne and his followers sat peacefully in their Old World armchairs, vicariously acting out their fantasies by following the colourful itineraries of Phineas Fogg and Captain Grant, others took to the road. Gauguin's own plans to travel to Martinique, Madagascar, Tonkin and Oceania fitted in with a general contemporary phenomenon. Public opinion in Western Europe was riveted on colonial expansion. Colonialism, of course, was spawned by a variety of motivations—commercial, personal and religious—which had one common denominator: the conviction that Western civilization was superior to all others, and that it was the white man's moral obligation to diffuse his ideas, religion and products—by persuasion or by force. Domestic political quarrels contributed to the tumultuous atmosphere; in France, the Tonkin affair, the rivalry with Italy over Tunisia and, later, the Fashoda incident had far-reaching ramifications. Rivalries between European nations were played out in the colonial sphere, and students all over Europe learned to colour in carefully their countries' possessions on planispheres. Much literature was written on the activities of explorers and missionaries.

Symbolism, viewed as a short-lived aesthetic movement that was essentially the concern of a few literary hacks, barely affected Gauguin. However, the movement took on a larger meaning, as proclaimed by André Fontainas, an active member, who, early on, revealed a gift for analyzing the art of his time: 'Symbolism is the group of young people who, from 1885 to 1900, and beyond, resolved to defend themselves against the ascendancy of a school whose uncontested leader was Zola.'[6] Ernest Reynaud extended the debate into the political realm: 'Symbolism took advantage of the disarray created by... the series of scandals that gave people the need for a change of air. Many people dreamed of nothing short of a complete upheaval. Symbolism brought together Boulanger's masses and the libertarian bourgeoisie. That is why we are witnessing a collusion of aesthetes and anarchistic workers.'[7]

It is in this larger context of aesthetic and intellectual fermentation that a writer like the young Barrès could be situated, even though he later revealed himself to be a staunch conservative. Claudel's *La Ville*, written in 1890, was a veritable indictment of the values of bourgeois society; and in his *Mémoires*

14   *The Breton Shepherdess*. 1886. Oil on canvas, 60 × 73 cm. Laing
Art Gallery, Newcastle-upon-Tyne

improvisées, he acknowledged the anarchistic leanings of his youth: 'I considered anarchy an almost instructive statement against the overcrowded and suffocating world around us.'[8] Gauguin was very much at home in this probing climate of cultural misgivings.

Michel Decaudin, an expert on the intellectual movements of the time, wrote of Symbolist poetry: 'Freed from passing fashion, Symbolism seemed like an unequalled effort to reach the essence of poetry, to liberate it from the descriptive, didactic and satirical functions it had hitherto assumed ... like those modes of expression which are not its exclusive possessions, such as eloquence, or hinder its creative movement, like the tyranny of prosody, in order to recognize that its true purpose is neither to describe nature nor give vent to the murmurings of the heart, but the intuition of a superior reality that is the very meaning of the universe, and to remind [us] that every poet is a visionary.'[9] These remarks apply as much to Gauguin and Redon as to Rimbaud and Mallarmé.

Professional obligations no longer held Gauguin to Paris, and, in 1883, he began a period of travelling that contrasted sharply with the ten previous years of complacent city living. Except for one rather mysterious trip to Spain, all the voyages that followed had two chief motivations: to find cheaper living conditions; and to find a market for his work. In addition, the Parisian environment was providing him little artistic inspiration. In 1884 he moved to Rouen, and shortly thereafter joined his family in Copenhagen, where he hoped to reconcile family life, painting and a lucrative activity. There he took a job as representative for a manufacturer of canvas cloth; but when this attempt to harmonize the various aspects of his life failed on all three counts, he returned to Paris, and a life of extreme poverty. He spent a few months in London, and then in Dieppe, where he saw Degas again, and made the acquaintance of the young Jacques-Emile Blanche who later became the appointed portrait painter for Paris's literary and fashionable set, as well as the unofficial chronicler of the art world. During these very lean years, Gauguin painted whenever he could afford to. In 1886 he left Paris for Brittany. The paintings of this first Breton sojourn marked the blossoming of the first phase of his artistic career.

Gauguin's move to Brittany was in no way revolutionary. Many of the most academic painters spent summers there, and some even settled permanently. In Pont-Aven, the village later made famous by Gauguin, an international colony of nearly forty artists had been building up since 1860. In 1885, Signac was in Saint-Briac; Renoir went there in 1806, while Monet was at Belle-Isle. But the works these artists brought back from Brittany could have been painted elsewhere. Gauguin was attracted by a 'wilder' Brittany, as well as by the hope of finding a cheaper, simpler lifestyle.

During his marine career, Gauguin may well have put in at Brest, but there is no reason to think that he explored the hinterland, as Pierre Loti had done.

In Gauguin's time, Brittany was considered by the rest of France as a province that had affirmed its spirit of independence at the time of the French Revolution. Memories of the Royalist insurgents were still vivid and even further revived by the publication, in 1829, of Balzac's novel, *Les Chouans*. Denise Delouche has astutely analyzed the role of literature in establishing an image of Brittany during Gauguin's time. Chateaubriand was the first to describe the province's particularities, and their portrayal dominated the entire century. Works like *René* or *Les Martyrs* were explicit: 'Armorica could only offer me heaths and woods, deep, narrow valleys crisscrossed by little rivers where no navigator ventured and whose waters rushed, unknown, to the sea: a solitary place, sorrowful, stormy, enveloped by fog, resounding with the noise of wind and whose rock-studded coasts are beaten by a wild ocean.' The famous *Mémoires d'outre-tombe*, written in 1849, was enjoying the first rush of popular acclaim during Gauguin's youth.

15   *Portrait of a Young Woman*. 1886. Oil on canvas, 46 × 38 cm. Bridgestone Museum of Art, Tokyo

16 *Still-Life with Charles Laval*. 1886. Oil on canvas, 46 × 38 cm. Josefowitz Collection

17 *The Inn-Keeper's Daughter*. 1886. Oil on canvas, 55.3 × 46 cm. Musée du Prieuré, Saint-Germain-en-Laye

18 *Boulders by the Sea*. 1886. Oil on canvas, 71 × 92 cm. Konstmuseet, Göteborg

19   *Snow*. 1888. Oil on canvas, 73 × 92 cm. Musée des Arts décoratifs, Paris

Other lesser known, but equally representative, contemporary texts emphasized Brittany's political individualism, its relatively exotic costumes and traditions, and its dialect; in this vein, a certain Baron Taylor wrote in the introduction to a book on Brittany called *Voyages pittoresques*: 'Brittany is for France what Spain is for Europe—a country apart, nourishing a people apart, without mixing or fusing with its surroundings.'[10] Gustave Flaubert and Maxime du Camp hesitated between Brittany and Corsica in their search for a 'beautiful land still devoid of bourgeois come to defile it with their admiration'.[11] Gauguin's motivations when setting out for Brittany—and, some years later, for Oceania—were surely akin to these.

One particularly interesting text—because it was written by an artist with a traditional background—is from the Notebooks of P.-J. David d'Angers. In 1844 he wrote of the *Christ* at Saint-Thégonnec: 'There is a monument topped by a figure of Christ on the cross with the Passion represented by a most primitive type of sculpture in the round, of a style that reminds me of Egyptian sculpture. For art, in its most elemental form, has the same character everywhere. This character is the expression of a deep conviction of men who speak up and affirm what they want to say. They dare! That is the secret of character: nothing is twisted, all the lines are straight, all the folds of the drapery are deep, as in the Byzantine style.'[12] This reference to Egyptian art is striking—especially as Gauguin, too, was interested in it, though perhaps a bit less by dint of the fact that it constituted an autonomous system with regard to Western art.

Gauguin may have been aware of Breton folk art before going to Pont-Aven, for there were examples of it in widely distributed publications and picture collections. However, picturesque depictions of rural life do not seem to have greatly influenced him. Another 'Breton' theme widely taken up by both

21　*The White Cliffs of Rügen* by Caspar David Friedrich. 1818. 90 × 70 cm. Oskar Reinhart Foundation, Winterthur

local and Parisian painters was the sea: harbour scenes, storms and naval battles. Marine references in Gauguin's work are rare, however. The ocean is depicted by a horizontal line in the background, suggesting calm and tranquillity. The only notable exception is *Above the Abyss*, in which an impression of dizziness and disequilibrium is created, not by the sea itself, but by the rocks, looking down on them from above. This plunging perspective produces the same effect as in a work by Caspar David Friedrich, *The White Cliffs of Rügen*. Nothing comparable is found in the countless pictures produced by such painters as Charles-Désiré Hue, Louis Garneray, Antoine Gudin, René-Paul Huet or even Claude Monet.

20　*Above the Abyss*. 1888. Oil on canvas, 73 × 60 cm. Musée des Arts décoratifs, Paris

Chapter III   The Pupil and his Masters

It would appear, from the few paintings uncontestably attributed to him, that Gauguin did not produce many works between 1883, when he decided to devote himself entirely to painting, and 1887, when he left for Panama with Charles Laval. Was his output constrained by his circumstances, when he lacked the means even to buy canvas and paints? Or did he destroy paintings that he considered experimental? Though the diverse works that have survived attest to both his impassioned drive to experiment and his courageous resolve to assimilate the art of his predecessors—in order to go beyond it—they are not simply scholarly exercises. Gauguin now sought to free himself from the influence of such masters as Corot and Daubigny, from whom he had borrowed both a general approach and specific methods. He also had to liberate himself from the precepts contained in the artists' manuals so prevalent at the time. His works from this period suffer from comparison with the boldness and seductiveness of his large, mature works, but paintings such as *Still-Life with Mandolin* (1885, Musée d'Orsay, Paris), the landscapes near Rouen or those from his first stay in Brittany (1886) reveal no awkwardness, and nothing leads us to think that Gauguin was dissatisfied with them. Many painters—Henri Moret, Maxime Maufra and Ernest Ponthier Chamaillard among them—who were attracted to Impressionism before falling under Gauguin's influence, adopted a similar approach and stuck with it for some time. Charles Laval and Emile Schuffenecker barely went beyond this stage at all. Their works are much sought after today; sometimes

14-18

a signature skilfully manipulated has led to a more flattering and profitable attribution to Gauguin himself. What distinguishes Gauguin's work from that of his followers, who were not necessarily without talent, was that he abandoned any approach that he judged inadequate, outmoded or incapable of conveying his vision.

Gauguin had discovered the work of Pissarro around 1872 through Gustave Arosa, or perhaps at the dealer Durand-Ruel's in the Rue Laffitte not far from Gauguin's office. When he actually met the elder artist several years later,[1] he was attracted to him both as an artist and a person, and invited him to his home. It is easy to imagine Mette Gauguin pleased to entertain a countryman, for Pissarro was a native of the Danish Antilles. In 1879 Gauguin decided to spend his holiday in Pontoise with Pissarro—an indication that he had begun to take his own painting more seriously. From then on, his job became merely a means of livelihood, and one that separated him from his art.

In 1879 Renoir decided to try his chances at the official Salon with his *Portrait of Madame Charpentier with her Children* (Metropolitan Museum of Art, New York). The painting was not only accepted but well received by a number of critics, and its success constituted the beginning of a certain public approval of Impressionism. But while Renoir appreciated the official acceptance of his painting, he was also cutting himself off from the possibility of continuing to exhibit with his friends. Pissarro's reaction to Renoir's defection was to seek to bolster the

22 *Tropical Landscape*. 1887. Oil on canvas, 90 × 116 cm. Bayerische Staatsgemäldesammlungen, Neue Pinakothek, Munich

23 *Young Breton Boy Fixing his Sabot*. 1888. Oil on canvas, 90 × 71 cm. Ny Carlsberg Glyptotek, Copenhagen

existing Impressionist group, while Monet became more reluctant than ever to accept new members. Degas was, as usual, uncompromising in his selections, but he did approve of Gauguin. Received by the official Salon in 1876, Gauguin, upon Pissarro's invitation, opted to participate in the fifth Impressionist show in 1880. He had, in fact, already shown a statuette in the fourth Impressionist exhibition of 1879, which, though it is not mentioned in the catalogue, did appear in Duranty's account of the show.[2] In 1880, Gauguin submitted a still-life and some landscapes and in 1881, when another exhibition was organized by the group—despite signs that it was splitting up—Gauguin once again took up Pissarro's invitation to participate (see the complete list of exhibitions, pp. 317-20).

When Gauguin chose Pissarro for his mentor, both because of the latter's art and natural aptitude for teaching—which, by the way, had already been of use to Cézanne—the elder artist was already widely

24 *Apple Picking*, by Camille Pissarro. 1886. Oil on canvas, 128 × 128 cm. Ohara Museum of Art, Kurashiki

experienced. For him, as for Renoir or Monet, the revolutionary art that they had been producing for more than ten years, and for which the term Impressionism was gaining recognition, was not at all a product of impulsive improvisation. Pissarro had studied drawing during his childhood in Paris, between 1842 and 1847. While in Venezuela, he spent time with the Melbye brothers, both artists, one of whom later emigrated to the Far East. Pissarro returned to Paris in 1855, in time to visit the Exposition Universelle where Ingres and Delacroix were triumphing, and Corot and the Barbizon School were beginning to make themselves known. Courbet capitalized on his recognition by organizing a personal show, a phenomenon altogether unusual for the time. At the insistence of his family, who supported him in his artistic endeavours, Pissarro began to work with Corot, studying the techniques of painting in order to be accepted by the strict jury of the official Salon. This he accomplished, first in 1859, and then fairly regularly beginning in 1865. All the while his own ideas, however, were becoming more libertarian.

In short, the artist that Gauguin admired was already a mature man, eight years his senior, a self-assured, uncompromising painter who had broken away from conventional principles of painting. His bold precepts had been developed slowly by long practical experience from a solid artistic base. We shall return to Gauguin's debt to Pissarro later; for now, let us point out that when, about 1882, Gauguin adopted a style heavily influenced by Pissarro, this conversion may have been, in some sense, overdue. Indeed, despite the fact that he had seen Pissarro's work at Arosa's and had visited several of the Impressionist shows which, since 1874, had taken place nearly every year, Gauguin had continued to paint in a heavy and rather conventional style derived directly from the minor masters of the Barbizon School. Whether consciously or not, Gauguin followed in accelerated fashion the same route that his chosen master had taken twenty years earlier. Later, relations between the two deteriorated.

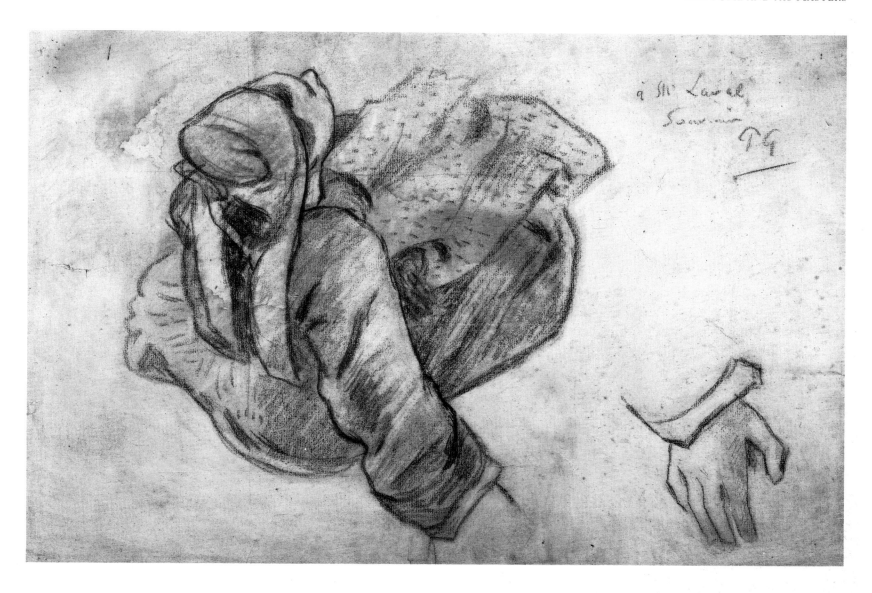

25 *Seated Breton Woman.* 1888 (?). Charcoal and pastel on paper, 33 × 48 cm. Dedication: 'à M. Laval/Souvenir/P.G.' ('to Mr Laval/souvenir of/P.G.') The following text appears on the verso: 'This drawing was used by Gauguin to adorn a ceramic sculpture of a woman gardening by Chaplet. This information was given to the Galerie Choiseul by Lenoble, son-in-law of Chaplet/15 April 18../Cotereau.' Art Institute of Chicago (Mr and Mrs Carter H. Harrison Collection)

Pissarro even condescended to some rather unkind remarks about his disciple, whom he considered unfaithful. But Gauguin always maintained great esteem and gratitude toward his teacher who provided him with a durable model of uncompromising commitment to an artistic career, which entailed great sacrifices for both himself and his family. It is true that—unlike Gauguin—Pissarro remained a devoted father; but in terms of bourgeois morality, the 'artist's calling' took precedence for both over the responsibilities of parenthood. Pissarro, who was from a devout Jewish family, had further proclaimed his social independence by marrying a Catholic, a decision that could only impress the unconventional Gauguin.

A small group of works of the area round Paris or Rouen shows Gauguin's affinity to Pissarro. Characteristic of these paintings are the heavily shaded undergrowth, near absence of sky, and an occasional peasant figure, in soft yet scintillating light. At the time, about 1880, when Renoir and Monet, and even Cézanne, were changing their styles, Pissarro

26 *The Laundresses at Pont-Aven*. 1886. Oil on canvas,
71 × 90 cm. Musée d'Orsay, Paris

27   *The Breton Shepherd*. 1888. Oil on canvas, 89.3 × 116.6 cm.
National Museum of Western Art, Tokyo

remained faithful to his. Only some time later did he adopt the Neo-Impressionist technique. Gauguin, too, was completely and sincerely, if belatedly, an Impressionist. In his work we can observe a division of brushstrokes, a love of light colours and vivid shadows and an absence of anecdotal motifs. The later Gauguin, with his monumental and mysteriously poetic figures placed in settings of stylized flora, stands in marked contrast to the landscape painter, capturing the sun's fugitive reflections over the Ile-de-France. This stage, so influenced by Pissarro, was essential for Gauguin's development.

All the great revolutionaries who, from 1880 to 1885, changed the art of painting—Cézanne, Seurat, Van Gogh and Gauguin—went through a purifying Impressionist period. And even the principals of the 1905 generation—Matisse, Braque, Delaunay, Picabia and others—dabbled in Impressionism. Now that Impressionism has become one of the popular movements in the history of art—which has sometimes made it suspect—we forget that it was once a vehement and venturesome break with tradition, rejected by the majority of people in its time.

Although Gauguin demonstrated allegiance to the Impressionist movement as a whole by adopting its style and exhibiting in its shows, his closest contact among these artists remained Pissarro, renowned artist and gifted teacher. It is, none the less, risky to speak of 'principles' with regard to the Impressionists. They have all too often—in the past and even today—been presented as instinctive painters who spontaneously, and nearly effortlessly, created charming, light-hearted, quickly brushed works that were utterly devoid of intellectual content or serious intention. Monet and Renoir greatly reinforced this point of view by remarks they made later in life, perhaps even in jest. But their works and their dates do not support this claim. If we examine canvases dating as early as 1866-70, it becomes clear that Impressionism at the time was already the result of a decade of work and research. Monet's *Le Déjeuner sur l'herbe* in 1866 (Pushkin Museum, Moscow), or *The Terrace at Saint-Adresse* in 1866-7 (Metropolitan

Museum of Art, New York), demonstrate his mastery of a difficult genre: the composition with several figures. Monet and his friends—and later Gauguin—rejected schematic composition and treatment of depth and space, as well as conventional handling of colour and preoccupation with the subject. Without theoretical proclamation, they elaborated a fully coherent, new approach to the representation of the world around them—an approach characterized by a lightened palette, divided brushstrokes, concentration on luminous reflections on vegetation, clouds and sea, as well as suppression of narrative themes. And if Impressionism's innovations had been only random, the movement would never have provoked such scandal when it appeared in full force at the famous exhibition of 1874. Although the prestige of Delacroix, the independent spirit of Corot, Courbet and Boudin and the boldness of Manet furnished ideas and provoked responses, Impressionism as a movement remained the creation—we could even say the property—of a small core of uncompromising artists. On the other hand, contemporaries such as Fantin-Latour, Félix Bracquemond, James Tissot and Alfred Stevens inherited the same possibilities, and participated in the same discussions, but stopped there. If, at the time, Impressionism gave rise to few theoretical pronouncements, it did take shape from debates waged between its artists, despite what they may later have said.

Gauguin was too young, between 1860 and 1875, to participate in this defining process. But his intuition and intelligence in studying the works of his elders allowed him to reconstruct their course. In any case, the relationship between Pissarro and Gauguin should not overshadow the debt he owed the Impressionists as a group, even if he did express regret that the shows were losing some of their vigour: 'I am an Impressionist but I only see my colleagues—men or women—rarely. The little church

28 *Blue Roofs*. 1884. Oil on canvas, 74 × 60 cm. Oskar Reinhart Collection, Am Römerholz, Winterthur

has become a common school which opens its doors to the first dauber who comes along.'[3]

We can attribute to Pissarro the idea, taken up again by Gauguin, of including figures in his landscapes, but Renoir also focused on this, especially about 1885. It was also during those decisive years of questioning that Monet painted the boat series with his stepdaughters and the *Women with Parasols* (1886-90), though for nearly twenty years he had given up depicting life-size or near life-size figures. After 1890, he once again gave up the practice, but the brief interlude was significant, to judge from the large size of his canvases as well as their boldness and diversity. At the same time, Gauguin was placing his Breton women in a natural setting, on the same scale as Monet. We shall return later to the affinities between his Tahitian landscapes and Monet's *Water-lilies*.

In order to appreciate the full significance of Gauguin's joining this controversial group, we must consider the Impressionists' actual status when, around 1880, he decided to show with them, thus placing himself publicly in their camp. The status that certain members of the group attained in their final years, as well as their posthumous popularity, should not make us forget the dire financial conditions, bitter derision and hateful attacks they had endured. In 1880, they were still being rejected by critics and the Parisian public, and were virtually unknown in the provinces and outside France. The reviews of their work, though hostile, were so scarce compared with the bulk of criticism devoted to such conventional subjects as the Salons, official exhibitions, inaugurations and competitions, as well as to painters now unknown, that it is doubtful whether they made any real impact. A few reproving lines on the work of Monet, Cézanne or Degas could only have offended the interested parties, without stirring up public curiosity, or attracting the attention of potential collectors.

At the time of Manet's death in 1883, the critics had not yet made peace with this artist who had opened the way to a new generation of painters.

Gustave Geffroy, who became the friend and defender of Claude Monet, and who later signed the first favourable reviews of Gauguin's work, wrote a cautious and ambivalent obituary to mark the occasion.

Even when he was closest to the Impressionist model, Gauguin gave his landscapes a distinguishing severity. There are few bright and sunny scenes, in the style of Sisley or Monet; and in his depictions of the area round Paris and Rouen—and later Brittany—there is little sky or water. Rather, he concentrated on dense, homogeneous vegetation, often in the form of undergrowth where the sun did not penetrate. *The Laundresses at Pont-Aven*, veiled in 26 a silvery harmony, and *Haymaking in Brittany* (Bridgestone Museum, Tokyo), of a more toned-down palette, share a note of sombreness not characteristic of his formative works, but common in those prior to Tahiti, with the exception of a few landscapes from Martinique. Gauguin was apparently striving to combine the delicate Impressionist technique with a somewhat wilder, poetic sense inherited from Courbet, Millet and the Barbizon School. Daubigny, Diaz, Rousseau and Cals were also drawn to wild undergrowth, muddy fields and bleak pastures; these painters are as far removed from the heroic, classical tradition in landscape painting as they are from the fresh-looking brightness of Boudin's beaches or Monet's and Renoir's suburban promenades. Gauguin's diverse landscapes reveal his taste for variety in nature. Did he appreciate the 'rustic' poetry of Armand Sylvestre and Pierre Dupont? Probably not. We know he had little sympathy for the Realist school of literature. It is more likely that his taste for variety was further proof of his independent spirit with regard to his fellow artists. Gauguin's strength lay in knowing how to strike a balance between the contributions of his predecessors and his own personal tastes, not always an easy task. He rarely improvised. On the contrary, the desire to assimilate a style often led to pastiche, as in *Blue* 28 *Roofs*, which clearly echoes Cézanne's *Views of Auvers* with its interlocking of blue and pink forms.

29   *Landscape near Pont-Aven*. 1888. Oil on canvas, 73 × 93 cm.
Bridgestone Museum, Tokyo

30 *Young Bretons Bathing*. 1886. Oil on canvas, 60 × 73 cm.
Hiroshima Museum of Art

31   *The Sculptor Aubé and Son*. 1882. Pastel on paper, 53 × 72 cm.
Petit Palais, Paris

Only the foreground, with its soil and shrubs, is treated with a thicker and freer paste than Cézanne's; the sky, with its blue and white streaks, brings to mind the work of Sisley.

29   One of the more refined and successful paintings of this group is the *Landscape near Pont-Aven*, which appears to have been done between the winter and spring of 1888. The mountain's charac-
84 teristic, hillocky form reappears in the background of several pictures, most notably the *Yellow Christ*. The horizontal lines of the landscape and the soft curve of the hill create an impression of serenity that is not broken by the vertical accents of the trees. The trunk of one of the willows at the left of the picture has the same tortured, irregular form as one of Gauguin's pieces of pottery. Despite the strong upward movement, the outlines are indistinct.

30   *Young Bretons Bathing*, which bears a somewhat faded date (86) and has often been erroneously dated from 1888, also constitutes an original derivative of the Impressionist model. This is a contemporary scene with a touch of the anecdotal, bathed in a delicate, Impressionist light. Bretons wrestling provided the inspiration for several paintings showing nude youths; and most of these rather clumsy works are dominated by the figures. In the Hiroshima painting, Gauguin also featured a skyless landscape of buildings and rivers. In this little-known and rarely reproduced work, we can recognize a modern version of a traditional theme, that of the nude in the landscape—a theme somewhat neglected by the Impressionists but revived by the generation that followed. Gauguin may have been measuring himself, perhaps unconsciously, against Seurat, whose *Bathers* had appeared in 1884, and perhaps also against Cézanne.

  Very early on Gauguin became interested in sculpture. Soon after his marriage, about 1873, he began spending time with Jean-Paul Aubé, the sculptor,
31 whom he drew with his son in pastel. Aubé is remembered for his monument to Gambetta; erected in the courtyard of the Carrousel, between the two wings of the Louvre, the grandiloquent sculpture set

off a controversy that resulted in its dismantling. In 1877 Gauguin's landlord and neighbour Jules Bouillot initiated him in the technique of sculpture. In 1879 Gauguin contributed a bust to the fourth Impressionist show, probably of his son, Emile (Metropolitan Museum of Art, New York). In the following year he showed one of his wife (Courtauld Institute Galleries, London), both innovations for the Impressionist exhibitions, which, until then, had contained only paintings and graphic works. (Degas did not show his *Large Dancer* until 1881.)

  At the time it was thought that every artist had to limit himself to one medium. Exceptions to the rule, such as Barye and Carpeaux, remained outsiders and even Daumier's sculptures were unknown to his contemporaries. Gauguin demonstrated his free spirit by devoting himself ardently to sculpture and, later, to ceramics.

  His first sculptures are of a slightly academic elegance. However, they do attest to such a mastery of marble that we might wonder whether they were in fact done in large part by Bouillot. But the bust of his son *Clovis* (Private Collection, Switzerland) and the *Singer at a Café-Concert* (Private Collection), which appeared in the Impressionist show of 1881, are treated more freely, and seem rather clumsy by comparison. The medallion evokes the Impressionist spirit in its linking of a female figure with flowers; the woman's face reminds us of Renoir's women. The use of several colours contrasts with the white marble of his busts, and foreshadows his later experiments in ceramics.

  Gauguin made the acquaintance of Félix Bracquemond (1833-1914) at the Impressionist show of 1886. Bracquemond was not only one of the best engravers of his day, but an influential member of the Parisian artistic scene. A friend of Manet, and one of the original exhibitors at the first Impressionist show in 1874, Bracquemond worked extensively in ceramics. In that field, he is particularly remembered for his decorations for the Service Rousseau, a ceramic collection created in 1866 and frequently reissued and shown for some thirty years afterward. The

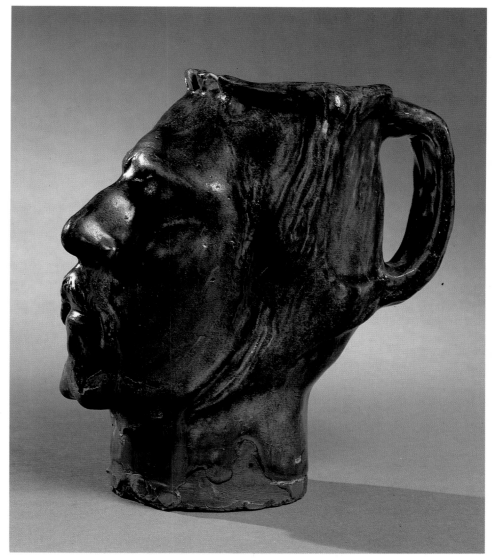

32 Vase decorated with scenes of Brittany. 1887. Glazed stoneware, H. 29 cm. Musées Royaux d'Art et d'Histoire, Brussels

33 Vase in the shape of a head. 1887. Glazed stoneware, H. 19.5 cm. Det Danske Kunstindustrimuseum, Copenhagen

Japanese-inspired designs of flowers and animals were of great interest to Gauguin. He befriended Bracquemond and bought a painting from him for 250 francs.

Bracquemond and Aubé introduced Gauguin to the great ceramic artist Ernest Chaplet (1835–1909), who worked for the renowned porcelain factory Maison Haviland. Gauguin decided to try his hand with ceramics, to earn money, and also because of a genuine interest in the technique. Until the end of his life, he experimented in the applied arts, refusing to limit himself to painting. In 1892 he wrote to Daniel de Monfreid: 'To think I was born to produce art works and that I've not managed to do so. Making stained-glass, furniture or porcelain would have suited me better than painting.' For some time, the applied arts had been found lacking by critics for their tendency towards pastiche and their lack of inventiveness. The Expositions Universelles and the founding of the Musée des Arts décoratifs in 1877 were now breathing new life into the applied arts and contributing to their renewal. The general movement was towards creating natural forms and reviving traditional techniques. Gauguin was not alone in dreaming of a sort of phalanstery where art and craft would be practised together.

Chaplet experimented with stoneware, but with little success. He drew his inspiration from utilitarian forms, his decorations emphasizing, rather than transforming, the shape of the piece. Gauguin met him in 1886, just before leaving for Brittany. They worked together again in 1887, and then went their separate ways, though remaining on good terms.

The dating of Gauguin's ceramic works has been complicated by the circulation of questionable works. Early pieces may well have been executed by Chaplet, with only their decorations created by Gauguin. Later works by Gauguin tended to be more free in structure than those by his mentor, Chaplet. As he became more experienced with clay, Gauguin began creating his own pieces from scratch, but he rarely used a potter's wheel. His works were usually between 13 and 27 cm high, their shapes often so imaginative as to defy description. But, at times, Gauguin's intentions with these works may have been betrayed by his lack of technical mastery. His decorations ranged from ornamental and abstract to vegetal. Certain works could be considered ceramic sculptures because of their unity of shape and motif. Some larger pieces contain several figures and the suggestion of a landscape, such as *The Gardener* (Private Collection, Paris). Gauguin was well aware of the unusual character of his works. He wrote to Bracquemond in January 1887: 'If you are curious to see me unload from the kiln all the little products of my greatest follies, come now. Fifty-five pieces in good condition. You will probably shriek when you see these monstrosities, but I think you will find them of interest.'

Unlike Chaplet, Gauguin showed little evidence of Oriental influence in his ceramic work, in the works shown in the Exposition Universelle of 1878, or at the Galerie Bing. However, he was definitely influenced by the Pre-Colombian pottery he had known since childhood. After his separation from Chaplet, the boundaries between pottery and sculpture broke down further. Thanks to the intervention of Theo Van Gogh in 1887, he showed works at the Boussod and Valadon gallery where they were noticed by Félix Fénéon, who had already commented on Gauguin's gift for sculpture: '[He] is above all a potter. He is drawn to stoneware, hard and contemptible as it is, for making wild, pug-nosed faces with large glabelle[4] and tiny, slanted eyes.'[5]

Merete Bodelsen and Jean d'Albis have suggested that Gauguin's experience as a ceramic artist may have led him to *cloisonnisme*. Whether for technical reasons, or because the decoration he chose dictated it, 'nearly all the vases made at the Rue Blomet from 1883 to 1885 contained incised decorations,... like Chaplet, Gauguin used *cloisonné* on his vases. It would be then, beginning in October of 1886 that he discovered aesthetic possibilities that could bring something fundamentally new to his painting style.'[6] Although these works seem less appealing and more disconcerting than his paintings, they did

32-34

attract a clientele at the time. Theo Van Gogh managed to sell a number of them.

Gauguin valued his ceramic work highly. He jotted down shapes in a notebook (Department of Graphic Arts, Musée du Louvre, Paris), and depicted pottery 52 in many of his paintings. In *Self-Portrait in Front of the 'Yellow Christ'*, the grimacing face of a Pre-Colombian-like vase is juxtaposed with the Crucifixion set in a Breton landscape, an image both Christian and Breton. Between this opposition of culture and religion is Gauguin himself. Later in life, he spoke 158 in great earnest (see p. 231) about *Oviri*, the work he wanted placed on his tomb.

Gauguin's visit to the Exposition Universelle in 1889 inspired him to write at length about his technical and aesthetic principles, which appeared in instalments in *Le Moderniste illustré* on 4 and 11 July 1889: 'Ceramics is not a frivolous art. From the most ancient times, it was much favoured by American Indians. God made man with a bit of mud. With a bit of mud we can imitate metal and precious stones— with a bit of mud and a bit of genius! Does this not make it an interesting substance? ... What comes out of the kiln takes on the character of the blaze and becomes more weighty for its passage through hell ... much of what is exhibited is dreadful, because a lighter firing is tidier and easier to do. It follows that ceramic decoration must be done in a way consistent with its firing. *For the ultimate basis of beauty is harmony*. Therefore dull, stylish subject-matter is not suitable to an unrefined substance. Dull colours next to primary colours are not harmonious. Look at Nature's artistry. The colours obtained in the same firing are always harmonious ... Sculpture, like drawing in ceramics, must be modelled "in harmony with the substance". I wish all sculptors would study this question of adaptation carefully. Plaster, wood, marble, bronze and clay, when fired, must not be modelled in the same way, for each substance has a unique nature in terms of solidity, hardness and appearance.'

This article would be worth quoting in its entirety. Although the ideas put forth may seem banal today,

they were quite unorthodox for the time, and attest to Gauguin's clear-sightedness.

Gauguin's work after 1880 was very innovative: going beyond models he had previously used or drawing inspiration from one or other of his contemporaries. His experiments manifested one of the fundamental traits of his artist's character: his independence from those he had temporarily adopted as mentors. Subscribing to the Impressionist group was in no way constraining for him, for he was never satisfied simply to follow the path laid down by his friends.

Unlike most of the Impressionists, Gauguin did not restrict himself to landscape painting but was drawn by the theme of a single figure set in an interior, against a neutral background. He considered the large study of a *Nude* from 1880 successful, not only 7 because Huysmans had noticed and liked it, but also because it demonstrated flexibility to adapt and his ability to master a traditional theme. But no sooner had the proof been given than he temporarily abandoned the theme in favour of others, still-life in particular. This motif, which had been somewhat neglected around 1860, was now attracting Manet, Cézanne, Fantin-Latour, and sometimes Renoir and Monet, but rarely Pissarro.

Gauguin's still-lifes are less innovative in the choice and the arrangement of objects on a table than in the setting of those objects in space. Sometimes the eye is stopped at the second plane by the abrupt introduction of a wall. *Flowers for a Bouquet* (formerly the Hahnloser Collection), *Interior, Rue Carcel*, 3 *Vase of Flowers* and *Still-Life in an Interior* (Private Collection, Switzerland) form a stylistic family, in which Gauguin eliminated all pictorial connections between the still-life and the separate background. In *Still-Life in an Interior*, the entire lower part of the canvas is filled with simple, familiar objects: a rustic basket, round pot, onions, dead fowl, wrinkled serviettes. The only element missing here from the complete repertory of the most traditional still-life is a black-handled knife placed diagonally in the arrangement. Cézanne was working in the same vein at this

34 Bowl decorated with Breton figure. 1886-7. Glazed stoneware,
15 × 24 × 11 cm. Det Danske Kunstindustrimuseum, Copenhagen

35   *Landscape* after Cézanne, fan-shaped. 1885. Gouache on paper,
28 × 54 cm. Ny Carlsberg Glyptotek, Copenhagen

time. Indeed, these objects had long been favoured by painters for their simple shapes and varied textures, as well as for their emotional and sometimes symbolic significance. The light, hatched technique is like that used in the Rouen landscapes. On the right side, the eye is drawn to a partition covered with a paper of floral decoration. The pattern of this paper appears in several of Gauguin's pictures, and in some by Cézanne, but it is impossible to ascertain whether it was simply a popular motif of the day, or whether Gauguin was somehow making reference to Cézanne. On the wall, beneath the signature, is a brown and reddish plaque, the presence of which is difficult to explain except as an element in the composition. In the upper left, a large rectangle, corresponding almost exactly to the golden section, contains back-lighted figures standing in front of a window, three women seen in profile, their heads lowered, and two children, one facing us, and one with his back turned. While no apparent link exists between these two areas, the homogeneous technique, uniform palette and even, if somewhat unreal, lighting help balance the composition. It is difficult to imagine that Gauguin's choice of subject-matter is entirely due to his desire to render a picturesque contrast in light. Starting with the motif of the straightforward still-life, in which familiar objects take on—as in Cézanne's pictures—a unique intensity, he set out to juxtapose them with the cluster of isolated, doleful figures. The picture's background has an oppressive quality which Robert Goldwater has justly linked to subsequent works by Edvard Munch and James Ensor.

This painting was probably done in Copenhagen, at the home of Gauguin's in-laws, who had not greeted the painter warmly. Six years later, when Gauguin took up the same theme in Tahiti (*Tahitian* 108 *Repast*), his improved state of mind and positive attitude toward his environment resulted in marked changes in the composition: now the figures are facing the still-life and their gaze suggests a link between people and objects.

In most of the still-lifes of this particular group, the connection between objects and defined or suggested space remains vague. Often, a bouquet introduced in the foreground creates a disequilibrium in the composition. Perhaps Gauguin was used to making use of Degas's experiments in breaking up space. He freed himself—with inevitable setbacks—from the carefully codified approach to still-life of the painting manuals. This was based principally on Dutch still-life painting and on the work of Chardin, which had recently returned to favour. Manet, Fantin-Latour and Cézanne, in his early works, had all arranged their objects according to traditional theories. After 1880 Cézanne chose still-life as a special forum for experimentation; Gauguin later borrowed his innovatory techniques of rising perspective and modelling with colour. However, Cézanne did not address the problem of linking figures and still-life, with the exception of the notable portrait of Gustave Geffroy painted in 1895. It was in this area that Gauguin demonstrated his kinship to Degas.

Gauguin never denied his admiration for Degas, of whom he spoke warmly in *Avant et après*, nor his fascination with the work of Cézanne. Cézanne was doubtless the only painter to have a lasting influence on Gauguin's works and whose 'formula'—to use 35 Cézanne's own term—Gauguin intentionally tried to assimilate. This may have been a source of irritation to Cézanne; but did he actually complain that Gauguin had 'stolen his little sensation' and 'carted it about on steamships'? If this anecdote, reported by Octave Mirbeau, is true, it should probably be attributed to Cézanne's sense of irony, rather than to any real feelings of dislike.

Cézanne's personality fascinated Gauguin. In a long letter to Schuffenecker dated 14 January 1885, Gauguin wrote a sort of meditation on the character of that artist-creator: 'Look at Cézanne, his basically mystical, Oriental nature—even his face resembles that of a Levantine elder—is misunderstood; he is drawn to mysterious forms, heavy and peaceful, like a man lying down to dream; his colour is grave like that of the Orientals; a true Mediterranean man, he spends entire days on mountain tops, reading Virgil and looking at the sky; and his horizons are high, his blues intense and his reds of an astonishing vibrancy. Like Virgil, whose works have many meanings, the text of his paintings can be interpreted in many ways; his backgrounds are both imaginative and real.' Though Gauguin was eulogizing Cézanne, this description could equally well be applied to Gauguin himself and to his own style. If we replace the refer-ence to Virgil with one to Maori legends, and the Levantine countenance with that of an ancient Incan, the description of the man could be of Gauguin him-self. What is surprising is that this letter was written well before his Oceanian period. Though he was writing in Copenhagen in the winter of 1885, in seek-ing to evoke an image of the painter from Aix-en-Provence, Gauguin was in fact describing himself seven years hence beneath the Tahitian sun.

Chapter IV   Breaking Loose

Times were hard for Gauguin in Paris, and in 1887 he again decided to flee the city where life had once been so comfortable. He left with Charles Laval for Taboga, an island not far from Panama, where his brother-in-law had started a business. This was Gauguin's first major voyage as a painter and, as for subsequent trips, his motivation was twofold: to earn money in a place where the cost of living was low, and to discover new sources of artistic inspiration in a faraway and 'primitive' land, already familiar to him from his youth.

His hopes of starting a business were quickly dashed. Accompanied by his faithful friend Laval, and with scanty resources, Gauguin was obliged to take work at the building site of the Panama Canal, where digging was in process. However, the building company was experiencing financial problems, which eventually led to a scandal with political repercussions. During a work slow-down Gauguin was laid off, so he and Laval sailed for French Martinique.

Numerous are the accounts of the charm of Martinique, the 'enchanted island'. A contemporary described it as 'one of the most precious pearls of France's colonial jewel box'. Similar accounts appear in the writings of Lafcadio Hearn, a man whose dates, personality and destiny bear an uncanny resemblance to Gauguin's. Like that of Gauguin, his background was a cultural mix—his father was Scottish and his mother Greek—and his need to flee the West, as well as his marriages with an American half-breed and then a Japanese, further linked him to the Parisian exile. They arrived in Martinique within days of each other, and they may well have met. Hearn described the island as a 'tropical dream' in terms that would have pleased Gauguin: 'Ah! The Tropics! They will always tug at my heart strings. God, my real work place was there, in the Latin countries, in the Antilles, and in Latin America... I left those enchanted shores only to be haunted by an irresistible feeling of regret.'[1] Hearn later played an important role in the dissemination of knowledge about the Far East in English- and German-speaking countries.

It seems that Gauguin had neither the time nor the opportunity to paint in Panama; Laval, however, did manage to make a bit of money by painting some rather conventional portraits. Gauguin never consented to this kind of compromise. The amount of work he produced in Martinique may sometimes be overestimated. Pictures by Laval, or by other members of the Pont-Aven School, may well have slipped into the established repertory with the help of a flattering label that increased their value. Some pictures thought to have been painted in Martinique may be authentic, but from a later period. In a letter to Schuffenecker, Gauguin mentioned a dozen canvases (in fact, he originally wrote a *dizaine*—about ten—and then scratched it out in favour of *douzaine*). Fewer than ten important, authenticated pictures from this period are known today.

These paintings betray barely a hint of the poverty and illness that were plaguing Gauguin's daily existence. Like the later Tahitian pictures, they emphasize instead the splendour of the tropical colours and lush vegetation as perceived by the artist's eye.

36 *Martinique Landscape*. 1887. Oil on canvas, 116 × 89 cm.
National Gallery of Scotland, Edinburgh

37 *At the Pond*. 1887. Oil on canvas, 54 × 45 cm. Rijksmuseum
Vincent Van Gogh, Amsterdam

38 *Mangos*. Martinique, 1887. Oil on canvas, 90 × 115 cm. Rijksmuseum Vincent Van Gogh, Amsterdam

39 *By the Sea*. 1887. Oil on canvas, 54 × 90 cm. Ny Carlsberg Glyptotek, Copenhagen

40   *By the Sea*. 1887. Oil on canvas, 46 × 61 cm. Private Collection, Paris

He also took note of the women's bearing and their clothing, and was fascinated by such customs as carrying objects on their heads: 'The observant artist who visits Martinique will be especially struck by the upright carriage and the quick, regular gait of load-bearing women. His first impression will be coloured by the sight of one of these women... Some of the girls are veritable caryatids.'[2] Gauguin painted these women, finding—in the tradition of Poussin and Delacroix—an antique beauty in their movements. In French Provence, too, he remarked on the 'Greek beauty'[3] of the women from Arles.

41 Randolf Caldecott, illustration for Henry Blackburn, *Breton Fold*, London, 1880, p.74

42 *Fire in the Borgo* (*Stanza dell' Incendio*) by Raphael. (Detail). c. 1514. Fresco, 670 cm. Vatican Palace Museum

43 *Footpaths*. Martinique, 1887. Oil on canvas, 72 × 92 cm.
Thyssen-Bornemisza Collection, Lugano

In fact, women do carry jugs on their heads in Brittany as in Martinique; and Raphael as well as Poussin had portrayed women in this graceful pose.

In several of these paintings, a body of water appears amidst the vegetation, whereas at Pont-Aven, as close as it was to the ocean, Gauguin had never dreamed of painting water. Several particularly architectural works evoke Cézanne's *Views of L'Estaque*, painted between 1883 and 1886, in which the flat surface of the sea divides two bands of land, and the whole composition is closed off by a wall of hills. The sea surrounded with land is a motif that recurs in such later works as *What Are We?* While 182 Gauguin's debt to Cézanne manifested itself in specific instances, it was less an influence he underwent than a lesson he adhered to. He referred to that lesson when deciding to introduce the sea into his landscapes. The serenity of certain paintings from Martinique, with their figures worthy of antiquity, brings to mind the work of Poussin. This, too, was less a matter of influence than of a common state of mind. In these pictures, as in later ones, Gauguin managed successfully to introduce a human figure into a natural setting, without disturbing either the scale or the unity of the composition. This was no small challenge, and one to which most of his contemporaries had not risen.

The dense vegetation is treated without shadows, as in the landscapes of the Ile-de-France and Normandy. But here the palette is entirely different, with violets, purples, a variety of greens and—particularly striking—a vermilion roof near the centre of the composition, once again evoking Cézanne. Van Gogh, who learned of these works several months later, was more taken with their colours than with 37 the composition. In *At the Pond* he was drawn to the blue dress and green bonnet of the Negress figure which pick up the cobalt blue of the sky and the green grass.

40 In a discussion of *By the Sea*, Jean de Rotonchamp emphasized the importance of Gauguin's Martinique experience: 'A painting from 1887 ... is evidence that the abandoning of Impressionist formulae was not

44 *Scene of Martinique* by Charles Laval. 1887. Oil on canvas, 62 × 92 cm. Private collection

determined by the theories set forth in 1888 by the Pont-Aven group... The exotic figures partially encircled by a line following their contours, [are] silhouetted against a blue sea... The tones are pure and clear, without optical mixing of colours. There is one exception—and this is characteristic of the transition: a bouquet of spices and red flowers placed in the foreground beneath some trees that are treated in the style of Pissarro.'[4]

Gauguin's work from the Martinique period was characterized by a search for new rhythms, a tendency to outline shapes and the adoption of a range of clearer, brighter colours. Conscious of the change his art was undergoing, he wrote to Schuffenecker on the eve of his return to Paris: 'Hold on; what I am bringing back is on form.' His time in Martinique was important on another count: it was the first time that Gauguin the painter had made contact with the tropical world of his childhood. He found there what was missing in Paris, and something even Brittany had not provided him with. Van Gogh understood it well, as he disclosed in a letter written to his sister between 29 July and 15 August 1888: 'Some time ago Theo bought a large picture from him portraying

45   *The Four Breton Women*. 1888 (?). Oil on canvas, 72 × 91 cm.
Bayerische Staatsgemäldesammlungen, Neue Pinakothek, Munich

46 *Breton Girls Dancing*. Pont-Aven, 1888. Oil on canvas, 93 × 92,7 cm. National Gallery of Art, Washington D.C. (Mr and Mrs Paul Mellon Collection)

Negresses in pink, blue, orange and yellow cotton dresses under tamarind, coconut and banana trees with the sea in the distance. Like *Le Mariage de Loti*, that description of Otaheite. The fact is that he has been in Martinique, and has painted amid the tropical scenery there.'[5] Everything was there: colours, vegetation, exotic people. To live and work there was Van Gogh's dream, too, and a dream that Gauguin sought to relive in other Martiniques. He had just seen paintings by Delacroix and Courbet at the Musée Fabre, Montpellier, and it is surprising that he did not comment on those works, some of which—Courbet's *Bathers*, for example—did later inspire him. However, at the time of writing to Theo Van Gogh in December 1888, Gauguin was dreaming of breaking with the tradition represented by these pictures. 'I am experiencing more and more nostalgia for the Antilles and, of course, as soon as I sell a few paintings, I shall go there ...' Gauguin's departure for Panama with Laval, in the hope of quickly earning enough money to paint freely, was incited both by a dream and by a wager. The wager proved fanciful, but the dream found concrete form in the exoticism and the light of the Tropics, a light that Gauguin was seeing for the first time through the eyes of a painter.

The works that followed Gauguin's return from Martinique suggest hesitation. The shadow of Pissarro was still present. However, Gauguin had acquired more artistic freedom and, especially after returning to Brittany, he began experimenting with unusual compositions and ways of centring images that seem to delineate a larger composition, as in the work of Degas, whose paintings seem to have particularly struck Gauguin's sensibility in this decisive year. Even Degas's subject-matter appears in some of Gauguin's pictures from Brittany, though here those legendary dancers from the Opéra have been transformed into Breton peasants in traditional costume. There are two pictures in this vein. One of them, *The Four Breton Women*, is customarily dated from Gauguin's first stay in Brittany, in 1886. However, the boldness of the composition and the sharpness of the outlines are reason for George Schmidt and Robert

45

Goldwater to contend that it was probably painted in 1888. The other picture, *Breton Girls Dancing, Pont-Aven*, depicts little girls in spontaneous poses. It was retouched at the request of Theo Van Gogh.

46

At this time Gauguin also took up another of Degas's principal themes, that of the nude; but he cautiously wrote, on 8 July 1888, to Schuffenecker: 'I have just done several nudes, which you will like. They are not at all [in the style of] Degas. The latest one is of a tussle between two children near a river, altogether Japanese, by a savage from Peru.' The fact that Gauguin felt the need to deny his affiliation with Degas, while suggesting other references, indicates that he may well have perceived that affinities did exist.

The two themes that dominated the spring and summer of 1888 were Breton women dressed in their finest robes and ornamental headdresses, and nude wrestlers; these came together in *Vision after the Sermon* (also titled *Jacob Wrestling with the Angel*). In linking these themes Gauguin gave them a spiritual dimension: the movements of the dancers have an air of ritual gesture, as for prayer; and the wrestling match is transfigured, becoming a metaphysical confrontation.

50

This is the pivotal picture that marked Gauguin's coming of age as a painter. The strangeness of the composition was altogether shocking for Gauguin's

47   Ford in Brittany. *c.* 1900. Postcard

48 Sketch for *Vision after the Sermon*. 1888. Pencil on white paper, 14 × 9.4 cm. Musée du Louvre, Paris

contemporaries; and the work remains disconcerting even for the modern eye. Though only one, rather rough study for the painting has come down to us it was clearly not the result of improvisation.

Light or black outlines, strongly applied, demarcate the surfaces with a precision that foreshadows the graphic technique of poster art and caricature of the 1900s. Before Gauguin, the only examples of such technique were in stained glass, where the outlines are imposed by the nature of the art, despite efforts by glassworkers to overcome those dictates. In Gauguin's picture, each fragment is covered with one pure colour, entirely devoid of gradations or nuance. Here is a refutation of Constable's theories, which Delacroix shared: 'Constable says that the excellence of the green of his fields lies in the fact that he composes them of a multitude of different greens. The lack of intensity and vitality in most landscape painters' greenery stems from their tendency to treat it with a solid colour. What Constable is saying here about the green of the fields can be applied to all colours.'[6]

Thus, Gauguin deliberately applied in this painting the practice which Delacroix and Constable carefully avoided. He even seems to have consciously chosen subjects whose curved outlines divide the whole pictorial surface into a compartmentalized network.

And the image is centred so arbitrarily that the picture appears to be a fragment of a much larger composition, accidentally cut off by the borders of the canvas.

Has perspective been entirely abandoned in this painting? The arrangement of planes suggests depth only if the viewer can mentally reconstruct the relative dimensions of the objects depicted. In fact, what we have here is the exact opposite of the painstaking system of transitions and colour variations exemplified by the landscapes of Poussin. How are the Breton women placed in relation to the ground? Where are the two biblical figures wrestling at the right of the canvas? Some time ago, these figures were traced to an engraving by Hokusai; for Gauguin, this would have constituted an indirect, perhaps even subconscious, way of placing them outside Western tradition. Are the wrestlers images projected on the wall? Is this a concretization of a description found in the sermon on which the painting is based? Or is it the 'projection' of a magic emblem, like those used in teaching catechism? It is a floating symbol, detached from the rest of the composition. This work was a precursor to the modern poster, in which the juxtaposition of two separate images has become customary.

The importance of this rupture is inestimable, for here Gauguin abandoned all reference to traditional procedures. He even renounced, with this work, any residual influence of the Impressionists, whose own renegade status persisted. It is true that in Gauguin's earliest works, and especially after 1885, there was a notable disregard for 'classroom' perspective, derived from revered masters and disseminated by basic manuals. The paintings from Martinique, with their compressed compositions and new or unusual arrangements, were even more strikingly antithetical to that tradition. Cézanne, Degas and Monet—and, before them, Manet—were moving in the same direction at that time. Still, while the groundwork for *Vision after the Sermon* had been laid, and the work can be considered the fruit of a period of maturation, it marks a sharp and singular break in Gauguin's

49 *Young Breton Bathers*. 1888. Oil on canvas, 92 × 73 cm. Kunsthalle, Hamburg

50 *Vision after the Sermon*. 1888. Oil on canvas, 73 × 92 cm. National Gallery of Scotland, Edinburgh

career as a painter. A romantic interpretation of the creative act—albeit applied more to poets and writers than to visual artists—might suggest that Gauguin painted this picture in a moment of exaltation. It is true that Van Gogh experienced such moments of creative exaltation in which his lucidity was diminished; Gauguin did not. Historians enjoy 'finding' traces or germs of an innovation with the advantage of hindsight. Such an exercise, while potentially enlightening, can never prove that the definitive order of events was inevitable. Many artists have been described as having 'promising beginnings', but often that promise goes largely unfulfilled. A case in point was that of Emile Bernard.

Gauguin described his newly finished picture in a letter to Van Gogh, written around 25 September 1888, in which he pointed out the painting's weaknesses, yet seemed overwhelmed by the strength of the work: 'I have just finished a religious painting which I very much enjoyed doing and am pleased with, despite the fact that it is poorly done ... There are Breton women praying, their costumes a deep black—luminous yellow-white bonnets. The two bonnets at the right are like monstrous helmets—a dark purple apple tree stretches across the canvas, its leaves drawn like a mass of emerald green clouds with yellow-green slits of sunlight. The ground is pure vermilion. At the church it descends and becomes reddish-brown... the angel is dressed in ultramarine-violet, and Jacob in bottle green. The angel's wings are pure chrome 1, its hair chrome 2 and its feet orange flesh. I think I have managed to give the figures a rustic and superstitious simplicity—The whole thing is very severe—The cow beneath the tree is very small, compared with its real size, and is rearing up—For me, the landscape and the fight in this picture exist only in the imagination of the people praying after the sermon, that is why there is a contrast between the naturalness of the people and the unnatural, disproportionate landscape that surrounds the fight.'

It is entirely understandable that Gauguin's contemporaries were disconcerted by a work that upset their way of looking at things. But the lack of comprehension extended even to his former colleagues. Pissarro wrote of this painting to his son Lucien on 20 April 1891: 'The Japanese and Chinese have practised this art, and their symbols are crudely natural; but they are not Catholic, and Gauguin is. I do not reproach Gauguin for making a vermilion background, nor for the two warriors fighting or the Breton peasants in the foreground; I reproach him for pinching this from Japanese and Byzantine and other painters. I reproach him for not applying his synthesis to our modern, completely social, anti-authoritarian and anti-mystical philosophy. Therein lies the crux of the problem. This is a step backward. Gauguin is not a visionary, but a shrewd character who has sensed the bourgeoisie's backward trend, in reaction to the grand sense of solidarity that is germinating among the common people—as yet unconscious but powerful, and supremely legitimate! The Symbolists are in the same category!'

Such a strong condemnation was hardly surprising. Though Pissarro, an innovator of his time, had just proved himself capable of changing his style by adopting the pointillist technique, he may well have balked at a second challenge coming so quickly. Indeed, accusing innovators of being reactionary is a common tactic of those not prepared to rise to their challenge. Pissarro's remarks have less to do with form than with theory, even ideology. If Gauguin had been aware of this commentary—which appeared in a private letter, but may have reflected conversations—he would surely have smiled at Pissarro's reference to him as a Catholic. Pissarro's suggestion was that Gauguin was reintroducing, in his own way, the mystical and sacred into painting, elements which his Impressionist confrères had sought to exclude. In these lines Pissarro seems to be acknowledging—perhaps unconsciously—that Gauguin was providing a remedy for what many observers argued was the weakness of Impressionist paintings from the Argenteuil period: their lack of 'reflection'. Redon rather unfairly referred to them as 'the bottom of the barrel', a judgment that indicates a curious insensitivity to these painters' sense of 'light verse' and hedonism expressed in *Views of Argenteuil* by Monet and Van Gogh's *Moulin de la Galette*. It is true, though, that Monet's and Renoir's figures—and even those of Manet—somehow lack inner life.

Until that time Gauguin had not introduced anecdotal or symbolic subject-matter into his paintings, in keeping with the tenets of Impressionism. In *Vision after the Sermon* the subject is imaginary and its meaning difficult to interpret. Albert Aurier, an early—and rare—contemporary admirer of Gauguin's work, described it thus: 'Far, very far away on a fabulous hill, whose soil appears as a gleaming vermilion, we see the biblical struggle between Jacob and the Angel. While these two legendary giants, transformed by distance into pygmies, fight their formidable battle, some naïve, interested women observe them, probably understanding little of what is happening over on that marvellous scarlet hill. They are peasants, and from the size of their white headdresses, spread wide like gulls' wings, the coloured patterns of their scarves and the style of their clothes, we gather that they are from Brittany. They have the respectful poses and wide-eyed expressions of simple creatures listening to extraordinary tales being affirmed by some revered, incontestable source. They could be in church, so silent is their gaze, so devout their posture: without doubt, in church, a vague odour of incense and prayer flutters about the white wings of their headdresses and the venerated voice of the old priest hovers over their heads ... Yes, without a doubt, [they are] in church, a poor church in some poor little Breton village ... But then, where are the mouldy pillars? Where are the milky walls with the tiny, chromolithographic Way of the Cross? Where is the pine pulpit? Where is the old parish priest whose droning voice we can surely hear, raised in sermon? Where is all that? And why the rising of that fabulous hill so far, far away, whose ground looks like gleaming vermilion? Ah! It is because the mouldy pillars, the milky walls, the little chromolithographic Way of the Cross, the pine pulpit and the old priest preaching have for some time

51   *Head of a Breton Peasant Woman*. 1888 (?). Graphite, red pencil and wash, 22.4 × 20 cm. Fogg Art Museum, Harvard University, Cambridge, Massachusetts

now been annihilated—they no longer exist but for the eyes and souls of these good Breton peasant women ... All these surrounding objects have dissipated into the vapours, disappeared: even the storyteller himself has disappeared, leaving only his Voice ... to contemplate, with such naïve and devoted attention, these peasants with their white headdresses; and it is that Voice, that provincially fantastic vision that rises up over there, far, far away ... '[7]

Whether painted from memory or imagination, the subject of Breton villagers coming out of Sunday mass is not typical of Gauguin; and we are led to wonder why he chose a theme so divorced from his customary concerns and habitual subject-matter. Despite his anti-clericalism, it would have been unlike Gauguin to make fun of the simple faith of Breton peasants. Although he rejected Catholicism as a religion, he had a definite sense of the sacred that prevented him from treating it with derision. On the contrary, he may have been struck by the seriousness and dignity of the religious ways of these women, even if they were marked by superstition. Gauguin shared little with a character like Monsieur Homais in Madame Bovary, who had become a symbol of narrow-minded anti-clericalism. It was not by chance that Gauguin chose for the subject of this picture one of the most mysterious passages of the Bible, and one of the least frequently represented—Delacroix's famous picture at Saint-Sulpice remains an exception. By battling the All-Powerful, Jacob affirms himself.

If we delve into Gauguin's personal preoccupations, we can construct an interpretation that accounts for his linking these two apparently unrelated motifs—Jacob and the Breton women. This boldly innovative painting may represent Gauguin's own struggle after a period of reflection that resulted in a veritable artistic conversion. After all, for Gauguin art was nearly sacred. Subsequent to his formative years under Pissarro's tutelage, Gauguin's approach to the visual underwent significant change. The figure of Jacob portrays Gauguin's artistic awakening, while other painters, like the Breton peasants in their ignorance, observed with stupefaction the birth of a new image. The style and the subject-matter of the painting overlap and merge, for the picture tells Gauguin's own story. There is a world of difference between Emile Bernard's exercise and the wilful, coherent inventiveness in Gauguin's work. On 8 October 1888 he wrote to Schuffenecker: 'This year I sacrificed everything: execution and colour, for style, for I wanted to force myself to do something besides what I know how to do.' Jacob's struggle was victorious.

When the painting was finished, Gauguin decided to give it to a church near Nizon; accompanied by Laval and Bernard, he took it there. On the white frame he had inscribed 'Don de Tristan de Moscoso', in memory of his great-grandfather. The parish priest of Nizon refused the work and Gauguin took it away with him. Once in Paris, he gave it to Theo Van Gogh, who was working in the Boussod and Valadon gallery. This marked the beginning of Gauguin's ascendance over younger painters. Shortly thereafter, in 1889, the painting was shown at the Salon des XX in Brussels. On 23 February 1891, at the sale organized by Gauguin himself in preparation for his next departure, it was one of the few works that fetched a decent price—900 francs, instead of the 1,000 that he had asked earlier in Brussels.

Chapter V   Towards a Stronger Identity

With *Vision after the Sermon* Gauguin established a workable system that he then set about implementing. Indeed, for him theoretical reflection often followed experimenting on canvas. As soon as he realized that he could construct coherent images while ignoring the hitherto sacrosanct rules of traditional perspective, his research quickly began moving out in different directions, and limitless new fields opened up. Several works painted in Arles and Paris during the winter of 1888-9 were indirectly influenced by *Vision after the Sermon* in that they benefited from the new artistic freedom that Gauguin was now fully exploiting. All of these pictures contain new techniques such as the breaking down of planes, use of diagonals, disequilibrium, and emphasis on a single detail—for example, flowers or fruit in 71 the foreground. In *Alyscamps*, for example, Gauguin introduced the handsome, strongly-centred Saint Andrew's Cross motif, often used by painters of the Barbizon School and, earlier, by the seventeenth-century Dutch landscape painters. The paintings of this period might be grouped as follows: those with isolated figures without a foreground but with precisely rendered surroundings, such as *Madame Rou-* 53, 54 *lin, La Belle Angèle, Madame Alexandre Kohler, Self-* 52 *Portrait in Front of the 'Yellow Christ'* and others; those with isolated figures and a strongly pronounced foreground; straightforward landscapes, sometimes with very small figures; and compositions containing several figures. This last type was rarer and presented more difficulties. Gauguin took it up recurrently throughout his life.

While the works from the period 1888-9 were varied, they had much in common. Especially during those years, Gauguin was a man who experimented constantly, seeking new approaches to the picture plane. The few paintings of a figure detached from the foreground constitute a definite group which challenged the model of portrait painting established some years earlier by Ingres. With monumental ease, that master had introduced different artifices for linking figure to setting: placing him in an armchair, by a fireplace or before a mirror. Another tradition in nineteenth-century portraiture consisted in setting the figure against a neutral or solid-coloured background, and was exemplified by Paul Delaroche, Paul Baudry, Alexandre Cabanel and especially Léon Bonnat, whose prestige was tremendous at the time.

It is important to remember that Gauguin set himself against both the Impressionist innovators and the academic tradition that still prevailed. Even Manet's portraits and figurative works employ a variety of approaches, including a neutral background, a decorative ground totally disconnected from the figure and, more rarely, ground linked to figure. The most innovative of Gauguin's immediate predecessors in this regard was Degas. However, the idea of placing a figure in the foreground of the picture, facing the viewer, probably came from Manet, whose *Luncheon at the Artist's Studio* and *Bar at the Folies-Bergère* come immediately to mind. Later, Edvard Munch picked up on this technique, either directly from Manet or via Gauguin.

If, from the point of view of representation, *Madame Alexandre Kohler, Madame Roulin* and *At the Café* (*Madame Ginoux*) are unconnected to their backgrounds, there are nevertheless links of a plastic order. In the case of *At the Café* an analysis of the pic- 72

52 *Self-Portrait in Front of the 'Yellow Christ'*. 1889. Oil on canvas, 38 × 46 cm. Private Collection, France

53 *La Belle Angèle*. 1889. Oil on canvas, 92 × 73 cm. Musée d'Orsay, Paris

ture based on geometric lines—an approach much favoured in the 1930s due to the influence of Cubism and the works of André Lhote—reveals the canvas's strong coherence: a highly complicated relationship between vertical, horizontal and oblique lines is easy to trace through the table, the billiard cue and other accessories. Although the value of this type of formal analysis is limited, in a few cases the relationships are so apparent that they are impossible to ignore. This can be seen as further proof—despite the fact that Gauguin's extant work includes very few preparatory studies—that he was not an improviser. In the case of *Madame Roulin*, for example, it is surely not coincidental that the slightly soft curves of the face and the lines of the clothes recur in the background landscape. The same coherence can be found in compositions containing several figures, notably *The* 55 *Schuffenecker Family*. In this case, syncopation and the shifting of planes, already introduced by Degas and Cézanne and seen in Japanese prints, do not adversely affect a plausible representation. There are only two examples of pictures that Gauguin con- 50, 53 structed of autonomous images: *Vision after the Sermon* and *La Belle Angèle*, a portrait of the wife of an entrepreneur from Pont-Aven. We know a good deal about the development of this portrait thanks to interviews with the model recorded by Charles Chassé.[1]

This portrait of a certain Madame Satre became 53 popular under Gauguin's title *La Belle Angèle*, and the popularity somewhat deflected attention from its highly unusual character, which even Van Gogh failed to catch. It is a bust-height portrait of a seated Breton woman, hands folded, wearing a black dress and lilac apron with pink and red flowers. There is something so fresh and country-like about the facial expression and the pose that it is most pleasant to look at.

The figure is painted within a defined area of the canvas, isolating her from the rest of the surface, which depicts wallpaper and a Peruvian idol. The statue is placed on an undefined base, either a chest or a shelf, on which Gauguin block-printed: LA

BELLE ANGELE. Such inscriptions, nearly always hand-written and quite small, are not uncommon in Gauguin's work.

To introduce two images into one painting with priority given to the medallion went contrary to every tradition in Western painting, although analogous themes existed in decorative painting, tapestry and book or magazine illustrations, where the practice was widespread. Perhaps Gauguin was familiar with such illustrations. But why deny him the incongruous innovation of transposing this technique to easel painting? Gauguin's objective here seems quite clearly to represent his model as sacred, which he achieves by using the mandorla and halo to form a segment of a circle cut off by the edge of the canvas. His model is posed in her loveliest attire, the traditional costume of Pont-Aven, and the cross almost exactly in the centre of the area containing the figure adds an harmonious detail, which may or may not have been intentional. Madame Satre is seen standing up, slightly sideways, set against a solid blue background; the area outside the circle represents blue wallpaper speckled with blue and yellow flowers. This motif appears in other paintings by Gauguin, including *The Inn-Keeper's Daughter*, which sug- 17 gests that one of the rooms in the Pension Gloanec was decorated with such wallpaper.

Several of Cézanne's still-lifes from the years 1885 to 1890 contain similar wallpaper backgrounds. In Cézanne's work, as in Gauguin's, there is this carrying over of an already transposed floral motif, creating a second-degree stylization.

The same is true of the Peruvian idol, whose exact function is difficult to ascertain. It may be a general religious symbol or a reference to Gauguin's childhood and his Incan ancestors. There is a hint of the affirmation of a sort of syncretism or religious relativism, since the idol belongs to a non-Christian faith and is placed here next to a cross. Perhaps, more simply, in this dramatically asymmetrical composition, Gauguin wished to introduce, with the outline of the Peruvian vase, a visual reference to Madame Satre's silhouette.

The history of this painting is significant. Gauguin offered it to his model, who declined it. We can easily understand how Madame Satre, whose knowledge of art was probably limited to the most traditional examples and to a kind of popular art known as 'Saint-Sulpice', would have been shocked by the icon. At the auction organized by Gauguin in 1891, the painting was bought by Degas, a fact which attests to his taste and independent spirit; Degas could admire Gauguin the artist even while disapproving of his personality. In the 1918 sale of Degas's collection, Gauguin's painting was bought by Ambroise Vollard. In 1927 Robert Rey, then curator of the Musée du Luxembourg and a prominent Gauguin scholar, asked Vollard to lend him the picture for one of his lectures at the Ecole du Louvre. Pleased by Rey's initiative, Vollard gave the painting to the Louvre's permanent collection.

When Gauguin became interested in working out compositions of several figures, he was venturing onto difficult ground. We should not be deluded by artists of preceding generations who apparently mastered this problem using academic techniques. Many painters, even the most illustrious, did not truly do so. Neither Ingres nor Courbet was comfortable with this challenge; Manet even less so. The Impressionists, with the exception of Monet in his early works and occasionally Renoir, avoided the problem altogether. Perhaps one reason for Gauguin's jealousy of Puvis de Chavannes was the latter's ease in organizing his compositions. Gauguin understood that the traditional approaches, even those used by artists he admired such as Delacroix, were no longer appropriate, for they were based on techniques he rejected, including depth, vanishing point perspective, relief and chiaroscuro.

Degas, too, had shattered set ways of doing things. His composition, like Gauguin's and Manet's, was based less on plausibility than on a desire to organize the surface and create an effect. Degas's and Gauguin's figures are often in positions that would be physically impossible to maintain; and the relationship between the figures no longer adheres to the

conventions which Puvis de Chavannes, for example, respected. Others soon began to divorce themselves from those conventions too: Seurat was among the first, and Hodler, whose artistic intentions were often close to those of Gauguin, exhibited *Night* in 1891 in Paris with considerable success.

Despite difficulties in establishing a chronology, it seems that this type of approach first appeared in the work of Degas. A painting such as the *Dancer with a Bouquet* (Art Museum, Rhode Island School of Design, Providence) is organized in a similar fashion to *Vision after the Sermon*. But rather than exploring the similarities between these two painters who knew and respected each other, let us simply note that they covered common ground in this difficult area.

Gauguin's relationship with Seurat was somewhat different. The two men apparently met in 1886, on the occasion of the eighth, and last, Impressionist show. The group was now quite different from what it had been at its inception. The original participants had either left the fold or gone through radical artistic changes. Seurat was at the centre of things in 1886 with his *La Grande Jatte*, which gave rise to jibes or, at best, reservations, even among the best-disposed critics. But he was not the only pointillist at the show: Pissarro was experimenting with the new technique, as were his son Lucien and the young Paul Signac. Gauguin foresaw the theoretical importance of Seurat's contribution, which was not limited to painting 'little dots' or separating brushstrokes. This technique fitted into a more general plan to rationalize the pictorial craft as well as to express feelings through facial lines and poses. Gauguin passed on to Seurat a series of 'precepts' written by an eighteenth-century Turkish poet and essayist, Vehbi Mohamed Zumbul Zade (Gauguin's spelling). In the text, recopied by Gauguin, these technical remarks appear side by side with assertions of a more philosophical nature, such as in the following passage: 'Discard black and that mixture of black and white they call grey ... seek for harmony and not contrast, for what accords, not for what clashes. It is the eye of ignor-

ance that assigns a fixed and immutable colour to every object ...' Or in this one: 'Calm and spiritual peace should emanate from your work. Each of your figures ought to be in a static position.' This precept was respected by both Seurat and Gauguin, but they differed in their ways of applying the following one: 'Study the silhouette of every object; distinctness of outline is the privilege of the hand that is not enfeebled by any hesitation of the will.'

The attention given to such a text corresponded to Gauguin's, and Seurat's, desire to found their art on principles which could be formulated; to this was added the practice, much in vogue at the time, of appropriating the secrets and teachings of Oriental civilizations. Seurat was fascinated by this text, and Gauguin even included long quotes from it in *Avant et après*.

The friendship between the two men was short-lived. Gauguin was suspicious of any theory that he had not set forth himself, and he doubtless had trouble abiding the fact that Seurat, eleven years his junior, was increasingly influential among the younger artists. Their actual falling out occurred as a result of a misunderstanding during which Seurat turned Gauguin out of Signac's studio, unaware that he actually had permission to be working there. But that quarrel merely crystallized a deep incompatibility: there was not enough room for two chiefs in one tribe.

At first, from 1881 to 1884, Seurat followed roughly the same artistic route as Gauguin. They both easily assimilated the Impressionist style, meeting its challenge to paint the most transient images where people, vegetation and sky were reduced to elements of Nature. But both Seurat and Gauguin, as well as Manet and Renoir, lamented the lack of order. Seurat was younger than Gauguin, but advanced for his age; despite his sarcastic remarks about *ripipoint*, an imaginary Neo-Impressionist character he in-

54 *Madame Alexandre Kohler*. 1889. Oil on canvas, 46.3 × 38 cm. National Gallery of Art, Washington, D.C. (Dale Chester Collection)

vented with Bernard, Gauguin was fascinated by Seurat's technique and experimented with divisionism in several canvases. Even if he did not actually see them, he must have been aware of the six large works that punctuated the carefully thought-out path that led Seurat through Impressionism and beyond. The first, *La Baignade* ('The Bath', 1882), is still infused with a soft, Impressionist light, but the shapes are clearly defined. *La Grande Jatte* (1884-6) represents the revival of a type of pictorial order modelled after Poussin but with contemporary fittings. In this painting classical references pervade an outdoor scene in which figures file by slowly, as if in a pagan procession. The static *Poseuses* (1887) idealizes the painter's craft, paving the way for Gauguin's *Annah the Javanese* (1893-4). *Parade* (1888) 146 introduces the entertainment theme, with diffused, artificial lighting, while retaining the static quality of the preceding works; *Le Chahut* ('The Rowdy Dance', 1890) employs artificial lighting, too, but here movement is introduced. Finally, *Le Cirque* ('The Circus', 1890) picks up on the entertainment theme and the movement, while defining a new sense of space. As in the work of Degas, these paintings represent parallel studies concerning fundamental problems.

The example of Degas, and also of Seurat—and probably a touch of jealousy—may have stimulated Gauguin to work on compositions containing several figures. The most characteristic of these is *The Schuffenecker Family*. As we have seen, Schuffe- 55 necker was Gauguin's old friend, professional colleague, and fellow Sunday painter. Whether Gauguin did this group portrait for the sake of friendship or because the family provided convenient and docile models is unclear. The picture is one of the first in which he tackled the formidable problem that had long discouraged painters. Manet and Fantin-Latour produced famous, but rare, examples of group portraits. For Gauguin, inexperienced and ill versed in academic tradition as he was, it constituted a courageous act. The composition is dominated by a pyramid-shaped mass formed by Mrs Schuffenecker and her two children, whose stately, almost hieratic, and perfectly balanced pose stands in marked contrast to the triviality of the rest of the decor. At the left of the painting stands Schuffenecker, staring admiringly at his wife. His facial expression, stance and folded hands suggest a note of caricature. It may not be coincidental that Schuffenecker's easel and canvas are seen from such an angle that nothing on them is visible. On more than one occasion, though, Gauguin depicted paintings by artists such as Van Gogh, Cézanne or Degas in his own works; and the right side of this canvas contains several such transpositions. Perhaps Gauguin wished to indicate, without saying so explicitly, that he cared little for his friend's work. One of the pictures depicted in the background of this canvas is a wood engraving by Kumisada Utagawa which also appears in a still-life belonging to the Oskar Reinhart Foundation, Winterthur. The painting hanging above it, whose right side is cut off by the stovepipe, has been attributed by some critics to Schuffenecker, but it was more likely by Cézanne or Gauguin himself. The windows of the studio, whose frames form a grid, separate the figures

56 *In the Greenhouse* by Edouard Manet. 1879. Oil on canvas, 115 × 150 cm. Staatliche Museen Preussischer Kulturbesitz, Nationalgalerie, Berlin

from the sunny, spring-like landscape visible through the centre window. The outdoor vignette consists of a house or church with a bright vermilion tiled roof set in lush greenery, not unlike one of Pissarro's landscapes from his Auvers or Pontoise period. It is tempting to read symbolic significance into these bars rising up between the landscape and the painters who seek to depict it. From then on, Gauguin, like Schuffenecker, turned his back on the chic realism of the Impressionist period, in favour of painting developed within the studio. Symbolic bars of this type appear in the work of Manet, notably *In the Greenhouse* and *The Balcony* (Musée d'Orsay, Paris).[2] Perhaps Gauguin was remembering Manet in this picture, but he may also have been referring to Fantin-Latour's *The Dubourg Family*, exhibited at the Salon in 1878. Though the treatment is entirely different, the spirit of the two paintings and their compositions are related. However, had Fantin seen *The Schuffenecker Family*, he would have been horrified by the clashing colours, sharp outlines and absence of shadows. Nevertheless, with her dignified stature and serious, meditative countenance—uncommon in

55 *The Schuffenecker Family*. 1889. Oil on canvas, 73 × 92 cm. Musée d'Orsay, Paris

Gauguin's work—Madame Schuffenecker is a worthy sister to the haughty Charlotte Dubourg.

89 A different example of Gauguin's drive to experiment is the *Still-Life with Three Puppies*. It is difficult to judge whether the curious juxtaposition of dogs, bowls and fruit is the result of clumsiness or conscious design. The objects have no logical connection to each other, unless the picture represents a riddle. Yet another note of incoherence is added by the mixing of styles: the fruit is treated in the manner of Cézanne, while the puppies evoke both Japanese art and, as pointed out by John Rewald, children's book illustrations. This naïve quality is not uncommon in Gauguin's work and foreshadows such later creations as Benjamin Rabier's comical animals.

58 Another work that stands out as bearing little resemblance to its antecedents is *Woman in Waves* (*Undine*), which was shown at the Café Volpini in 1889 and reproduced as an engraving. The carefully studied arabesque here prefigures Art Nouveau. *Woman in Waves* 'is above all a pretext for the interweaving network of arabesques that spreads out over the whole height of the canvas—in which the suppression of the sky allows for a reduction of depth'.[3] Gauguin named the painting somewhat later, as if he wished to confer a poetic dimension by relating it to the Undine of La Motte-Fouqué,[4] the symbol of the *femme fatale*, taken up again by Giraudoux. One of the many literary references to this theme is a lovely verse by André Chénier: 'Son beau corps a roulé sous la vague marine' (Her beautiful body rolled beneath the wave).

Gauguin's painting, which may have derived from Rodin's *Danaïde*, subsequently inspired several works by young Aristide Maillol.

Was Gauguin influenced, or merely preceded, by Emile Bernard in his drive to define a new artistic formula? Even recent critics have been preoccupied by this question. Very early on, Bernard claimed credit for his contribution to the development of the new style that was born in 1888 in Pont-Aven. Over the years—and even during Gauguin's lifetime—some critics did credit Bernard with the innovation. Roger

57 *The Dubourg Family* by Henri Fantin-Latour. 1878. Oil on canvas, 146 × 170 cm. Musée d'Orsay, Paris

Marx, a foremost critic of his time, claimed in 1892 that the day of representing the real, which had recently become the fashion, was so widely accepted that it risked becoming conventional and banal and that a new artistic movement was forced to produce the opposite of its predecessor, to advocate the ideal and the unreal. Marx credited Emile Bernard, whose work was then being shown at Durand-Ruel's, as the initiator of this aesthetic, today called 'Symbolism'. The critic went on to say that Bernard presents an entirely imaginative conception, as his precursors had, using a technique that deforms in order to depict better and to emphasize further moral character and feeling. Marx characterized Symbolist art, like its ancestor Roman art, as essentially decorative, owing to its deliberate simplification of what it portrays.

Claude Anet, who later became known as a novelist, wrote in 1901 in *La Revue Blanche* how important it was to set matters straight concerning the chronology of influence of one painter on another. He took pains to clarify the fact that Denis, Sérusier, Gauguin and others had followed Bernard in his new direction of art. Anet concluded that it would thus be appropriate to refer to Bernard as 'the father of French Symbolism', a title Roger Marx had already attributed to him a decade earlier.

It is possible that Roger Marx and Claude Anet were indoctrinated by Bernard. Or perhaps they were more concerned with analyzing symbolic intentions than matters of style. Gauguin was far away, and, having irritated his rare admirers with his arrogance and his bad manners, he had few friends left in Paris. When he got wind of some of these texts and of Bernard's claims to precedence, his response was an ironic dismissal in a letter to Maurice Denis in June 1899: 'Everyone knows that I did truly rob my Master Emile Bernard.' Over the years Gauguin's posthumous glory grew, gradually eclipsing the reputation of Bernard, whose own work was marred by an increasingly reactionary academicism. Still, Bernard persisted, in his numerous written works, to claim credit for initiating a movement that was already becoming historic. We can understand Bernard's consternation when, in the spectacular 1937 exhibition at the Palais de Tokyo in Paris, entitled *Chefs d'œuvres de l'art français*, a Breton landscape bearing Gauguin's signature turned out to be his. Right up until his death in 1941, Bernard doggedly—and sincerely—argued his case. The matter deserves to be re-examined. (For a discussion of Gauguin's influence on younger artists, the Nabi School, the reader should consult the conclusion of the present work.)

Emile Bernard was born in 1868. By adolescence his artistic talent was evident, and at seventeen he entered Cormon's studio at the Ecole des Beaux-Arts. There he met Louis Anquetin and Toulouse-Lautrec who, along with Van Gogh and Picabia, were among the more unlikely students of an artist whose greatest work, *Cain*, is a masterpiece of academic painting. In 1886 Bernard was dismissed from Cormon's studio. He began dabbling in Pointillism, then at its inception, and travelled to Brittany where he met Schuffenecker and Gauguin. It seems that certain of his paintings and drawings, which demonstrate a strong

drive towards simplification and stylization, can be dated as early as 1887, a year in which Gauguin's graphic techniques had not yet reached such a high level of stylization. In August 1888, when he was not yet twenty, Bernard met Gauguin and Laval at Pont-Aven, where he painted *Breton Women in the Meadow*, a series that appealed so much to Van Gogh that he did a copy of one of the paintings. These are clearly predecessors of *Vision after the Sermon*.

Bernard's output during the three or four years he worked with Gauguin—who, it is essential to remember, was twenty years his elder—was far from homogeneous. The verso of his still-life, *Still-Life with Stoneware Jug*, bears the proud inscription 'Premier essai de synthétisme et de simplification 1887' (First attempt at Synthetism and simplification); but the inscription was added after the fact, and the date on the front of the painting is illegible and poorly assimilated into the thick, enamel-like colour. In this picture the palette is muted, the shapes modelled by the shadows. The clear reference to Cézanne introduces doubt as to the painting's date. The same applies to *Bathers*, which is also dated 1887. Perhaps this picture's clumsiness stems from the fact that it represents the efforts of an eighteen-year-old fledgeling painter. The distortion of the body suggests the influence of Cézanne, but this time his style seems almost caricatured. In the famous *Madeleine at the Bois d'Amour*, poetic content takes precedence over plastic inventiveness. The model for this painting was Bernard's sister, with whom Gauguin was infatuated, though she later married Laval. This is a dreamy portrayal of a woman lying in a forest—strongly evocative yet containing no specific story-telling elements. Gauguin's *Portrait of Madeleine Bernard*, for which he also used Bernard's sister as his model, is a more lively picture in which emphasis is placed on the young woman's face. The upper section of the background shows a

58 *Woman in Waves (Undine)*. 1889. Oil on canvas, 92 × 72 cm. Cleveland Museum of Art (Gift of Mr and Mrs William Powell Jones)

59 *Breton Landscape* by Emile Bernard (1868-1941). Oil on canvas, 55 × 49 cm. Private Collection, France

the coherent organization of the pictoral surface in *Vision after the Sermon*. Pictures like Bernard's *Breton Women under Umbrellas* (Musée d'Orsay, Paris), in which the Synthetist characteristics are more pronounced, are from 1892. The orderly, even rigid

60 *Bretons in the Field* by Emile Bernard. 1888. Oil on canvas, 74 × 92 cm. Private Collection, France

fragment of a painting on the wall, in which the ballet slippers suggest that the artist was Degas. Bernard himself described the circumstances surrounding these two paintings: 'Gauguin did the portrait of my sister, whereas I painted her in the Bois d'Amour in a reclining position suggesting that of a fallen tree. Of course, both these pictures were but caricatures of my sister, though Gauguin's was truly a portrait—which, though not a faithful rendering, was none the less stylistically interesting—behind an old-style landscape of Pont-Aven which is now in the Musée de Grenoble. Naturally, Gauguin was smitten by my sister's sweet nature, and longed to carry her off, but my father intervened just in time.'[5]

It is clear that Bernard used stylized forms and flat areas of colour in his work, abandoning a traditional approach to perspective, before Gauguin did. He may possibly have even influenced Gauguin in these areas. However, in Bernard's work these elements appear to be part of a temporary, exploratory phase. In *Breton Women in the Meadow* (1888) the silhouettes are juxtaposed as in a bas-relief, quite unlike

61 *Still-Life with Stoneware Jug* by Emile Bernard. 1887. Oil on canvas, 46 × 55 cm. Musée d'Orsay, Paris

rhythm of the composition is reminiscent of Seurat's *La Grande Jatte*. Bernard's subsequent output, though abundant and varied, led—with a few notable exceptions, particularly in the field of graphic art—back towards academicism, while Gauguin continued along the innovative path to the apotheosis of a new approach to painting.

Gauguin and Bernard were not alone in their struggle to define this new painting. Louis Anquetin shared their preoccupations. Early in his career, Toulouse-Lautrec showed an interest in accentuating outlines, as well as opting for unconventional compositions and treatment of space. Although it is difficult to date Lautrec's early works with certainty, 63 a painting like *The First Communion*, painted in the spring of 1888, constitutes, with its simple graphic techniques and tilted perspective, an essential piece of evidence in this case. Van Gogh's role in the development of this approach should not be underestimated either, which is aptly illustrated in this passage from one of Van Gogh's letters to Theo, dated October 1889: 'I am trying as much as possible to simplify the list of paints—therefore I very often use the ochres as I did in the old days. I know quite well that the studies in the last package, drawn with such great shadowy lines, were not what they ought to have been; however, I beg you to believe that in landscape I am going on trying to mass things by means of a drawing style which tries to express the interlocking of the masses. Do you happen to remember that landscape by Delacroix—"Jacob Struggling with the Angel"? And there are others of his! For instance, the cliffs and those very flowers of which you sometimes speak. Bernard has really done some perfect things in this respect.'[6]

From all this it is clear that Bernard did play a significant role in the development of a new style of painting. But Gauguin, with his infinitely more flamboyant personality, had a greater impact.

In several written accounts, Bernard in fact claimed dual paternity, associating or dissociating—depending upon the case—two elements in his art. The first he called Synthetism, a term that pertained to matters of form; the second he referred to as pictorial symbolism, which had to do with a picture's literary and poetic significance. In the afterword of a collection of letters he had received from other artists, compiled much later and published only in 1927, Bernard defined his ideal quite precisely, accusing Gauguin of being a 'blind perpetuator of procedure' who conserved 'from Symbolism only the outer, decorative fittings without investing them with spiritual content'. With these declarations Bernard demonstrated that his current artistic views had become totally incompatible, not only with Gauguin's but also with those of the artists who subsequently developed and interpreted earlier ideas. In a previously unpublished text, he repudiated his early works: 'Ignorant people have always liked raw colours. It is not surprising that they appreciate so-called modern art. There is perhaps not much difference between yesterday's chromolithographic prints and today's posters, so much in vogue.' In that same text, Bernard revealed his present reactionary mentality by offering up one of the academic school's oldest recipes: 'To tone down a shade of umber, go back over the whole colour, if it is warm, with matt burnt umber.'

The rivalry between Gauguin and Bernard should not overshadow the fact that for at least two years the two men were on very good terms. In September 1888, Bernard wrote Van Gogh an enthusiastic letter which Van Gogh subsequently mentioned to Theo: 'His [Bernard's] letter is steeped in admiration for Gauguin's talent. He says that he thinks him so great an artist that he is almost afraid, and that he finds everything that he does himself poor in comparison with Gauguin.'[7] In 1889 Bernard was one of the principal contributors to the exhibition at the Café Volpini, showing works under his own name as well as the pseudonym Ludovic Nemo. He also became closer to Van Gogh; it was he who informed Albert Aurier of Van Gogh's suicide, and the funeral inspired him to do a painting. In an artistic atmosphere characterized by impassioned discussions and reversals, Bernard appeared as a younger brother,

62   *Portrait of Madeleine Bernard*. 1888. Oil
on canvas, 72 × 58 cm. Musée de Peinture et de
Sculpture, Grenoble

63   *First Communion* by Henri de Toulouse-
Lautrec. 1888. *Essence* on carton, 65 × 37 cm.
Musée des Augustins, Toulouse

64 *The Chapel of Tremalo* by Emile Jourdan. *c.* 1910. Oil on canvas, 74 × 78 cm. Musée d'Art, Pont-Aven

convinced of his artistic calling, but ever doubtful.

The relationship between Bernard and Gauguin was still so cordial between 1890 and 1891 that Gauguin, who had first planned to leave alone, invited the younger artist to accompany him to Madagascar, which had been declared a French protectorate in 1885. Numerous articles had appeared in the press describing the variety of peoples living there. When Gauguin changed his mind about the trip, Bernard suggested they leave together for Tahiti, instead. The two men apparently quarrelled on the occasion of the sale organized by Gauguin, on 23 February 1891, to raise money for the trip. In fact, the sale was publicized by several articles singing Gauguin's praises, and one by Albert Aurier explicitly mentioned Gauguin as the leader of the school. Nothing could have irritated Bernard more, especially in light of the fact that it was he who had first brought Gauguin's work to Aurier's attention. Their falling out was violent and definitive, for Bernard could not bear to be thought of by younger painters as Gauguin's follower. The exact circumstances of their quarrel are difficult to establish, but the fundamental reasons are clear. John

Rewald summarized them thus: 'What neither Gauguin nor Bernard cared to admit in the heat of resentments and recriminations was that the style they had created in Pont-Aven had been born of their close collaboration. Their friendship had been based on a continual give and take in which each tried out his new ideas on the other, in which they stimulated, criticized, and complemented each other, in which each had become more conscious of himself through comparison with the other. Advice had been liberally given and received. Their relationship had afforded to each an opportunity to escape the agonizing solitude in which one has to ask and answer questions by oneself. That some ideas originated with Bernard there can be little doubt, but the art of painting is not based solely on ideas. What counted now that their new formula had been solidly established was not so much the past but the present and the future. This present saw Bernard entangled in a vague mysticism and in the rediscovery of the principles of old masters, whereas Gauguin resolutely pursued the road on which they had started together. As to the future, it was to reveal Gauguin constantly searching for new and ever more powerful means of expression, while Bernard increasingly abandoned the promising conquests of his youth.'[8]

Bernard's later work should not, however, be dismissed as a simple return to academicism. His rich personality found expression in writings which demonstrated his wide cultural knowledge and passionate interest in questions of an artistic nature. This was perhaps one of the reasons for the stagnation of his work as a painter. Cézanne suggested as much in a letter to his son, dated 26 September 1906: 'He is an intellectual congested by memories of museums.' Every word of this quip is important: for Cézanne, the word intellectual denoted someone devoid of both a visual sense and sensitivity in general. Bernard had in fact visited Cézanne in Aix in 1904, after having approached Gauguin and experienced a sort of mystical conversion. They had a number of open conversations, and Bernard painted some landscapes that betray Cézanne's unmistakable influence.

Cézanne wrote some of his most famous letters to Bernard, particularly the one containing that much-quoted maxim: 'Treat nature in terms of spheres, cylinders and cones.' Rare is the book on modern art that has not referred to this phrase, as both a key to Cézanne's own style and an announcer of Cubism. Perhaps too much has been made of this. It is seldom pointed out that the tone of Cézanne's letters varied greatly according to whom he was addressing and if he wrote to Bernard in a theoretical and solemn tone, perhaps he was pandering to what he perceived as an 'intellectual's' special needs.

Even after their falling out, and perhaps in spite of themselves, Gauguin and Bernard still shared a number of aesthetic ideas, doubtless developed during their numerous conversations. Their reflections on their work and lucidity with regard to their place in history contrasted sharply with the Impressionists' expressed lack of interest in theory, which, in fact, was largely an affectation, for Monet and Renoir certainly meditated on their art, especially after 1880. Gauguin and Bernard wrote much over the years, and Bernard's ideas became richer, more systematic and more coherent. He saw himself as the historian of a poetic and pictorial movement of which he was one of the initiators. The undated text entitled *Le Symbolisme pictural*, as well as the long *Mémoire* published in *Maintenant* (1947, n° 7) reiterate in clearer language ideas he had already expressed more spontaneously in a series of articles published by *Mercure de France* in 1895. Among other things, he recognized the value of 'primitive' arts ('expressions of truth'), folk art and pictures from Epinal, which at the time were too rare to constitute anything other than curiosities. Bernard was especially interested in religious, mystical and Gothic art, which was both spiritually charged and, according to contemporary opinion, had the merit of achieving a synthesis of the arts. He saw in medieval art a model, not of style, but of intention. Bernard contested the primacy of painting as it had been practised for the preceding three centuries; he advocated a return to crafts, taking the example of the Pont-Aven period: 'Because of its decorative character, Synthetism quickly became a practical art ... we created tapestry, sculpture, stained glass, illustration, and wood, copper and zinc engraving ... Vollard soon became the patron of these pursuits.'[9] (Maillol practised weaving before sculpture.) Bernard passed on this commitment to crafts as an integrating force in the arts, as well as the conception of the Gothic cathedral as an artistic 'model', to some of the Nabis, particularly Maurice Denis and Charles Filiger.

These ideas, which were circulating at the end of the nineteenth century, came together in the Créteil Abbey Group, led by Albert Gleizes and active between 1906 and 1908. The Gothic cathedral theme was taken up as one of the principal motifs of the Weimar Bauhaus. In fact, it was the subject of a woodcut that appeared on the cover of the first Bauhaus manifesto in 1919. The woodcut was the work of Lionel Feininger, who had visited Paris several times between 1907 and 1911 and knew Gleizes's work. The extent to which Gauguin's and Bernard's ideas in artistic matters remained complementary, regardless of their differences in personality, was made evident by their mutual wide-ranging influence on such subsequent generations of artists.

Chapter VI   A Stormy Alliance

Upon returning from Martinique in November of 1887, Gauguin renewed his contacts in Paris, in particular with Bernard and the Van Gogh brothers. Like Gauguin, Vincent Van Gogh had had a rather late start as a painter, first moving and changing occupations several times: he started out as a picture dealer in The Hague, London and Paris, became a tutor in two English schools, and then trained and worked as a missionary in Belgium. He eventually rejoined his brother Theo, who had settled in Paris and was working for the Boussod and Valadon Gallery. The brothers moved in avant-garde circles, and in about 1886 they met Gauguin, Bernard and Père Tanguy, the picturesque colour-grinder who exhibited works of little-known artists in his shop. In fact, for a long time Tanguy's was the only place in Paris where one could see paintings by Cézanne. In January 1888, Theo Van Gogh, who was by then director of the Montmartre branch of Boussod and Valadon, took in paintings and ceramic works by Gauguin on consignment.[1] This marked the beginning of one of the most famous and dramatic relationships ever to exist between two painters. Vincent had already abandoned the realistic subject-matter of his early period, with its sombre colours and stark images that descended directly from the Hague School and the work of Jean-François Millet. After a brief stay at Cormon's studio, he discovered Impressionism via Pissarro and Signac. He lightened his palette, added silvery shades, and adopted a less heavy-handed technique along with Impressionist-inspired motifs. He even experimented briefly with divisionism.

In a matter of months, Van Gogh covered the same artistic itinerary that Gauguin had taken ten long years to complete. Both had clear-headedly assimilated the teachings of Impressionism, though they understood very well that by 1888 the movement was already a thing of the past. Monet and Renoir were questioning their approach to art; Cézanne and Seurat, each in his own way, had struck out on new paths. Gauguin's landscapes from Martinique, with their brilliant colours and clearly outlined forms, reveal a carefully constructed, new style. As for Van Gogh's works from the winter of 1887-8, they have much in common with his strongly graphic early works. Sometimes the approach to perspective is straightforward and traditional; sometimes the picture plane is compressed. Even before leaving Paris for Provence, Van Gogh was replacing the delicate, watercolour-like tones of his earlier palette with strong colours, applied with long, clearly defined brushstrokes. Two portraits, one of Père Tanguy (Private Collection and Musée Rodin) and the other of an Italian cabaret owner, *La Segatori* (Musée d'Orsay), were painted while he was still in Paris.

Gauguin stayed only three months in Paris before setting out for Pont-Aven in late January or early February 1888. Only weeks later Van Gogh left Paris as well, but in the opposite direction, towards Arles. They were both seeking a more frugal lifestyle than could be found in Paris, as well as more favourable working conditions. Van Gogh chose 'the equivalent of Japan, the South' (quoted from a letter of 4 or 5 June 1888),[2] while Gauguin opted once again for

65 *Landscape near Arles*. 1888. Oil on canvas, 72 × 92 cm.
Nationalmuseum, Stockholm

66 *Van Gogh Painting Sunflowers*. 1888. Oil on canvas, 73 × 91 cm. Rijksmuseum Vincent Van Gogh, Amsterdam

Brittany, explaining in a letter to Schuffenecker, dated March 1888: 'You have Paris within you, and I the countryside. I love Brittany. I find primitiveness and wildness here. When my clogs sound on this granite earth I hear the muffled tone, strong and flat, that I am looking for in painting' (see p. 126). The two artists may originally have considered leaving together. In any case, Van Gogh, suffering greatly from loneliness, soon called on Gauguin to join him. When he learned of Gauguin's dire financial situation, he asked Theo to send each of them a monthly pension in exchange for his own work and one painting by Gauguin each month.

There is something pathetic in Van Gogh's entreaties to his brother and to Gauguin. Until now, historians have tended to emphasize the commercial aspect of the proposition. It is true that Theo had managed to sell a few of the works that Gauguin had left with him, and that Gauguin was tempted by the prospect of a steady monthly income, however modest. Vincent and Theo considered that the two painters could save money by pooling their resources, and that eventually other artists, such as Laval and Bernard, could join them. But the idea of an artists' colony, existing under Theo's patronage, was not born only of financial considerations. It was a shared dream. Bernard Zurcher has observed that 'Gauguin's reply was ambiguous. He agreed on principle, but in fact, he himself was nurturing a plan similar to Vincent's ... no doubt he was a bit jealous of Vincent, who was younger than he—a fact on which he never ceased to harp—trying to establish a "studio in the south" with his brother's money ...'[3]

The correspondence between the two artists reveals considerable hesitation on both sides. Still, Gauguin believed in the importance of collaboration. As if to justify his decision, he called up an image from his sailing days, which Vincent carefully relayed to Theo: 'He says that when sailors have to move a heavy load, or weigh anchor, so as to be able to lift a very heavy weight, and to make a huge effort, they all sing together to keep them up to the mark and give them vim. That is just what artists lack!' (quoted from a letter from Gauguin to Van Gogh, referred to by Vincent in a letter to Theo, dated June 1888).[4] But in another letter, this time to Schuffenecker on 16 October 1888, Gauguin coldly appraised Theo's intentions: 'Believe me, as taken as [Theo] Van Gogh is by me, he would not decide to support me in the Midi for the sheer pleasure of it. He has studied the Dutch market and means to push our work exclusively, and as hard as he can.' Vincent redoubled his arguments, but then, faced with Gauguin's hesitation, pulled back. As for Gauguin, he countered that he could not leave Pont-Aven before settling his debts. Vincent's letters appear warm and sincere alongside Gauguin's cold, business-like replies. In fact, the friendship they had struck up in Paris—little known to us for lack of written documents—had probably not gone beyond exchanging ideas on art in cafés or artists' studios. Gauguin may have sensed that, given Vincent's unyielding, violent personality, living together could only lead to disaster.

Gauguin's hesitation may also have had an artistic—and psychological—basis. In the past, he had been quite willing to collaborate with other artists; but as an artist he needed to preserve his originality and his ego. As it happened, he was in a period of intense research. His work had been enriched by the vision of Martinique's landscapes. Upon his return to Paris, he had found a fomenting atmosphere in which young and mature artists alike were exploring new territory. He was lucid enough to sense Van Gogh's power of invention. The portrait of *La Segatori*, for example, attests to a phenomenal capacity for originality, not only with relation to academic norms, but also to the work of Lautrec, Degas and Seurat. Gauguin may well have found the magnitude of this talent disturbing. Eager to protect himself, he—perhaps subconsciously—set out to assert himself, first in the Parisian milieu, then with regard to Van Gogh. He may well have felt safer in Brittany, surrounded by young artists he could dominate, than venturing on to new ground in Provence. The spring and summer months of 1888 in Pont-Aven were perhaps the most decisive of Gauguin's entire career:

67 *Self-Portrait—'Les Misérables'*. 1888. Oil on canvas,
45 × 55 cm. Rijksmuseum Vincent Van Gogh, Amsterdam

it was then that he developed—not effortlessly, but with determination—his own unique style; *Vision after the Sermon* constituted the flowering of that maturation process. It was also at that time that he became a 'master', dictating to young Paul Sérusier the 'lesson' that Sérusier, in turn, transmitted to a new generation of young Parisian painters, the Nabis (see p. 295). Having thus affirmed both his own convictions and his role as leader, he was free to confront the challenge of being near the inventive, demanding and tumultuous Van Gogh, without feeling either personally or artistically threatened by him.

An incident exemplifying this ambivalence, which also suggests the misunderstandings that followed, relates to Van Gogh's idea of exchanging portraits. At first, Gauguin and Bernard were to pose for one another and send the two paintings to Van Gogh. The idea was to emphasize the cohesion of their work and to take stock of their respective progress. Lonely as he was, Van Gogh must have relished the idea of having his friends near, if only in effigy. But the other two artists did not share his enthusiasm. In September 1888 Gauguin wrote: 'I am looking at little Bernard, and somehow I do not yet have the key to understanding him. I could do the portrait from memory, I suppose, but in any case it would be an abstraction. I don't know, perhaps tomorrow it will come to me, all of a sudden.' Bernard, who until then had barely touched portraiture and was doubtless unsure of himself, also put Van Gogh off. The disappointed Van Gogh discussed Bernard's refusal in a letter to Theo: 'But he says he *dare not* do Gauguin as I asked him, because he feels afraid in front of Gauguin' (September 1888).[5] In the end, each artist painted his own portrait against a plain wall on which appears a rough sketch of the other. Gauguin did not present himself in a flattering light, which led Van Gogh to remark that the picture contained 'not a shadow of gaiety'. He compared the two paintings favourably, though: 'The Gauguin is of course remarkable, but I very much like Bernard's picture. It is just the inner vision of a painter, a few abrupt tones, a few dark lines, but it has the distinction of a real, real Manet. The Gauguin is more studied, carried further ... gave me absolutely the impression of its representing a prisoner.'[6] It is interesting to compare this with an equally outrageous caricature Van Gogh painted of himself.

Gauguin spent only two months with Van Gogh in Arles, and, as we know, their time together ended dramatically. Before that time, the two men had hardly known each other. In addition, Van Gogh had suffered greatly from eight lonely months in Arles, devoid of artistic discussion. His letters reveal his deep need for affection and guidance, as well as his thirst for artistic and intellectual exchanges. On the one hand, he looked to his brother and to Gauguin to

68 *Self-Portrait* by Vincent Van Gogh. 1888. Oil on canvas, 62 × 52 cm. Fogg Art Museum, Harvard University, Cambridge, Massachusetts (Bequest of Maurice Wertheim Collection)

69 *Alyscamps* by Vincent Van Gogh. 1888. Oil on canvas, 73 × 90 cm. Rijksmuseum Kröller-Müller, Otterlo

was convinced that his own work had progressed tremendously since he had left Paris. As soon as Gauguin saw Vincent's recent canvases, he understood how much further his colleague had gone in what had been shared territory before Arles: flat areas of colour, in strong unnaturalistic shades, boldly outlined, or sometimes almost caricatured forms, and compositions that were at times conventional, at times astonishingly innovative. If Gauguin feigned indifference it was in keeping with his persona. Later, when he wrote in *Avant et après* that at Arles Van Gogh was still bogged down by the precepts of Impressionism, he was betraying both his intellectual integrity and his memory: 'At the time when I arrived in Arles, Vincent was in the full current of the Neo-Impressionist school, and was floundering about a

help fill that emotional and intellectual void, but on the other, he was touchy and very conscious of the originality of his work. His tendency to excessiveness was heightened by undernourishment and the effects of alcohol. At first, he greeted Gauguin warmly, although his visitor responded to his overtures with irritation, repeating one of Cézanne's pet phrases: '[they're] trying to collar me'. Furthermore, to Van Gogh's disappointment, Gauguin was unimpressed with the Provençal landscape, comparing the light and vegetation unfavourably with those of the Tropics. In January 1889 Vincent reported to Theo that Gauguin had declared Arles the foulest place in the Midi. Not long before that, in 1887, Signac had written to Pissarro: 'No, I am not carried away by this place...' [7] Twenty years later, Maurice de Vlaminck, who painted his most violent Fauvist landscapes on the shores of the Seine, noted ironically that he was most at ease working in the Midi when the light resembled that of the Ile-de-France.

Gauguin had come to Provence somewhat grudgingly, on account of the insistence of the Van Goghs, to whom he felt obliged, and also because he was tired of Brittany. He imagined himself teaching Vincent, not being taught by him. However, Vincent

70 *Café Terrace at Night* by Vincent Van Gogh. 1888. Oil on canvas, 81 × 65.5 cm. Rijksmuseum Kröller-Müller, Otterlo

107

71 *Alyscamps*. 1888. Oil on canvas, 92 × 73 cm. Musée d'Orsay, Paris

72 *At the Café* (*Madame Ginoux*). 1888. Oil on canvas, 73 × 92 cm. Pushkin Museum, Moscow

week. It may be somewhat arbitrary to speak of an isolated 'Arles period'; however, as Bernard Zurcher has pointed out, ' ... the two artists settled down to a sort of "pictorial duel", canvas against canvas, on similar though not identical subjects.'[9] Van Gogh worked several times at Alyscamps, the famous old cemetery at Arles, which Maurice Barrès used in *Le Jardin de Bérénice* as the setting of the heroes' promenades. Twice Van Gogh organized the pictorial surface so that the borders of the path, seen from above, disappear diagonally, while the tree trunks, interrupted by the two edges of the canvas, scan the canvas with their blue vertical lines. These parallel trunks constitute a sort of grill, separating the viewer—or perhaps the painter—from that serene place at the end of the path. The raised perspective, arbitrary choice of colours, and absence of shadows are direct references to Japanese prints. For his own *Alyscamps*, Gauguin chose a more banal point of view in the path's axis, and a more conventional approach to the composition: three women in traditional costume appear in the centre of the picture, which also contains a profusion of partially yellowing vegetation, and in the background is the steeple of the church of Saint-Honorat. The strong, yet subdued colours, the open lines with their soft curves, and the large expanse of silvery sky create a climate very different from the one in Van Gogh's painting. However, Gauguin's treatment of this theme brings to mind another of Van Gogh's pictures, *Café Terrace at Night*, done a few weeks before Gauguin's arrival but certainly known to him. In both these pictures, the basic composition, format, and use of a central vanishing point are nearly identical. In fact, Gauguin's painting might be seen as a response, even a contradiction, whether conscious or not, to the *Café Terrace*. Alluding to the novel by Guy de Maupassant, Vincent wrote to his sister in early September 1888: 'the beginning of *Bel Ami* happens to be a description of a starlit night in Paris with the brightly lighted cafés of the Boulevard, and this is approximately the same subject I have just painted.'[10] Elsewhere, in a letter to Theo of Septem-

[margin: 69, 71, 70]

73 *L'Arlésienne* by Vincent Van Gogh. 1888. Oil on canvas, 65 × 49 cm. Rijksmuseum Kröller-Müller, Otterlo

good deal and suffering as a result of it; not because this school, like all schools, was bad, but because it did not correspond to his nature, which was far from patient and so independent. With all these yellows and violets, all this work in complementary colours—a disordered body of work—he accomplished nothing but the mildest of incomplete and monotonous harmonies. The sound of the bugle was missing from them.'[8]

Only about a dozen paintings by Gauguin from Arles are known to us, and this seems a logical number, given what we know about his pace. Van Gogh, on the other hand, completed five or six canvases per ber 1888, Van Gogh explained his intentions in painting the café: 'I have tried to express the idea that the café is a place where one can ruin oneself, go mad or commit a crime.'[11]

Element for element, Gauguin's picture of a typical outing in a calm, country garden, dominated by a church, constitutes the antithesis of Van Gogh's night world, with its unwholesome distractions and the disastrous destiny they portend for its victims. The contrast can also be seen in the two artists' methods. In the same letter to his sister, Van Gogh wrote: 'It amuses me enormously to paint the night right on the spot. They used to draw and paint the picture in the daytime after the rough sketch. But I find satisfaction in painting things immediately.'[12] This painting, done from life, emphasizes another important difference in approach: Van Gogh painted only what he saw, whereas Gauguin, while greatly stimulated by his environment and much inclined to use models (whom he sometimes mentioned in his correspondence), tended instead to recompose, embellish, and generally transform his images. At Arles, Van Gogh was greatly influenced by Gauguin, and tried to adopt his style. In November 1888, he wrote to Theo: 'I am going to set myself to work from memory often, and the canvases from memory are always less awkward, and have a more artistic look than studies from nature, especially when one works in mistral weather.'[13] Until then, Van Gogh had retained the Impressionist method; and such a reversal opened new horizons for him. In another letter, also dated November 1888, he spoke of drawing a garden 'as in a dream'. After Gauguin's departure, Van Gogh returned to his own, highly personal dialogue with reality, as described in a letter to Bernard: 'As you know, once or twice, while Gauguin was in Arles, I gave myself free rein with abstractions, for instance in the "Woman Rocking", in the "Woman Reading a Novel", black in a yellow library; and at the time abstraction seemed a charming path. But it is enchanted ground, old man, and one soon finds oneself up against a stone wall.'[14] Nothing could describe more aptly the whole of Van Gogh's paint-

74 *L'Arlésienne (Madame Ginoux)*. 1888. Coloured crayons and charcoal, with white chalk highlighting, 56.1 × 49.2 cm. Fine Arts Museum of San Francisco (Achenbach Foundation for Graphic Arts, gift of Dr. T. Edward and Mrs Tallah Hanley)

ing. The world of dreams and enchantment was cruelly closed to him; in order to create he needed hard reality before his eyes, or in his hands. Gauguin's world, on the other hand, was an imaginary one. This is the context in which they used the word abstraction, which appears repeatedly in their correspondence; non-figurative art was still a few years down the road, even if seeds of it can already be discerned in these two artists' experiments.

The differences between the two artists' methods were also reflected in their tastes in art. In late November 1888, Gauguin wrote to Bernard: 'Vincent and I rarely see eye to eye, especially in regard to painting. He admires Daumier, Daubigny, Ziem and the great [Théodore] Rousseau, all people whom I cannot bear. On the other hand, he detests Ingres,

Raphael, Degas, all of whom I admire. I always tell him he's right, just to keep the peace. He likes my work very much; but each time I do a painting, he finds one or another thing wrong with it.' We can well imagine the tone of their discussions: Van Gogh, ever a perfectionist, unreservedly expressing his opinions; Gauguin, smouldering, but side-stepping an opinion he did not share, to avoid unnecessary quarrelling. Nevertheless, their choice of objects of admiration is revealing: Van Gogh leaned towards observers—realists—while Gauguin preferred painters whose personal style predominated over faithful representation. A visit to the Musée Fabre in Montpellier, which was rich in important works by painters of the preceding generation—Delacroix, Courbet, and the Barbizon group—provoked renewed discussion.

A concrete example of this fundamental difference in the two artists' methods is provided by their two 73 portraits of Madame Ginoux, the brothel-keeper. Van Gogh finished his painting in three quarters of an hour, while Gauguin had scarcely finished a sketch. However, Van Gogh's picture shows an attempt to assimilate Gauguin's *cloisonnisme*. As for Gauguin's 72 painting, *At the Café*, it superimposes Madame Ginoux's portrait on a depiction of the interior of a café which was inspired by a picture by Van Gogh. Van Gogh later used Gauguin's sketch for this portrait in doing his own, which, according to his custom, he placed against a solid background. The following year, Gauguin wrote to him: 'I saw the painting of Madame Ginoux, very beautiful and curious. I like it better than my drawing. Despite your illness, you have never worked with such lucidity.' Whether Van Gogh considered this an unalloyed compliment 75 is not clear. In another picture, *Landscape near Arles*, it was Gauguin who adopted Van Gogh's flamboyant palette. This painting creates a startling first impression. A closer look reveals that the shapes in

the foreground are somewhat vague, while the overlapping planes and tight play of vertical and horizontal lines in the background suggest the influence of Cézanne. Gauguin was in full possession of his powers here. Robert Goldwater affirms that '... this picture is exceptional—and important. It makes us realize that Gauguin, for all his fierce independence of character and style, was an artist who, without copying, understood and absorbed what he needed from the work of the great men around him.'[15]

The artistic confrontation between Gauguin and Van Gogh at Arles is also manifest in two important works: Gauguin's *Old Women of Arles*, and Van 76 Gogh's *Promenade at Arles—Souvenir of the* 77 *Garden at Etten*. Most historians consider that Van Gogh's picture derived from Gauguin's, as evidenced by the off-centre focal point, formed in both cases by the figures of two women placed far to the canvas's left side. But, while Van Gogh's painting is treated with small, light brushstrokes, Gauguin's stark drawing and colour scheme could be seen as a concession to his colleague's style. Thus, the question of precedence must be left in abeyance.

Not since *Vision after the Sermon* had Gauguin so 50 strongly stylized a painting, using strong colours, compressed perspective and caricatured forms. To look for 'sources' or traces of the influence of others on this picture is pointless. Gauguin's capacity for innovation was very much a part of him, even if it was further stimulated by his rivalry with Van Gogh. This picture can almost be seen as an exercise in style, with its multiplication of triangular shapes, the path tilting up at the left, like a toboggan, and the park bench seen from above, plunging down sharply. Until then neither Degas nor Cézanne had so completely abandoned the traditional approach to perspective, as dictated by Alberti. Such a sharp departure from that convention had, thus far, only been seen in caricature drawing—and even that genre had, in 1888, not yet attained the level of simplification it would in later years, thanks to the work of Gauguin, as well as that of Henri-Gustave Jossot, Ostoya and Juan Gris. This picture also contains the seeds of

75 *Landscape near Arles*. 1888. Oil on canvas, 91 × 72 cm. Indianapolis Museum of Art

76 *Old Women of Arles*. 1888. Oil on canvas, 93 × 72 cm. Art Institute of Chicago (Mr and Mrs Lewis L. Coburn Memorial Collection)

77 *Promenade at Arles—Souvenir of the Garden at Etten* by
Vincent Van Gogh. 1888. Oil on canvas, 73 × 92 cm. Hermitage,
Leningrad

Toulouse-Lautrec's posters. Gauguin especially liked this work, and made a print of it.

The persistent tackling of similar themes could only deepen the feeling of rivalry between two such unyielding personalities. Their interweaving experiments brought out their differences more than their affinities. The tension between them increased; despite Vincent's protests, Gauguin resolved to leave. Gauguin's much later description of the drama that ensued—so often recounted—was for a long time the sole known account. [16] He wrote, in *Avant et après*, that Van Gogh had tried to kill him. On 23 December 1888 the crazed artist purportedly tried to attack Gauguin with an open razor in his hand; then, rebuffed, he severed his own ear and gave it to a prostitute. His fragile mental state, aggravated by drinking and undernourishment, had been further weakened by the preceding two months of intense artistic activity. Ultimately, his fear of being abandoned by Gauguin, and by his brother, who had recently informed him that he was engaged to be married, precipitated the crisis. Gauguin's previous decision to return to Paris was only reinforced by the incident.

Gauguin was at Le Pouldu when he learned of Van Gogh's suicide on 27 July 1890. He immediately wrote a cordial note to Theo, but otherwise did not appear especially affected by the news. He had abandoned the idea of taking Vincent with him to the Tropics some time earlier. Theo, however, had not forgotten the idea, and telegraphed Gauguin in Brittany: 'Departure assured for Tropics, money follows, Theo, Director.' When the money failed to arrive, Gauguin at first suspected a farce, but he soon understood that Theo, too, was mentally deranged. In fact, he died several months later on 21 January 1891; and Gauguin certainly regretted the loss of this man who had managed several of his rare commercial successes. Although Gauguin opposed the idea, Vincent's old friends resolved to carry out Theo's dream of organizing a major retrospective of Van Gogh's work. The project resulted in only a modest show at the 1891 Salon des Indépendants. It was during this Salon that Seurat died violently of diphtheria. We have no record of any reaction on Gauguin's part, but it is known that the two men had little sympathy for each other, and in addition, Gauguin was in the midst of preparing for his departure.

Chapter VII   The Artist at Work

While not admitting any responsibility for the break with Van Gogh, Gauguin nevertheless found himself in very low spirits when he returned to Paris. Without a home of his own, he had recourse, yet again, to the hospitality of the more or less willing Schuffenecker. But the arrangement was not only for financial reasons; he needed the company of another painter, preferably a receptive one.

While still in Arles, he had received an invitation to participate in an upcoming exhibition of the XX group in Brussels. Since 1884, this group, headed by the lawyer and art critic Octave Maus, had organized exhibitions, accompanied by concerts and literary discussions. The academicism of the official institutions imposed the same artistic constraints in Belgium as in France; it was also in 1884, only months after the creation of the XX group, that the Salon des Indépendants was founded in Paris. Most non-academic artists, especially the Impressionists and Neo-Impressionists, were invited to the XX's events, where compositions by Gabriel Fauré, Vincent d'Indy and Johann Sebastian Bach were performed. Members of the XX were well informed of the latest artistic developments in the Parisian avant-garde world, and, as early as 1890, they offered Cézanne one of his rare opportunities to exhibit his works in public.

The unfortunate experience in Arles, which had dashed all hopes for the creation of a 'studio of the south', may have pushed Gauguin to seek consolation in Brussels. However, because the participants included older artists such as Pissarro and Monet, as well as the principals of Neo-Impressionism—Seurat, Signac and Henri Cross—with whom Gauguin had broken off previously good relations, he had no illusions of being considered the leader of the Parisian group. In the end, he was unable to go to Brussels for lack of money, and, while he may have hoped to receive favourable critical reviews, his paintings were in fact poorly received there.

During his brief stay in Paris, Gauguin produced only one important work, the *Portrait of the Schuffenecker Family*, as well as some ceramic works. He 55 soon decided to return to Pont-Aven to rejoin his friend Meyer de Haan. Paul Sérusier, who had been fascinated by Gauguin's teaching during his first visit to Pont-Aven in September 1888, and had brought back the famous *Talisman*, decided to seek him out 209 again, first at Pont-Aven, then at Le Pouldu. Although Sérusier borrowed certain stylistic characteristics 80 from Gauguin, the symbolist and mystical connotations of his work are quite distinct from Gauguin's.

Gauguin's thoughts now turned again to Paris, where the Exposition Universelle, the major cultural event of its time, was being organized. There was no chance of being included in an official show, although the critic Roger Marx had managed to introduce a few Impressionist works in an exhibition entitled 'A Centennial of French Art'. As it turned out, chance and Schuffenecker's enterprising spirit combined to allow Gauguin to exhibit several works inside the fair and, perhaps more importantly for him, to establish a public image as the leader of the group.

78 *Haymaking*. 1889. Oil on canvas, 92 × 73 cm. Courtauld Institute Galleries, London

79 *Two Breton Girls by the Sea*. 1889. Oil on canvas,
92.5 × 73.6 cm. National Museum of Western Art, Tokyo

80 *The Barrier* by Paul Sérusier. 1890. Oil on canvas, 50 × 62 cm. Musée d'Orsay, Paris

A buffet-restaurant had been set up in the exterior galleries of the Palais des Beaux-Arts. It was surely not by coincidence that Schuffenecker arranged to meet the manager of the café who also ran the Café Riche, a meeting place for boulevard painters. According to an account given by Théodore Duret, Gustave Caillebotte had organized monthly dinners there, which

81 *Breton Man and Woman* by Charles Laval. 1888. Oil on canvas, 38 × 48 cm. Josefowitz Collection

he called the Impressionist Dinners.[1] For some unknown reason, probably financial, the mirrors that the proprietor had intended for mural decorations in the main dining room never materialized. Schuffenecker persuaded Volpini simply to cover the walls with fabric and allow him and his friends to hang their paintings there. Gauguin was still in Pont-Aven when Schuffenecker wrote to him with the good news. He promptly replied: 'Bravo! You have succeeded. Go and see Theo Van Gogh and arrange things until the end of my stay. But remember that this is not an exhibition for the *others*. Let us arrange to have this for a small group of friends and, in this context, I would like to be represented by as many works as possible. Therefore, please make sure that everything is done with my best interest in mind, according to the amount of space available.'

Gauguin's first projected list of participants looked like this:

'Schuffenecker . . . . . 10 paintings
Guillaumin . . . . 10 »
Gauguin . . . . 10 »   40 paintings
Bernard . . . . 10 »

Roy . . . . 2 »
The man from Nancy 2 »   10 paintings
Vincent . . . . 6 »
_____
50 paintings'

The 'man from Nancy', Léon Fauché, and Louis Roy were two young artists whom Gauguin had just met, and won over, at Pont-Aven. 'Vincent' referred, of course, to Van Gogh. Theo Van Gogh, who kept his brother's work during his stay in the Midi, refused to contribute anything without even consulting Vincent. Although Vincent subsequently supported Theo's decision, his letter was not without a note of regret. The final list of participants, according to the catalogue, looked like this: Paul Gauguin, Charles Laval, Léon Fauché, Emile Schuffenecker, Louis Anquetin, Georges Daniel, Emile Bernard, Louis Roy and Ludovic Nemo (Bernard's pseudonym). Guillaumin had disappeared from the original list, probably

82 *Still-Life with Japanese Print*. 1889. Oil on canvas, 72.4 × 93.7 cm. Tehran Museum of Contemporary Art

because he was thought to be too close to the Impressionists. At the same time, a place was made for the loyal Charles Laval, as well as for Daniel de Monfreid, a young painter who, under the name Georges Daniel de Monfreid, was a faithful disciple and devoted friend of Gauguin's, especially after the latter's departure for Oceania. Monfreid concocted his own surname. According to some sources, he was born Georges Daniel in 1850, the son of an American called Read, a director of Tiffany's, and an actress from Perpignan called Caroline Bertrand, whose husband, a certain Jacobi, had conveniently disappeared in Latin America.[2] Other sources contend that Daniel's father was Leopold II, king of Belgium. Toulouse-Lautrec may also have exhibited with the group; we only know that he expressed the wish to do so. Although his name is not mentioned in the catalogue, it should be remembered that an exhibition is rarely exactly true to its catalogue, which must inevitably be printed in advance. This catalogue, with its eight reproductions, was exceptionally large and luxurious for its time.

Although it was a group exhibition, the dominant character was clearly Gauguin. It was the first time he had presented such a large group of works in public. He had selected fifteen paintings, one pastel and one watercolour, and was the only participant to have two reproductions in the catalogue. With the exception of one work from Martinique, *Mangos*, all the paintings shown were done in Brittany or Arles. He did not include any earlier works in which his technique still showed traces of Impressionism. Besides Gauguin, the other best represented artists were Schuffenecker who, after all, had originated the whole project, and Emile Bernard, one of whose two works was presented under his pseudonym, Ludovic Nemo.

The catalogue also contained this mention: 'Visible upon request: Album of Lithographs by Paul Gauguin and Emile Bernard.' This album was actually composed of lithographs on zinc, a sheet of zinc being less costly and easier to use than a lithographer's stone. The artists' intentions were doubtless to earn a bit of money with the sale of the album, but their motivations were artistic as well. Gauguin based his prints on existing works—mostly of women from Martinique and from Arles, and of Breton scenes—as if seeking to distribute representative samples of his current work. However, his choice of themes for the album was uncharacteristically domestic—most of them portrayed women in situations with sentimental connotations. The titles of the prints, often inscribed on the plate, reinforced this orientation; one of them, *Human Misery*, would be appropriate for the whole album. Another especially evocative title, *Dramas of the Sea*, appears twice: the first example is a print depicting three Breton women standing atop a cliff overlooking a stormy sea. Their bearing denotes prayer and lamentation, a common theme in traditional Breton painting. The other print of the same name refers to an episode in Edgar Allen Poe's *Descent into the Maelstrom*, Baudelaire's translation of which had been published in 1856. In this print, depicting two brothers in distress, the composition is curiously inscribed within the shape of an inverted fan. Perhaps in creating this print Gauguin had in mind one of Victor Hugo's most famous poems, *Oceano Nox*:

> *Où sont-ils les marins tombés dans les nuits noires?*
> *O flots! Que vous savez de lugubres histoires!*
> *Flots profonds! redoutés des mères à genoux!*

(Where are those sailors, fallen in dark nights? O waves! What dismal stories you know! Deep waves! Dreaded by kneeling mothers!)

It is difficult to judge the full extent of the show's success, and its repercussions. Its title, 'Groupe Impressionniste et Synthétiste', was certainly intriguing. To describe an exhibition as Impressionist in 1889 was still cause for suspicion; as for the word 'Synthétiste', it was familiar only to a few initiates. There were some favourable reviews. But Félix Fénéon, who had already shown interest in Gauguin—particularly in his ceramic work—was

38

hesitant; he even went so far as to challenge Bernard and Laval outright to free themselves 'from this painter whose work is too arbitrary or at least the result of such a particular frame of mind that newcomers can hardly use it as their starting point'.[3] Fénéon was usually more perceptive in his observations. In fact, contrary to his admonition, many young painters found a useful 'starting point' in Gauguin's work. Fénéon also commented on Gauguin's artistic debts: 'It is likely that the manner of Anquetin, with its impenetrable contours and flat and intense tones, was not without some influence upon Paul Gauguin; but this influence is of a purely formal nature, for it seems that not the slightest sensation inhabits these intelligent and decorative works.'[4] In this regard, John Rewald has remarked that 'Gauguin, who did not know Anquetin, never forgave Fénéon for this statement, although the critic, while wrong in fact, was right at least insofar as Anquetin's *cloisonniste* style was perfectly known to Gauguin through Anquetin's co-cloisonnist Bernard.'[5] Gauguin was considered the leader of the group, and despite the show's commercial failure, he was consoled by the fact that his revolutionary principles were now being adopted by a growing number of young artists.

Another well-known critic, Albert Aurier, had little to say about individual works in the show, but commented favourably on 'this interesting undertaking'. Fénéon went on: 'Fortunately, I have been informed that individual initiative has just attempted that which administrative idiocy, forever incurable, would never have consented to undertake. A small group of independent artists succeeded in forcing their way, not into the Palais des Beaux-Arts itself, but into the fair, and in creating a tiny rival of the official exhibition. Oh! The installation is a bit primitive, very bizarre and, as everyone will doubtless comment, bohemian!... But what can you expect? If those poor devils had had a palace at their disposal, they certainly would not have hung their pictures on the walls of a restaurant!'[6]

Before leaving again for Brittany, the place that clearly represented a refuge for this uprooted artist in search of himself, Gauguin wrote articles on the Exposition Universelle. These were his first printed texts, appearing in a number of small magazines, including *Le Moderniste illustré*, on 4 and 6 July 1889. In them, Gauguin discussed the fair in general and, specifically, the Fine Arts Pavilion. His writing style already contained that very particular combination of polemical verve and personal reflection that characterized his subsequent, longer works, *Avant et après* and *Noa Noa*. The articles discussed such diverse subjects as the Musée de Cluny ('At the Cluny we can see wooden sculpture, faïence, curios etc... marvels'), and steel architecture, particularly the Eiffel Tower, which Gauguin defended against the

83 Profane sculpture of the sixteenth century (?). Chapel of Tremalo near Pont-Aven

84 *The Yellow Christ*. 1889. Oil on canvas, 92 × 73 cm. Albright-
Knox Art Gallery, Buffalo (General purchase funds, 1946)

85 *Breton Calvary—Green Christ*. 1889. Oil on canvas,
92 × 73 cm. Musées Royaux des Beaux-Arts, Brussels

virulent attacks of even the most independent spirits, such as Huysmans and Verlaine. Anticipating twentieth-century tastes, he argued that metallic constructions were intrinsically beautiful, and that they did not need to hide their structures and true appearance beneath exterior decoration. He reaffirmed his interest in ceramics which 'is not a futile exercise'. He attacked the tyranny of academic art, asserting that 'the Musée du Luxembourg is a dishonour for France'. Further, he solemnly denounced the official attitude toward independent art, 'which official painters follow with an anxious eye, and which discerning people, thirsty for pure, real art, look at with interest. All of twentieth-century art will derive from them. And you, Messieurs of the Institute, wish to pass over them in silence. We would have liked to see a separate section at the Exposition for independent artists. We are amazed that the government and the City of Paris persist in obeying so slavishly the bidding of Bouguereau and his cronies.' At the time, few people had spoken out so clearly concerning the rejection of living artists by the authorities. Albert Aurier expressed the same idea in slightly less explicit language: 'A small section is lacking in the Palais des Beaux-Arts for the few independent artists who, unknown to or scorned by the public, silent and indifferent to financial gain, recognition and immediate popularity, are working far from the official schools and academies, researching and developing a new kind of art, that will, perhaps, be the art of tomorrow.'[7]

Gauguin left for Pont-Aven, and shortly afterwards for Le Pouldu, a small, remote port already familiar to him from previous visits. The number of painters living and working at Pont-Aven had probably not increased since he first went to live there, but now that Gauguin had become the leading figure in a group of revolutionaries for whom art was the subject of endless discussion, both serious and facetious, he preferred to isolate himself at Le Pouldu with a few of his most faithful disciples.

It was there that he met, quite by accident, the young Parisian writer, André Gide. Although Gide never showed much interest in Gauguin's work, nor in modern painting in general, he later recounted their meeting in *Si le grain ne meurt*.

In Brittany Gauguin found a much-needed land of welcome. The fact that he returned there repeatedly proves its irresistible attraction for him, so succinctly and poetically expressed to Schuffenecker in the letter dating from March 1888, cited earlier, where he spoke of his love of Brittany, and the clumping sound of his clogs that imitated the muted tones he sought in painting. An interesting note about this letter—the original of which has been lost—concerns the transcription of the word *ton* (tone), which was changed by subsequent editors to *son* (sound); although this latter transcription is more logical with regard to the wooden clogs, it would eliminate the allusion to Baudelaire that *ton* evokes.

Gauguin's second stay in Brittany constituted a decisive phase in his artistic career. But it is difficult to determine to what extent the land itself influenced his work. No important works were produced during his first stay there in 1886. *Four Breton Women*, 45 previously thought to have been painted during that time, was almost certainly done between 1886 and 1888. But if, in 1886, Brittany as a unique physical environment had little apparent effect on his work, he did observe and faithfully render many decorative details that were new and exotic to him: the traditional clothes and headdresses, characteristically pointed church steeples, calvaries, and steeply sloping rooftops. He may have made sketches of these details, or simply committed them to memory. It should be remembered that all these picturesque aspects of Brittany were abundantly—and profitably—portrayed in the works of contemporary 'traditionalist' painters. But the impassable gulf that exists between Gauguin's Breton paintings and traditionalist images is not only attributable to differences in style. Gauguin's most important Breton works— *Vision after the Sermon, The Yellow Christ, Breton* 50, 84 *Calvary—Green Christ* and *La Belle Angèle*—have a 85, 53 sacred significance that none of Dagnan-Bouveret's or Jules Breton's praying figures possesses. Gauguin had little interest in facile indications of the sacred, such as hands joined in prayer, or burning candles. Instead, he invented new symbols. In the particular 79 instance of *Little Breton Girls by the Sea* (National Museum of Western Art, Tokyo), a nuance of pathos emanates from the girls' faces, one of whom appears to be mentally deficient. Another mentally handicapped character appears in *Human Misery*, as well as in other works, both from Arles and from Brittany.

Ironically, it was Gauguin's image of Brittany, created at the end of the nineteenth century, that ultimately entered into the collective unconscious, to such an extent that today it is exploited by local tourist agencies. But to say that Gauguin had explored the deeper mysteries of the Celtic soul would be an exaggeration. He reserved that effort for the Polynesian civilization, an image of which he managed to project as more real—at least more acceptable—than European life.

Gauguin's interest in Brittany was genuine, deep and respectful. The character of Bécassine, the ridiculous, feeble-minded young Breton created in 1905 by Joseph Pinchon was simply a distortion of Gauguin's figures. Still, the artist's interest in Brittany was transient. He adapted the visual and spiritual environment of Pont-Aven to his needs, and then moved on. For each of his departures from Pont-Aven there were specific, circumstantial causes. But the underlying reason was two-fold: first, he required regular artistic nourishment from the Parisian culture; and second, once the initial novelty wore off, Brittany was not a sufficiently exotic environment to spark his creativity. After all, for someone who had known Peru, Algeria and Martinique, the Breton landscape could hardly seem substantially different from that of the Ile-de-France: both the rural lifestyle and the religious customs were the same. Furthermore, Gauguin was certainly not attracted by the conservatism of the Bretons, nor by the climate. He needed a more drastic change of scenery—both visual and cultural.

Gauguin's earliest works contain no specific references to the aesthetics of Japanese prints. These, and other visual arts from Japan, became known to the West around the middle of the nineteenth century. But at that time, because the Oriental style of representation was too far removed from Alberti's sacrosanct principles of perspective, few artists had taken them seriously. Only after 1860, with the work of Manet, Whistler and Bracquemond, did the first real interest in *japonisme* develop. This rise in interest corresponded both to the arrival in Europe of a wave of prints and objects from Japan, following the 1858 opening of Japanese ports to Western ships, and to the challenging, by Western artists, of traditional rules governing the creation of pictorial space. In short, those Japanese 'models' arrived just at the right time.

When, after 1885, Gauguin began collecting Japanese prints—he hung them on the walls of his studios and pasted a few into the manuscript of *Noa Noa*—Japanese prints had already been in vogue for more than twenty years. Artists such as Gauguin, Anquetin, Toulouse-Lautrec, Van Gogh, Lucien Pissarro, Bernard and, later, Bonnard constituted a second generation of artists who acquired a taste for things Japanese. Opportunities to see Japanese prints were plentiful; the principal dealers who handled them, S. Bing and Mayashi, were constantly renewing their stock. In 1888 Bing published the influential book *Le Japon artistique*.

For Van Gogh, and probably for Gauguin as well, Japan had two connotations: the first related quite precisely to artistic technique, while the second touched upon the more general realm of myth. For Van Gogh especially, Japan was a country of light and of very special colours, for which the South of France constituted a sort of substitute. We know from his correspondence that he had read *Madame Chrysanthème* by Pierre Loti, *L'Art japonais* by Louis Gonse, and, doubtless, *Les Promenades japonaises* by the Goncourt brothers. He was fascinated by that exotic, far-away country, observing in particular that artists there lived communally; he longed to take up the Japanese practice of exchanging works between painters. Van Gogh incorporated Japanese prints into

86   *Still-Life with Fruit*. 1888. Oil on canvas, 43 × 58 cm. Pushkin
Museum, Moscow

a number of paintings, all of which he dated from his period in Paris, with the exception of the *Self-Portrait with Bandaged Ear*, which was painted in Arles. During his stay in Paris, he also did three known copies of Japanese prints. However, as has been astutely pointed out by Akiko Mabuchi in her remarkable book on Van Gogh and Japan, the 'influence' of Japanese prints on that artist's work was almost exclusively limited to his years in Paris, spilling over very little to his work from Arles.[8]

Gauguin's attitude toward Japanese prints was similar to Van Gogh's; it is likely that the subject came up frequently during their discussions and influenced their reading. Until 1889, Gauguin's response was to insert direct references into some of his pictures: in *Still-Life with Horse's Head* (Private Collection), there is a porcelain figurine and two typical fans,[9] which constitute either cultural references or a sort of private wink, destined for a small group of initiates. In *The Schuffenecker Family* of 1889 as well as in a *Still-life* of the same year (Private Collection), Gauguin used the same device as Manet did in his *Portrait of Zola* (1867), in which a folding screen and Japanese print decorate the room, as if to evoke the artist's and his model's common interest in Japanese art. This sort of referential *japonisme*, also used by Van Gogh in his *Portrait of Père Tanguy with Japanese Prints* (Private Collection, Paris), is reminiscent not only of Japanese art itself, but also of works by Manet and Monet, from the previous twenty years. These two artists, like Gauguin, did not make stylistic transformations of their Japanese 'models', but merely simplified them as dictated by their pictorial format. Van Gogh, on the other hand, transformed the flat surfaces of the prints he depicted in his paintings into bloated, often distorted areas. In later works, Gauguin carried out similar transformations.

Another painting by Gauguin, *The Wave* (Private Collection), was strongly inspired by the famous print by Hokusai, or by Hiroshige's *Whirlpools*, and also recalls Monet's *Views of Belle-Ile*, a series he began in 1886. As for the customary comparison between the motif of Jacob wrestling with the angel, from the painting by the same name, and a print by Hokusai, it is defensible if we admit that Gauguin interpreted his model very freely. Still, Gauguin had clearly seen and analyzed Japanese prints, as evidenced by the following passage from an autumn 1888 letter to Emile Bernard: 'You talk with Laval about shadows and ask me if I disdain them ... in so far as they are an explanation of light, yes. Look closely at the Japanese, who draw admirably, and you will see life outside and in the sun without shadows. They use colour only as combinations of tones and various harmonies, yet give the impression of heat ....' Gauguin himself often eliminated or introduced shadows freely, according to the construction of his picture. In the same letter to Bernard, he defended that precept: 'As shadows are the *trompe l'œil* of the sun, my inclination is to eliminate them. But if a shadow enters your composition as a necessary form, that is altogether different ... Therefore, my dear Bernard, introduce shadows if you consider them useful.'

Japanese prints also made use of flat areas of colour, *cloisonnisme*, an elevated point of view, distorted proportions in the foreground, and diagonal compositions. For our purposes, it is important to consider this art form as one significant influence on Gauguin's work. Medieval stained glass, contemporary popular imagery, Egyptian art, ceramic decoration and Pre-Colombian art also provided him with paths that led beyond Western tradition. In Gauguin's use of Japanese references, as in Van Gogh's, the importance of exoticism should not be underestimated.

The period 1889-90, just before his departure for Tahiti, was marked by important accomplishments. Several of Gauguin's most successful paintings, including *La Belle Angèle*, *The Yellow Christ* and *Breton Calvary—Green Christ*, which is in fact a Pietà, were done during his second stay in Brittany, where he felt comfortable working. These two latter works exemplify the characteristic techniques of this period: strongly marked outlines, flat areas of colour,

129

87   *Still-Life with 'Friend Jacob'*. 1888. Oil on canvas, 27 × 35 cm.
Private Collection, Switzerland

130

88 *Still-Life, Apples, Pear and Ceramic Jug.* 1889. Oil on canvas, 28 × 36 cm. Fogg Art Museum, Harvard University, Cambridge, Massachusetts (Gift of Walter E. Sachs)

a full if somewhat off-centre composition, and strong verticals and horizontals, softened in the lower right part of the canvas by a curved, feminine presence. In *The Yellow Christ*, the crucifix is set against a rural landscape, with hills and rooftops similar to those depicted in other Breton paintings; *Green Christ* is set by the sea, with the horizon placed high on the canvas, leaving only a limited expanse of sky.

In choosing such subject-matter, Gauguin encountered another difficulty, already apparent in *The Schuffenecker Family*. His style gave rise to distortions, sometimes of caricature-like proportions, which could have been shocking in this religious context. But, in fact, there was absolutely no intention of mockery in these, or in any of Gauguin's paintings. He was certainly not a devout Catholic, but his anti-clericalism did not really become apparent until later in life, following his quarrels with the bishop from the Marquesas Islands. But in these pictures, as in *The Vision after the Sermon*, he did not seek to poke fun at the simple yet sincere faith of Breton peasants. These two paintings demonstrate, rather, a kind of timidity in the presence of images of a faith that he could not share, but did indeed respect. Having decided to depict these scenes from the Passion, he hesitated, and then opted for second-degree representation, that is, the representation of a representation. The artist himself hid behind two works of art, two sculptures surrounded by real people who had come to bear witness to their faith. These sculptures have a clumsy, 'primitive' quality that fits well with Gauguin's own style.

Gauguin distinguished his works from the traditional, familiar depictions of the Crucifixion, as well as from the proliferation of pious images in circulation at the time. He may have known the striking *Crucifixions* by Grünewald that Huysmans had recently rediscovered (in 1888) and spoken of so enthusiastically. Gauguin's and Huysmans's paths crossed on more than one occasion.

Gauguin used real models for his two religious images. *The Yellow Christ* was taken from a large wooden polychrome statue in the chapel of Tremalo,

84
83

near Pont-Aven; tradition has it that he had also seen, in the open air, at Pont-Aven, a calvary painted yellow. The artist may well have combined the two images. The Pietà, habitually depicted at the base of large Breton calvaries, was inspired by the one in the village of Nizon, also near Pont-Aven. The importance that Gauguin attached to these two paintings is attested by the existence of several drawings—either studies or souvenirs—and a woodcut. A sketch of the calvary, entitled *Sacred Images*, appears in the manuscript of *Avant et après*, and a copy of the engraving is pasted into *Noa Noa*, on page 182 of that work.

Although these paintings were distinct works originally, they actually constitute a diptych, either in fact or in theory. Their dimensions are identical (92 × 73 cm). In fact, they might be considered to form a triptych with another work, *Christ in the Olive Grove* (Private Collection). This third picture has customarily been considered to be a self-portrait, whose symbolism refers to a handwritten note, presumably by Gauguin, conserved by his admirer, Albert Aurier:

> *Christ*
> *Douleur spéciale de trahison s'appliquant à Jésus*
> *aujourd'hui*
> *et demain*
> *petit groupe explicatif*
> *le tout sobre harmonie*
> *Couleur sombre et rouge surnaturel.*

('Christ, Special suffering for treason applied to Jesus today and tomorrow small explanatory group everything sober harmony Sombre colour and supernatural red.')

Gauguin, the prophet of a new kind of art, abandoned by his own people, identified with Christ sacrificing himself for his mission, portraying him looking anguished in the olive grove. Shortly afterwards, he painted another self-portrait in which he superimposed his own image on one of the *Yellow*

52

Christ; at the right of the picture he inserted a Peruvian idol, as a reminder of his other spiritual roots.

In 1889 he had already painted a self-portrait in 98 which he portrayed himself as sacred. This picture was painted directly on a panel in the dining room of Marie Henry's inn, at Le Pouldu, and shows Gauguin with a halo above his head. He further beatified himself by painting a somewhat satanic portrait of his friend and rival Meyer de Haan on an adjacent panel.

In 1896, Gauguin completed a new self-portrait, 162 subtitled *nearing Golgotha*. At this time the rejection by his Parisian 'friends' was affecting him greatly. It was difficult to express an assimilation more clearly. Behind his façade of the mocking painter, Gauguin was convinced of the loftiness of his mission and the sacrifices it imposed. His childhood memories of catechism were enhanced—or, rather, subsumed—by the mystical, theosophical ideas, tinged with occultism, that were circulating at the time and had captured the imaginations of several of his close associates, in particular Filiger and Sérusier.

Several works from 1888-91 demonstrate once again to what extent Gauguin analyzed and made use of Cézanne's style, which Gauguin was one of the first to discover. It should be remembered that, until his first exhibition at Vollard's in 1895, Cézanne's work circulated confidentially, and could only be seen at Père Tanguy's shop. Maurice Denis confirmed that fact: 'The author of these pages confesses that, in about 1890, when he first began visiting Tanguy's shop, he thought of Cézanne as a myth, or perhaps even the pseudonym of an artist specializing in other fields, and that he even doubted his existence.'[10]

88 *Still-Life, Apples, Pears and Ceramic Jug* is a true pastiche of a work by Cézanne, with its colourful, thickly-painted fruit, painted in a style quite unusual for Gauguin. The crockery is painted a lovely light 86 blue; the outlines are undistorted. But another *Still-Life with Fruit*, dedicated to Charles Laval ('à mon ami Laval, P. G., 88') contains some distortion, and a slight tilting of the picture plane. Gauguin's debt to Cézanne is even more evident in yet another still-life,

89 *Still-Life with Three Puppies*. 1888. Oil on canvas, 91.8 × 62.6 cm. Museum of Modern Art, New York (Mrs Simon Guggenheim Fund)

Flowers and a Bowl of Fruit on a Table (Museum of Fine Arts, Boston). Here the splitting up of the background into vertical zones is unusual for Gauguin, who habitually preferred to divide canvases horizontally. The painter has managed to bring together, in the background, light blue, rose, dark green and yellow. The distortion of the cup and the fruit at the right, the way in which the table-top tilts forward to coincide with the picture plane, the fact that certain objects project shadows while others do not, all

90 *Still-Life Fête Gloanec*. 1888. Oil on canvas, 38 × 53 cm. Musée des Beaux-Arts, Orléans

91 *Portrait of a Seated Woman*. 1890. Oil on canvas, 65 × 55 cm. Art Institute of Chicago (Joseph Winterbotham)

92   *Still-Life with Fruit Bowl, Glass and Apples* by Paul Cézanne.
c. 1875. Oil on canvas, 46 × 55 cm. Private Collection. Gauguin put
this painting, which belonged to him, behind Marie Derain, but
enlarged it, in doing her portrait (pl. 91)

attest to Cézanne's—and, to a lesser extent, Degas's—influence on Gauguin's work during this time.

A similar, and even more stylized, arrangement of objects on a table seen from above can be observed 90 in the still-life known as *Still-Life Fête Gloanec*, which bears the signature 'Madeleine B'. Gauguin painted this picture as part of a group birthday gift for Marie Henry, owner of the Pension Gloanec, from the painters who lodged there. Knowing that the gift would not be well received, he attributed its boldness to the inexperience of Madeleine Bernard, Emile's sister. This painting can be dated fairly precisely, on or just before 15 August 1888, giving us a clear indication of the evolution of his work just prior to the painting of *Vision after the Sermon*. The composition is divided into three distinct parts, each seen from a different point of view: the edge of the pedestal table, seen from directly in front; the table top, seen from above; and the flowers and vases, seen from the side. Again, this picture suggests the influence of Cézanne and Degas, more than that of Japanese prints. The downy texture of the flowers and the unusual juxtaposition of colours—indigo, orange and various shades of green—also recall Degas, in particular his *Milliners* series.

Gauguin always recognized the unique character of Cézanne's work. As early as 1884, he described the works he saw at Père Tanguy's shop as 'marvels of an essentially pure art'. Much later he wrote: 'Cézanne owes nothing to anyone, he is satisfied to be Cézanne' (*Racontars de Rapin*, 1902). Thus, when painting his 'exercises' after Cézanne, he forced him-89 self to conform to a discipline. *Still-Life with Three Puppies* is a veritable exercise in which Cézanne's style is fused with that of Japanese prints. Other still-lifes by Gauguin, painted in the same period, are quite different.

Portrait of a Seated Woman constitutes an em- 91 phatic tribute to Cézanne. A young Breton woman named Marie 'Lagadu' also posed for Sérusier. The facial traits are not sharply caricatured like those in *La Belle Angèle* or in the *Portrait of Madame Ginoux*, 53, 72 but, rather, recall the gravity of the *Portrait of Madeleine Bernard*. As in many other of Gauguin's 62 portraits, Marie Derrien is seated in front of a painting. In this case the painting is a still-life by Cézanne 92 that Gauguin owned, which was characteristic of the years between 1880 and 1885. The distortion of shapes, and the use of colours, instead of shadows, to create relief, exemplified by Cézanne's painting, were borrowed by Gauguin, as well as by the Nabis and the Cubists. In the painting depicted here, Cézanne used the most humble and placid of themes, the bourgeois still-life, as a medium for allowing his quiet boldness to abolish four centuries of conventions for representing space. It is not surprising that this was one of the rare paintings that the artist signed. Gauguin had seen this still-life in Paris and brought it with him to Brittany. When Schuffenecker offered to buy it from him in June 1888, he replied: 'This Cézanne... is an exceptional pearl and I have already refused 200 francs for it; I cherish it and, except in case of absolute necessity, I will only part with it when my last shirt is gone.' Gauguin was so impressed with this painting that he transposed it to his portrait of Marie. In fact, the original Cézanne measured a modest 46×55 cm, and Gauguin enlarged it to fill the whole background of his large canvas. The same Cézanne was glorified yet again by Maurice Denis, who placed it in the centre of his *Homage to Cézanne*, surrounded by Odilon Redon and the Nabis. Because of Gauguin's intervening painting, the *Homage to Cézanne* became an indirect homage to him, too.

Chapter VIII   Dreams of Distant Shores

Gauguin's need for evasion could no longer be satisfied by Brittany, nor by the Midi. He longed to flee the Old World, to free himself of its complacency and unchallenged values, and, at the same time, find new artistic stimulation. On a more mundane level, he was continually in search of a simpler, cheaper place to live and work. He had experienced extreme poverty, and, despite the occasional sale that brought in a bit of money, his extravagant tendencies prevented him from living cheaply in Paris. His failed excursion to Martinique had not discouraged him. He began seeking out information about the most distant and exotic French colonies. In April 1889 he wrote to Emile Bernard: 'I have decided to leave for Madagascar... I have obtained information... from Madame Redon, among others, who comes from [the island of] Bourbon [Réunion], and knows Madagascar very well. She says that with 5,000 francs you can live there for thirty years if you want to.' A few months later, Gauguin wrote to Odilon Redon: 'I have just had a conversation with my neighbour who lives in Madagascar... and now I am quite confused. He says that unless one goes far inland, the cost of living is high, and that there is little fruit, etc. Please discuss this seriously with Madame Redon and send me precise information along with your best advice. You know exactly what I want to do there, and, therefore, what is best. Young Bernard wishes to go with me, but he has no money. So you see, this trip is quite a complicated affair.'

In autumn 1889 Gauguin undertook proceedings to go to Tonkin, but wrote to Bernard that 'the replies are currently rather negative. The people they send to the colonies are generally those who do silly things, like pick safes, or some such... and for me, a simple Impressionist artist, a rebel, it is impossible.'

Gauguin wrote again to Odilon Redon in September 1890: 'The reasons you give me for staying in Europe are more flattering than actually convincing. My decision to leave is made, but since arriving in Brittany, I have modified it somewhat. Madagascar is too near the civilized world. I am leaving for Tahiti, and I hope to stay there for the rest of my days. I think that my work, which you respect, is but a seed that I can cultivate there in that wild and primitive place. For that I must have peace. What does it matter that the glory will belong to others?'

During his short career as a sailor, Gauguin had probably not put into Tahiti, but he had crossed the Pacific, which he saw again in 1887 on his trip to Panama. At that time, the Panama Canal was being built, initiated by the then French diplomat, Ferdinand de Lesseps, with the objective of strengthening France's position in Oceania. In 1884 Paul Deschanel, future President of France, published a book called *La Politique française en Océanie à propos du canal de Panama*, with a preface by Ferdinand de Lesseps. Deschanel quoted Pierre Loti extensively when describing 'the penetrating charm, intense poetry, stirring sweetness of Tahiti, that new Cythera, with a seductive and sensual wind that caresses this enchanted island'.[1] Behind its scientific and administrative façade, Deschanel's book reinforced the image, already propagated by Pierre Loti,

93 Paul Gauguin about 1891. Photograph taken in Paris by the artist Boutet de Monvel, in the studio at Rue Vandamme

of a land without social taboos, where Nature bestowed its gifts freely on its inhabitants. Gauguin must have seen one or another of the numerous travellers' or missionaries' journals, novels, magazine or dictionary articles circulating about Tahiti. However, it is certain that he did not discover Jacques Antoine Moerenhout's major book, *Voyage aux îles du grand océan* (Paris, 1837), until later; he drew on it heavily for *Ancien Culte mahorie*, published about 1892.

Tahiti was sometimes presented less idyllically. In *Les Missions Catholiques en Océanie*, Tournefond pointed out: 'Our poets, Chamfort, Delille, Victor Hugo and others, sang the praises of these blessed islands, and our philosophers thought they had finally found, and could observe at their leisure, uncivilized peoples, those children of nature that J.-J. Rousseau had made so fashionable. Alas! As navigators reached those much-vaunted lands, their enthusiasm disappeared ... a multitude of islands appeared, one after the other, with their crude and cannibalistic Black men ....' Soon came 'a crowd of adventurous men, society's waifs, who had rebelled against every law in Europe'. [2]

This second image of Oceania, as a land inhabited by ferocious savages, was almost as widespread as that of the 'new Cythera'. Two writers, totally dissimilar but both contemporaries of Gauguin, exemplify that contrast. Villiers de L'Isle-Adam, in *Tribulat Bonhomet* (1887), recounts at great length the adventure of a young Englishman who died 'a most tragic death during a mission in Outer Oceania' (p. 224). At the other extreme of the Parisian literary milieu, Emile Goudeau, founder of the cabaret Le Chat Noir, wrote *La Vache enragée* (1885) in which a Communard returns from deportation to New Caledonia and describes the indigenous population as cannibals: 'What kind of people are the Melanesians? Brutes! We should do away with them all. They're monkeys' (p. 158).

It is true that, in another passage, the protagonist has a quite different sort of dream: 'in front of the coconut seller, he dreamed of exotic retreats, tropical solitude, full of giant coconut trees that would be friendlier to him than inhospitable city houses' (p. 57).

It is possible that the other destinations that Gauguin considered were simply stopgaps, and that an Edenic image of Tahiti was always in the back of his mind. Van Gogh wrote to his sister on 30 March 1888: 'So I can imagine, for instance, that a present-day painter should do something like what one finds described in Pierre Loti's book *Le Mariage de Loti*, in which a picture of nature in Otaheite is drawn. A book which I warmly recommend to you to read.' [3]

It is unlikely that Gauguin waited for Van Gogh's 'recommendation' before reading the book, in which

Tahiti, the exotic paradise, was portrayed as an ideal place for fulfilling an artistic destiny. Like most of his contemporaries, Gauguin had read Loti's books, and he had discussed them at length with Van Gogh. He certainly sensed the affinities between himself and Loti, whose contemporary success as a novelist and travel writer has been all but effaced by history.

Under his real name, Julien Viaud, Pierre Loti, who was two years younger than Gauguin, led a double life as novelist and naval officer. His brother, Gustave, was a navy surgeon; between 1859 and 1870 he produced the first photographs ever taken of Tahiti and sent them home to his family in France. Young Julien was attending Naval Academy at the very moment Gauguin was turned away. In a letter to his sister, Julien confided: '... when I am a sailor, I shall have everything I've dreamed of for so long, the unknown and travelling.'[4] From Brest, where he was stationed in the Naval Academy's training vessel, he took advantage of his leaves to explore Brittany as an amateur painter. He wrote: 'Decidedly, this is a charming place, and I have never felt such a desire to paint as since I have been here.'[5] He looked forward to departing on 'a magnificent voyage to those far-away lands that have fascinated me since my childhood'.[6] Like Gauguin—whom Loti may well have crossed in a naval operation during the Franco-Prussian war—Loti yearned not only for a change of scenery, but to discover a 'primitive' world: 'I am beginning to hope that the world is less civilized than we generally think it to be'[7]; and, while passing by Easter Island in 1872, he produced numerous drawings of those famous statues that, since the expeditions of Captain Cook and the French navigator Jean-François de Galaup, had so captured Europe's imagination. Loti gave his sister the material for three articles which appeared in *L'Illustration* on 17, 24 and 31 August 1872. He stayed in Tahiti, where he had a relationship with a native woman and was given the nickname Loti, a Tahitian word for a kind of flower. His first book, *Le Mariage de Loti*, written in 1880, was the fruit of that experience. Subsequently, his military career permitted him to discover many other countries, including Senegal, China, Indochina, Japan and Egypt, each of which inspired a book. He was particularly receptive to the unique beauty of those countries and their people; and his few affairs there later surfaced in his novels. But this admirer of Chateaubriand experienced melancholy and disillusionment everywhere he went, except in Tahiti, of which he wrote: 'I love everything about it, each memory I brought back, everything that reminds me of it; I had dreamed so much of it long ago that I feel attached to it by childhood memories; now I have two homelands: Tahiti and Saintonge. I love those forests of coconut trees as much as our own forests.'[8] In all honesty, we should add that Loti participated enthusiastically in the 1885 destruction and plundering of the Ma-Kung temples in China.

In short, for Gauguin, Loti represented someone who had achieved his childhood dreams of travelling to far-off lands, but in the secure, comfortable context of a military career. Gauguin wrote to Bernard in June 1890: 'Loti saw Tahiti as a writer with a fortune, and his own ship at his disposal.' Loti obtained glory by transposing images from those voyages into his art. Gauguin's artistic achievement did not attain the same renown during his own lifetime. In fact, he was afraid of the price attached to fame. Quoting Carlyle, he wrote to Van Gogh: 'You surely know of those fireflies in Brazil that are so bright ladies pin them in their hair in the evening. Glory is beautiful, but—there you have it—it is to the artist what the hairpin is to those insects' (known through a letter from Vincent to Theo Van Gogh of 13 August 1888). Gauguin and Loti shared certain personal beliefs as well, notably a rather vague form of pantheism and a rejection of rationalism and naturalism. Pierre Loti's acceptance speech to the Académie Française in 1892 was interpreted by his contemporaries as a 'condemnation of naturalism'.[9]

Gauguin had certainly seen Polynesian objects in Paris. Thanks to the efforts of Robert Goldwater and Philippe Peltier, we know much about contemporary collections that were open to the public. Beginning in 1850, the Musée de la Marine, which

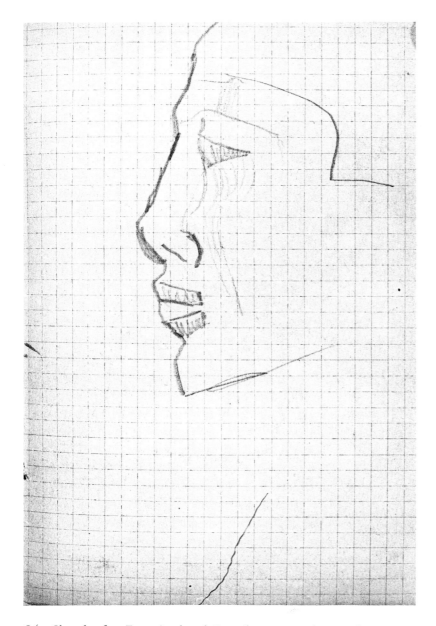

94   Sketch of an Egyptian head. Pencil on squared paper from notebook, 14 × 9.4 cm. Department of Graphic Arts, Musée du Louvre, Paris

Musée de l'homme, was founded. Peltier sums up the atmosphere: 'At the 1889 Exposition Universelle, in the "villages indigènes" set up on the Champ-de-Mars in Paris, Tahitian and New Caledonian dwellings were reconstructed. For the first time, Oceanian objects were seen in their natural context. However, they were clearly from *elsewhere*, and provoked a feeling of strangeness: what predominated was exoticism, the dream of a world in its natural state, a return to civilization's infancy, or to an Eden lost for ever.'[11] Earlier presentations, in particular those of the 1878 Exposition, had apparently given more emphasis to the invention of forms by those 'primitive' peoples.

In all likelihood, Gauguin visited the Musée de la Marine and may also have seen the exhibits at the Exposition Universelle of 1878 and the Musée d'Ethnographie. We know for certain that he saw the exhibits at the 1889 Exposition; the Café Volpini, where his own works were exhibited, was inside the fair, and we have already mentioned the articles he published in relation to the event.

Drawing his inspiration from the numerous Polynesian sculptures at the fair, Gauguin later painted a figure of a Caribbean woman on a panel in the dining room of Marie Henry's inn at Le Pouldu. The figure was crudely drawn, almost caricatured, and quite unlike anything in his previous repertoire. On another panel he painted *Self-Portrait with Halo*, no 98 less stylized, but with a fluency and elegance that contrast sharply with the clumsiness of the Caribbean woman.

The 1889 Exposition Universelle required extensive preparations, for it was a prestigious event for the young Republic. It gave France the occasion to assert itself among nations after the war with Prussia in 1870, and was also the centennial celebration of the French Revolution. The exhibition occupied the area extending between the Champ-de-Mars, the Esplanade des Invalides, the embankments of the Seine and the Trocadéro. Supposedly six days were needed to visit everything. Gauguin, who had not yet definitively decided on his destination, would have

was installed in the Louvre, exhibited Polynesian works. Peltier has observed: 'At the Exposition Universelle of 1878 three distinct categories in the primitive arts became apparent, represented by three different areas, the Palais des Sciences anthropologiques, the Palais des Colonies and the exhibition of ancient arts.'[10] In that same year, the Musée des Missions ethnographiques opened its doors, and in 1882 the Musée d'Ethnographie de Paris, ancestor of the had the occasion to visit a number of exotic pavilions. Each colonial power set out to present a full picture of its empire. There were Indian and Chinese pavilions, an Incan temple, an Egyptian bazaar, a reproduction of a 'pagoda from Angkor which protects the simple huts of the inhabitants, whom we see going about their everyday lives, wearing their national costumes; Polynesians, Cambodians, Tonkinese....' [12] This sweeping display of exoticism was presented side by side with a retrospective of French art as well as an international presentation of scientific and technical achievements in every field of industry. Such a juxtaposition of images could only reinforce the general public's belief in the power of progress and the West's mission to 'civilize' the rest of the world. The fair itself, as well as similar exhibitions that had been mounted during the preceding years, reiterated those ideological convictions. Gauguin did not agree with this view, and his visit to such pavilions could only have confirmed his intention to flee the Old World in order to find a purer place to live and work.

We have already discussed the rejection of the all-powerful cult of progress and mechanization, of which the Eiffel Tower, built for the Exposition, was the consummate symbol. The ideological discussions that preceded and accompanied this exhibition aided and abetted this cultural rejection, which was fuelled by opinions issuing from diverse sectors of society. Gauguin's position was shared by the writer Paul Claudel, who frequented the Symbolist milieu and the Tuesday gatherings at Mallarmé's in the Rue de Rome. His conversion dates from 1886. Beginning in 1893, with his first stay away from France as vice-consul in New York and in Boston, Claudel read books on Indian and gypsy folklore, [13] which he drew on for his play L'Echange, at the very same moment when Gauguin was referring to a book by an ethnographer in writing his own Ancien Culte mahorie. Later, in China, Claudel led 'a life of deliberately chosen estrangement and solitude'. [14]

One of their contemporaries, Charles de Foucauld, undertook, in 1883-4, an exploratory expedition into

95 *Caricature of a Head*. Pencil on squared paper from notebook, 14 × 9.2 cm. Department of Graphic Arts, Musée du Louvre, Paris

inner Morocco before becoming a Trappist monk in 1886, then leaving for Palestine to live the life of an ascetic and finally settling in the Sahara. Like Gauguin's, Foucauld's escape was instigated by ethnographic research, and, as in the case of Claudel, by a conversion to Christianity of a sort that, although orthodox, was marginal. The same was true of the erudite religion of Huysmans, and the polemical furor of Léon Bloy, who became a Soldier of God.

Gauguin never subscribed to a creed, but it should be remembered that his attitude and departure for Tahiti represented a kind of asceticism, as well as a total commitment, and were as much a matter of moral as of aesthetic necessity.

Gauguin's desire to break away should not be interpreted as the revolt of a misfit. His case is no different from that of other great innovators who seriously broke with the cultural mores of their milieu: they were not simpletons, ignoramuses or failures. Cézanne, Arthur Rimbaud and Alfred Jarry were all exemplary students who had been awarded prizes for their academic performance. Mallarmé, Claudel and Apollinaire read extensively. Seurat, Matisse and Kandinsky had exceptional knowledge of the visual arts, both past and present. Monet, who has too often been portrayed as a gruff man of limited outlook, in fact possessed a fine library which he consulted regularly. Théodore Rousseau was hardly the simpleton he has been made out to be. As for Gauguin, we have already seen that he had acquired a solid literary and artistic background. The challenge to Western values posed by these modern artists was not promulgated by 'brutes', but by highly educated individuals who had already assimilated those very values and were therefore in a position to perceive their limits.

Gauguin hesitated about leaving right up to the last moment. On 15 April 1891 Jules Renard noted in his *Journal*, only days after Gauguin's departure: 'Daudet, in brilliant form, describes the embarkation of Gauguin, who wishes to go and live in Tahiti to be away from everyone, yet never actually leaves. Finally, even his best friends began saying "You must leave, dear old boy, you must leave".' Although Renard was never known for his kindness, this account of Gauguin's hesitations and his apprehension about leaving is substantiated by others. Leaving meant depriving himself of a stimulating circle of friends and admirers, whose attentions both irritated and flattered him. Jan Verkade, a young Dutch artist introduced to Gauguin by Jacob Meyer de Haan in February 1891, wrote: 'After speaking to me at length

about modern painting, he [Meyer de Haan] took me to a little restaurant in the Rue de la Grande Chaumière, across the street from Colarossi's studio. Gauguin, whom I recognized immediately by de Haan's description, was eating supper. He raised his eyes as we entered, with a look that seemed to say: "What imbecile is de Haan bringing to see me this time?" Though, in fact, he was somewhat younger, Gauguin looked like a fifty-year-old man who had seen hard times but managed to come through. He had long black hair that covered his entire forehead and a short, stubbly beard that exposed a mouth with sensual but resolute lips, as well as yellowish cheeks. The most striking thing about his face were the heavy eyelids which gave him a tired look. But his large, hooked nose somewhat counterbalanced this impression and suggested energy and perspicacity. 'I was presented to the master and to the other "regulars", most of them foreign painters, and I ate supper. Gauguin was very quiet, and soon got up and left. When he had gone, de Haan spoke at length once again about Gauguin's work, illustrating his lecture by covering the table with all sorts of drawings. I went home full of enthusiasm.' [15]

Jan Verkade stayed in Paris for some time, becoming a loyal member of the Nabi School. He later entered the Benedictine abbey in Beuron, Germany, where he took up mural painting.

In order to pay for his trip and have something set aside to live on, Gauguin needed to find some money. When it came to financial matters, he vacillated between cunning and naïvety. In 1889, at Le Pouldu, he made the acquaintance of a certain Countess of Nimal [16] who, together with the Minister of Finance, Maurice Rouvier, promised to set up a sale of his work to the French government, in particular his wood relief *Be in Love and You'll Be Happy*. Gauguin hastened to tell Schuffenecker and Bernard the good news. But the affair never materialized. Even so, Gauguin dedicated a large *Still-Life* to the Countess, on which the name was scratched out but remains legible. This strange Countess of Nimal, a collector of contemporary art, has been largely

101

99

ignored by historians, despite the fact that she claimed to be the mother of an illustrious twentieth-century personality, General Maxime Weygand. Her fleeting interest in Gauguin might have to do with the intervention of Georges Daniel, who was prob-

ably Weygand's half-brother, and the son of King Leopold II of Belgium. In any case, it seems that the Countess of Nimal supported both Weygand and Daniel financially.

In 1890 Gauguin thought he could count on the promise of a certain Doctor Charlopin to buy 5,000 francs' worth of paintings if Charlopin managed to convert a patent into cash. This, too, proved to be a vain hope. Then there was the telegram from Theo

96 *Madame la Mort*. Frontispiece for Rachilde's *Théâtre*, 1891. Charcoal on paper, 23 × 30 cm. Department of Graphic Arts, Musée du Louvre, Paris

97 *Hour of Innocence*. 1891. Oil on canvas, 89.5 × 130.2 cm.
Chrysler Museum, Norfolk, Virginia (Gift of Walter P. Chrysler, Jr.)

98 *Self-Portrait with Halo*. 1889. Oil on panel, 79.2 × 51.3 cm.
National Gallery of Art, Washington, D.C. (Chester Dale Collection)

99 *Still-Life with 'Countess of Nimal'*. 1889. Oil on canvas, 49 × 55 cm. Private Collection

Van Gogh (see p. 116), whom Gauguin had reason to trust, since he had already managed to sell several of his works. If Gauguin appeared more affected by Theo's death than by Vincent's it was because Theo had been one of his rare links with the world of commerce. Gauguin got in touch with Maurice Joyant, future biographer of Toulouse-Lautrec, and Theo's successor at Boussod and Valadon, where some of Gauguin's works were still being kept on consignment. But this had no financial repercussions.

He began to think seriously about auctioning his work at the Hôtel Drouot, although he knew that for such a venture to succeed he would have first to consolidate his reputation. The ever-modest Pissarro wrote to his son, with a note of bitterness: 'If you only knew with what triteness and superficiality Gauguin behaved in order to get himself elected (and that is the word) to the position of "genius".'

Gauguin realized he had to have a good article published to publicize the event. His faithful friend Charles Morice considered that he was not well enough known to write the article himself and,

accompanied by Gauguin, he went to Mallarmé for advice, perhaps with the secret hope that the great writer would deign to write the piece himself. Mallarmé suggested they ask Octave Mirbeau, who was not yet known as a writer of fiction, but widely respected for his journalistic skills. Although he generally sympathized with the Realist movement, Mirbeau, motivated either by personal interest or by professional gain, agreed to write the article. He may even have felt sorry for Gauguin. He wrote to Monet that he had received a letter from Mallarmé concerning Gauguin's distressing situation, his living in the extremest poverty, and wanting to flee Paris and to go to Tahiti, in order to start again. To help him out, Mirbeau agreed to write an article in *Le Figaro*— which, he claimed, was not easy—on the occasion of the sale of thirty of his paintings. Mirbeau's letter to Monet is of particular interest, not only for the information it provides about Gauguin's personality, but also because it proves that, despite the fact that he was moving away from Impressionism, Gauguin was anxious to have Monet's opinion of his work, a message Mirbeau duly transmitted. He recounted Gauguin's visit to him, relating his impression that Gauguin was intriguing: both curious to look at and tormented by art. Gauguin was anxious, according to Mirbeau, to get Monet's reaction to his development in using ever simpler forms to express complex ideas. Mirbeau admitted to liking *Vision after the Sermon* and Gauguin's ceramic work.

We have substantial information about the contents of the auction, which took place on 23 February 1891. As for the exhibition at Volpini's, Gauguin had chosen paintings from Paris, but this time he also included works from Martinique, the Midi and his various stays in Brittany. There were thirty paintings in all, including his most famous works to date: *Vision after the Sermon, Alyscamps, La Belle Angèle*, 50, 71, 53 and others. They were grouped arbitrarily, and, for some unknown reason, *Vision after the Sermon*, which was listed in the catalogue as no. 25, was, according to the minutes, actually sold as no. 6.[17] The day after the auction, Gauguin wrote to his wife:

'The sale took place yesterday and went well. It was not as successful as the exhibition held the day before, but the moral success was immense, and I think it will soon yield results.' Gauguin wanted to encourage Mette, while at the same time letting her know that he would not be able to send her any money from the sale. The total sales came to 7,350 francs, less expenses. Gauguin had surely hoped for

more, but considering his controversial status in the Parisian artistic milieu, and the fact that only one painting went unsold, the final result was satisfactory. The prices ranged between 250 and 900 francs, comparable to what Gauguin had been getting for works sold through Theo Van Gogh. We know the names of the purchasers, and in some instances we might wonder whether they enhanced the prices more out of friendship than from a genuine taste for the work itself. Among the buyers were Degas, who bought two works, including *La Belle Angèle*; Méry Laurent, Mallarmé's friend; Count Antoine de la Rochefoucauld; Georges de Bellio, owner of *Impression, Sunrise* by Monet and patron of the Impressionists, bought two paintings; the Natanson brothers, founders of *La Revue Blanche*; Daniel de Monfreid, under the name Daniel, took two paintings; Roger Marx; the Count of Chollet, who bought *Alyscamps* and *Above the Abyss*, and later *Two Tahitian Women on the Beach*, as well as building up a fine collection of Impressionist and Pointillist paintings; and Ker-Xavier Roussel, who took a Breton painting on behalf of his Nabi friends.

71, 20
114

Mallarmé, who was ill and could not attend the sale, sent a short note of excuse: 'My dear Gauguin, an attack of influenza, without serious consequences I hope, deprives me of the pleasure of shaking your hand, as well as seeing once again—with a farewell glance—the beautiful things I so love. Have you been satisfied, or, at least, gleaned from the sale hope for your departure? During this past winter I have often thought of the wisdom of your decision. Your hand! All this is not so that you will reply, but that you know I am yours, from near or from far.'

100

As we have already seen, this auction was the occasion of the falling out between Gauguin and Bernard. In March, Gauguin left for Denmark to say goodbye to his family, though he did not consider the farewell definitive. Possibly encouraged by the celebrity the sale had earned him, he wrote to the Ministry of Finance requesting an official mission to facilitate his settling in Tahiti. The letter, which has been preserved, reads as follows:

100 *Stéphane Mallarmé*. 1891. Aqua fortis, 18 × 14 cm. Annotated: 'Morice, I read him, admire him and like him, Paul Gauguin.' Bibliothèque d'Art et d'Archéologie, Paris
'This portrait is a masterpiece. Gauguin has taken note of everything: pointed ear, arched eyebrows, the straight, porcupine hair of the professor. Mallarmé taught us every Tuesday.' (Paul Claudel, *Journal*, 13 February 1942.)

101 *Portrait of Jacob Meyer de Haan*. 1889. Oil on wood, 80 × 52 cm. Private Collection

102 *Still-Life with Ham*. 1889. Oil on canvas, 50 × 58 cm. Phillips Collection, Washington, D.C. (Purchased from Paul Rosenberg, New York, 1951)

15 March 1891

Dear Monsieur le Ministre,

I wish to go to Tahiti in order to pursue a series of paintings of that country, to portray its character and light.

I have the honour of asking you, Monsieur le Ministre, to kindly, as you did for Monsieur Dumoulin, entrust me with a mission, *free of charge*, which would facilitate, with the advantages it would provide, both my studies and transport.

Yours sincerely,

35 Rue Delambre · Paul Gauguin

The expression 'to portray the character and light' of the country was not an arbitrary formulation. Beneath its apparent banality, it suggests the two underlying themes of his Tahitian quest: to find new sources of inspiration, relating to the 'character' of the country; and to develop new means of expression, appropriate to that inspiration, characterized by the 'light'.

Gauguin soon received a well-disposed reply to his demand, accompanied by a discount of 30 percent on the price of his ticket. In view of the rather unconventional character of his work, this prompt and favourable response suggests that a letter of recommendation from Clemenceau to the Minister may have had the desired effect. Also, the Minister in question was the same Rouvier who had already heard of Gauguin via the Countess of Nimal.

In keeping with tradition, Gauguin's friends organized a banquet in his honour, on 23 March, at the Café Voltaire. The guests included artists such as Odilon Redon and Eugène Carrière, and writers such as Jean Moréas, Charles Morice, Jean Dolent, and Alfred and Rachilde Vallette. Gauguin's disciples—Sérusier, Mogens Ballin, Léon Fauché, Jens Ferdinand Willumsen, Daniel de Monfreid and others—were also present. Mallarmé gave a carefully composed speech: 'Gentlemen, to get right to the point, let us drink to the return of Paul Gauguin; but not without admiring that superb conscience which drives him into exile, at the very peak of his talent, to renew himself, in far-away lands, and within himself.'

Again for the sake of tradition, Gauguin's friends put together a benefit show, in his and Paul Verlaine's honour. It was held at the Paul Fort Theatre on 27 May, some time after Gauguin's departure on 1 April. Gauguin was purportedly disappointed by its poor financial showing.

On 10 May 1891, just a few weeks after Gauguin had passed through Marseilles, Arthur Rimbaud arrived there and died shortly thereafter. Verlaine had certainly spoken of that 'visionary' in front of Gauguin, and may even have given him a copy of *Une Saison en enfer*, published secretly in 1887. Gauguin wrote an article about Rimbaud in his review, *Les Guêpes*: 'Rimbaud was a poet, subsequently considered a useless creature by a segment of society, as are all artists' (18 June 1899). Indeed, these two had the same adversaries. But Gauguin did not realize the fundamental difference that separated him from Rimbaud: for Gauguin flight was an indispensable stimulus to creativity, while Rimbaud's departure resulted in permanent silence.

Chapter IX   Looking for Eden

When Gauguin boarded ship at Marseilles on 1 April 1891, he was convinced that Tahiti would be the answer to all his dreams. The crossing took nearly two and a half months. We know little about that time, except what we can glean from the few surviving letters he wrote. On 4 May 1891, he wrote to Mette: 'For the last thirty days I have done nothing but eat, drink and everything else, lamely watching the horizon. A few sharks stick up their fins from time to time by way of greeting, and that is all. Fortunately I am able to think sometimes of you and the children.' In that same letter, he complained of his fellow passengers: '... very decent people who have only one fault, an altogether common one, I'm afraid, and that is to be perfectly mediocre'. From this it would seem that he had at least some intercourse with the other passengers. He may have read, or drawn, though we have no trace of any drawings. It would not have been the first time that he went for several weeks—even months—without touching a pencil or a paintbrush. For us, unaccustomed during the past century to artists capable of suspending creative work for any significant length of time, it is difficult to imagine Gauguin living on a boat for two and a half months without touching a sketchbook. If he did not read, or draw, or engage in interesting conversation, he certainly had time to think, quite probably about his work. His Tahitian output quickly confirmed the principles of which *Vision after the Sermon* was the first manifestation, and it may well be that the long crossing, during which he was con-

demned to solitude and reflection, allowed him to crystallize his intentions.

He had a bit of money and an official letter confirming his mission, which gave him access to the island's polite society. Immediately upon arriving in Papeete, whether deliberately or through laziness, he let himself slide into a life of socializing that was hardly conducive to serious work. In fact, a few of his written pieces express his disappointment at finding in Tahiti a caricature of the French social world, while what he really wanted was to 'soak myself once again in Nature's purity, see nothing but savages, and live their life' (*L'Echo de Paris*, 23 February 1891).

Perhaps that disappointment explains why the first paintings from Tahiti—which were, incidentally, all 104 portraits—are considered by some to represent something of a regression. Their style is less assertive, their composition less ambitious. In July 1891, Gauguin wrote to his wife: 'It has now been three weeks since my arrival, and I have already seen so much that I am troubled. It will be some time still before I shall be able to paint a good picture.' Shortly thereafter, for both economic as well as professional reasons, he left Papeete for Paea, and then Mataiea, fifty miles from Papeete, on the ocean. There, his opportunities to see Europeans were rare. He still complained of his difficulty in working, but perhaps we should not overestimate such complaints, given his tendency to accentuate difficulties to his wife. In the summer of 1891, he wrote to Mette: 'I have begun working, but not without difficulty; I always have trouble getting down to work in a new place. Little by little I shall get used to each new thing, and each person.' He had; in fact, written a similar letter shortly after arriving in Brittany.

Gauguin's output during his first stay in Tahiti was tremendous. It has been contended that during the first six months he painted nothing, but this is doubtful; he himself spoke of 'sixty-six more or less decent canvases'. Even if we set aside those paintings that cannot be dated with certainty, there remain more than sixty works from this first Tahitian period. Despite Gauguin's complaints, typical of any active artist, he seems to have become altogether master of his medium. The volume of work produced during this time is all the more remarkable because the subject-matter, unlike that of the paintings done previously in France, is imagined, rather than taken from life. In addition, these pictures were done painstakingly and over time. Gauguin never worked briskly like Renoir, or feverishly like Van Gogh; his pace was rather similar to Cézanne's, although the latter master rarely invented his motifs, but selected them carefully. During this time, Gauguin's powers of invention were much more fertile than during the preceding years, when imaginative scenes were relatively rare in his work. If we compare this body of work with that of Cézanne or Seurat, who were also

104   *Young Girl with Hat.* 1891. Oil on canvas, 36 × 40 cm. Musée d'Art moderne, Troyes (Pierre and Denise Lévy Collection)

just emerging from their Impressionist periods, we find that all three artists had made great strides in developing their own style, but that Gauguin's was by far the one most based on imagined themes.

It is not always possible to correlate Gauguin's disappointments and financial difficulties with his output. There is no question that constraints such as holding down a clerk's job or sustained illness prevented him from working as much or as serenely as would have been desirable. But, as with Van Gogh or Cézanne, a kind of moral certitude kept him going. One could hardly transgress accepted values with such energy and determination as Gauguin did without a sense of purpose.

103   Tahitian Archipelago, postcard

105   *Matamoe—Landscape with Peacock.* 1892. Oil on canvas, 115 × 86 cm. Pushkin Museum, Moscow

106 *Reverie*. 1891. Oil on canvas, 92 × 73 cm. Nelson-Atkins Museum of Art, Kansas City (Nelson Fund)

107 *Arearea—Joyousness*. 1891. Oil on canvas, 75 × 94 cm. Musée d'Orsay, Paris

108   *Tahitian Repast*. 1891. Oil on canvas, 73 × 92 cm. Musée d'Orsay, Paris

109   *Ia Orana Maria—Virgin with Child*. 1891. Oil on canvas, 113.7 × 87.7 cm. Metropolitan Museum of Art, New York (Bequest of Sam A. Lewisohn, 1951)

110   *Ta Matete—The Market*. 1892. Oil on canvas, 73 × 92 cm. Kunstmuseum, Basel. Several alterations are visible, particularly round the shoulders

111   *Ta Matete*. Detail of plate 110

As if he were seeking to challenge the former great creators of images more than his own contemporaries, he took on every theme, from portraiture, to landscape, still-life, genre scenes and religious subjects. He used every formula: isolated figures in a natural setting or an interior, compositions with two or more figures arranged in a frieze, or on shifted planes, or landscapes peopled with numerous small figures. From this vast body of works perhaps a dozen stand on their own as pictures whose format, composition and iconography exclude the possibility that they were studies, or preparatory works.

One of the principal characteristics of these works is the scarcity of empty spaces; the whole surface of the canvas is decorated. Neither ground, nor sky, nor sea—which appear, but only as thin strips near the top of the canvas—is represented by a large, uniform surface which would offer the eye a realm of tranquillity. The decorative motifs of the clothing blend in with the flat, homogeneous treatment of the painting's surface. Each canvas is divided, like a puzzle, into more or less equal-sized segments. This approach contrasts sharply with Cézanne's, whose *Views of l'Estaque* and later depictions of *Mont Sainte-Victoire*, from the 1880s—which Gauguin had seen—juxtapose empty areas with highly worked ones (Cézanne compared them to playing cards); it was not until after 1895 that Cézanne introduced a more homogeneous fragmentation of the painted surface. In this area, Gauguin sought inspiration rather from tapestry, medieval stained glass and Oriental miniatures. Even at the time, the similarity between Gauguin's neatly segmented and outlined areas and the art of stained glass was pointed out. On 18 February 1891, before Gauguin's departure for Tahiti, Octave Mirbeau wrote in *Le Figaro* that his 'most recent works have the mystical opulence of a cathedral's stained glass window'.[1] Here *cloisonnisme*, which in stained glass or enamel was imposed by the medium, did not constitute merely a decorative device (as it did in the work of some of his disciples, such as Filiger, Ranson and others). Gauguin used strongly defined outlines to set off the large shapes of his composition and to emphasize figures or objects without introducing relief. Because of this technique, his work has often been described as 'decorative'. But Gauguin's style was flexible and dynamic: it was the servant, not the master, of expression and a part of his quest for poetic meaning. The same analogy exists between Gauguin's fluid use of this technique compared with the rigid formula used by Emile Bernard and other painters of the Pont-Aven School, as between the free and imaginative fragmenting of forms in analytical Cubism and the tendency of synthetic Cubism to begin with an abstract cylinder to suggest a bottle. In this area, Gauguin was clearly a predecessor of analytical Cubism.

Gauguin never gave up creating relief with shadows; nor did he entirely banish half-tones or shading. He used some old recipes from traditional painting when he felt he needed them. In *Te Nave Nave Fenua—Fragrant Earth*, which was one of his

112 *Tahitian Man.* 1891. Graphite, black and red chalk on paper, 32.5 × 27 cm. Art Institute of Chicago (Gift of Mrs Emily Crane Chadbourne)

142

162

most systematically treated pictures, the vegetation is created with shades of greens and blues which, in some areas, take on the delicacy of watercolour, while the group is divided into carefully outlined flat areas. It is true that the woman's body is shaped by rather arbitrarily arranged patches of shading—one cannot determine where the light is coming from—but these replace what would otherwise have been ungraceful flat areas of colour on the skin itself. The same is true of the imaginatively manipulated shadows.

107 The same freedom of application can be seen in *Arearea—Joyousness*. Each element of the composition is treated differently: the red dog, a veritable heraldic figure, the two women, the tree at the right and the group in the background all constitute unrelated blocks, linked only by an elegant balancing of the planes and colours, which are sometimes applied in flat areas, sometimes shaded.

The still-lifes of this period no longer rely on Cézanne, but at times still suggest the influence of Degas. The large bouquet of flowers with the figures grouped on the side in *Te Tiare Farani—Flowers of France* (Pushkin Museum, Moscow) uses an approach derived from Degas. Perhaps this formal reference to the Parisian milieu has to do with the nostalgic character—unusual in Gauguin's work—of the subject-matter.

108 Another work from this period, *Tahitian Repast*, contains no references to Gauguin's immediate predecessors; only the knife placed diagonally on the table recalls traditional approaches to the genre. Still-life had experienced something of a renaissance during the 1860s, with such proponents as Manet, Fantin-Latour, Cézanne and Bonvin. But this painting's ancestors predate that generation; it was sixteenth- and seventeenth-century painters who tended to place a figure near a heavily laden table. In this painting, Gauguin plays with perspective and light. Each of the four planes—the edge of the table, its surface, the figures and the opening at the right—is seen from a different point of view. The observer's eye is directed upward, but shadows are projected in

113 Old photograph with which Gauguin was familiar and which he confused with one of an Egyptian bas-relief (double exposure). Photograph courtesy of Patrick O'Reilly

various directions. The link between the figures, the fruit and the objects on the table is established by the children's gazes; this link was missing, perhaps deliberately, in earlier paintings.

In the paintings from Tahiti, direct references to secondary sources have all but disappeared: there are no more traces of Japanese prints or Breton calvaries, no more fragments of pictures by Degas or Pissarro. By now, Gauguin had lost the need to use explicit references to someone or something else. On the other hand, indirect or transposed borrowing was more common than before, and often derived from photographs of works he had brought with him, many of which were done by his guardian, Gustave Arosa. In a letter to Odilon Redon, he affirmed: 'I have brought with me a whole series of photographs and drawings which will speak to me every day'; and he added, interestingly: 'as for you, I have a memory in my head of all that you have done, more or less.'[2]

Many of these pictures were of Western works, but there were also sculptures from Angkor and friezes from Borobudur, the great Javanese temple. However, Gauguin's approach to these elements was new; he no longer inserted direct, legible references

114 *Two Tahitian Women on the Beach*. 1891. Oil on canvas,
69 × 91 cm. Musée d'Orsay, Paris

115 *Parau Api—Women on the Beach* (The supposed translation is 'What News?'; but some sources have given this painting, which is very similar to that of plate 114, the same title as the earlier work.) 1892. Oil on canvas, 67 × 91 cm. Staatliche Kunstsammlungen, Gemäldegalerie, Dresden

to them, but, rather, assimilated them into the very substance and meaning of his own work. In *Ia Orana Maria—The Virgin with Child*, for example, the costumes, physical types and vegetation remove the painting from a Western context. Further, by placing the two women praying to the Virgin and Child in poses typifying Buddhist rather than Christian piety, Gauguin accentuates the exotic character of the scene. His purpose may be to suggest Christianity's universality, or, perhaps, to embody a sort of syncretism. The angel at the left provides a discreet Western reminder, treated with Botticellian elegance.

There are other examples in which a simple pose can take on an 'exotic' significance. For example, Gauguin liked to represent figures either seated or half-reclining on the ground. This position necessitates leaning, either on an elbow or on some object. On at least ten different occasions, he placed the figure with its arm very straight and hand flat on the ground, causing a rather stiff raising of the shoulder. For this unusual position his model was probably a photograph of Borobudur.[3] Such a position, doubtless considered rather ungraceful, was all but unknown in Western movement, where the only examples were of injured or crippled figures. A good example of a fairly complete repertory of possible positions is provided by the sixteen bronze statues of the Parterre d'Eau at Versailles, representing rivers. They are all in leaning or reclining positions. There is not one example of a straight arm like the one favoured by Gauguin. Even Manet, whose capacity to ignore visual clichés was renowned, had nothing new to offer in this domain. As in the case of the praying pose in *Ia Orana Maria*, the fact that the borrowed element was Javanese heightens its significance.

The search for 'sources' of gestures, positions or accessories in these paintings has been carried quite far, notably by Richard Field and Bernard Dorival. The sources of compositional schemes have been explored somewhat less, and require a certain amount of prudence. For some time, it was observed that the famous painting representing a market scene,

Ta Matete—The Market, was inspired by an Egyptian frieze. But it also resembles a photograph taken in Tahiti, which Gauguin was probably able to look at.

To present Gauguin as either a plagiarist or a clever arranger of borrowed images would be to misinterpret totally the facts. Without engaging in pastiche or plagiarism, he sought to place his own values—and his own poetic world—on an equal footing with those that were 'hallowed by posterity'. Thus, *Ia Orana Maria* was a uniquely Tahitian version of a Virgin and Child or a conversation of saints with gift-bearers, just us those by Hans Memling were uniquely from Bruges. In Gauguin's time, the Louvre exhibited Memling's *Virgin by Jacques Floreins* and the *Mystical Marriage of Saint Catherine*. That artist's 'primitive charm' (as it was described at the time) and particular style must have caught Gauguin's eye. After his trip to Belgium, which, incidentally, was subsequent to the painting of *Ia Orana Maria*, Gauguin wrote to Daniel de Monfreid: 'I saw the Memlings in Bruges; what marvels, and then, when we see Rubens afterwards (enter Naturalism) everything falls apart.'

Two Tahitian Women on the Beach and *Parau Api* (also entitled *Women on the Beach*)—What News? are transpositions of *Women of Algiers* by Delacroix. *Manao Tupapau—Spirit of the Dead Watching*, with its strange black creature in the background, is a Tahitian *Olympia*. Gauguin was well aware of the innovative value and scandalous repercussions, some thirty years earlier, of Manet's painting. Thanks to Claude Monet, Gauguin had to copy Manet's *Olympia* upon entering the Luxembourg; he had a photograph of it with him in Tahiti. When, during the reign of Napoleon III, Manet transposed a Renaissance Venus into a contemporary context, the gap suddenly closed up, both in terms of time and psychological distance, between the model and the viewer. Just as Cézanne placed his *Modern Olympia* in a romantic boudoir with frills and flounces, Gauguin interpreted a motif which extended beyond Manet to all the Venuses and all the Majas who once provoked scandal, but were by now generally

109

110, 111
113

114, 115

116
124

116 *Women of Algiers* by Eugène Delacroix (Detail). 1834. Oil on canvas, 180 × 229 cm. Musée du Louvre, Paris

accepted in the artistic realm. When Gauguin placed Venus or Olympia in a Tahitian hut inhabited by phantoms, the gap became, once again, both physical and psychological, separating the viewer from the subject-matter by a whole constellation of beliefs. We shall come back to the mythical, but distinctly Tahitian, significance with which Gauguin wished to infuse this painting (see pp. 179-82).

142 In the same way, *Te Nave Nave Fenua* is an obvious transposition of a Venus, or a Flora, or an Eve in terrestrial paradise. The Western theme carries its unique meaning and its own range of cultural references, evoking the masterpieces of history. But the

stylistic elements, as well as the iconography, undergo transformations in Gauguin's work. These changes, which can look like direct challenges, were rarer between 1880 and 1888—or, rather, Gauguin was measuring himself in general against either his contemporaries or his immediate predecessors, such as Manet, Cézanne, Pissarro and others. From then on, Gauguin referred to established artists, and even if he demonstrated a certain independent spirit in his preferences—as in the case of Memling and Rubens—he could not altogether escape the hierarchy of values proper to his time, according to which seventeenth-century Italian painters and Nicolas Poussin reigned supreme. Poussin was the obligatory reference point of the entire Ecole Française, the founder of the national tradition, and the only French name capable of challenging the giants of the Renaissance; he alone could reconcile David, Ingres and Delacroix and give academic painters their raison d'être. Poussin's work was based on precise principles and methods, and depended on a carefully codified formal and iconographic repertoire. Gauguin had no trouble becoming familiar with the gist of it, either with the help of theoretical books like Charles Blanc's *Grammaire des arts du dessin*, or, more likely, by observing the extraordinary collection of forty works by Poussin in the Louvre. (The only significant later Poussin acquisition was *Inspiration of the Poet*.)

No original painter of Gauguin's generation—with the exception of Seurat in his *La Grande Jatte*, and Puvis de Chavannes—had sought to vie with Poussin on his own territory. Manet, Monet, Renoir and Degas did not seek to organize figures in harmony with nature. The relationship between Cézanne and Poussin, based perhaps on some sort of Oedipal rivalry, emerged only after 1890. But, beginning in 1886 and especially in Tahiti, Gauguin painted increasingly ambitious compositions containing several figures in a natural setting. In these pictures, he emphasized the vertical and introduced a sacred motif, sometimes reinforced by a procession or a statue of a deity in the background. All these traits

167

were typical of Poussin as well. More specifically, we can observe the transposition of the right-hand sec-

168 tion of Poussin's *Rebecca and Eliezer* in Gauguin's
167 *Nave Nave Mahana—Fragrant Days*. Other links between these two paintings are based more on reminiscences. In Tahiti, Gauguin had seen men carrying bunches of pandanus leaves on their shoulders, which surely reminded him of those harvest bearers from another promised land depicted in Poussin's *Autumn*.

Of the paintings dating from 1891-3, a dozen contain direct references to Poussin; others contain suggestions, as if Gauguin had intended to use elements and then abandoned the idea. This is true of his large painting of 1898, *Where Do We Come From? What* 182 *Are We? Where Are We Going?*. Just as *japonisme* made its appearance in Gauguin's earlier paintings, here we can trace Poussin's influence.

Still, it should be pointed out that to interpret the Tahitian paintings as Polynesian transpositions of Western paintings is to ignore the titles that Gauguin carefully bestowed on his works, as well as the explicit interpretations he wrote for some of them. Several recent authors, familiar with Polynesian civilization, have emphasized the near-ethnographic significance of Gauguin's paintings. But to assess the legitimacy of this point of view we must first establish how much Gauguin knew about Maori culture.

Chapter X   Tahitian Lore

When he left France for Oceania, Gauguin hoped to find a total change of scenery. He imagined himself plunged into an exotic civilization which he had learned about from French ethnographic museums. He was soon disappointed. In Papeete, he discovered European society at its least appealing. The Europe he was trying to escape had been transplanted here in a grotesque and puerile form—colonial snobbery—which was not what he had expected. European and Chinese tradesmen were as numerous in Papeete as the indigenous population, and relations between them were not simple. An almost symbolic coincidence was that Pomare V, the last king of Tahiti, whom Gauguin so looked forward to meeting, died the day after the artist's arrival. Gauguin reacted bitterly to this news for he considered it tolled the death knell of Maori traditions, its customs and ancient grandeur, and opened the way for the triumph of Western imperialism with its soldiers, commerce and officialdom. Gauguin may have deluded himself about Pomare V's knowledge of Maori tradition, but the fact remains that the king's sudden death, at the moment of the artist's arrival, constituted a setback for his investigation into Maori culture.

Pomare's funeral was a grandiose affair, organized according to European custom, but there is no indication that Gauguin took advantage of the occasion to sketch groups of Tahitians gathered together. Neither did he seek to obtain commissions for portraits; if he said so in letters to his wife, it was to prove to her that he was indeed seeking ways to earn a living. (In a similar situation in Martinique, Gauguin had abandoned the task of earning a living by portrait painting to his companion Charles Laval.) There were a few incidental portraits of friends or neighbours, such as those mentioned by Lieutenant Jénot (a French naval lieutenant who befriended Gauguin on his arrival in Tahiti), including the *Young Girl with a Hat*, with its delightful harmony of straw yellow and pale blue. Even more remarkable is the *Portrait of Suzanne Bambridge*. The strength of her physical presence, the full-face, immobile pose and sumptuous garb (perhaps of Chinese origin), combine to invest this painting with the majesty of seventeenth-century ceremonial portraits—which, incidentally, Van Gogh had also evoked in his *Portrait of the Postman Roulin*. The parsimonious use of shading, on the face and the hand, was perhaps introduced as a concession to Gauguin's model, who was certainly accustomed to more traditional norms of representation. In the left-hand part of the background there is a wallpaper-inspired flower motif which appears in other Tahitian works, as well as in earlier paintings; a similar motif can be observed in the background of *Self-Portrait—'Les Misérables'* and *La Belle Angèle*. This motif also appears often in Cézanne's still-lifes.

Despite the fact that this portrait was commissioned (it netted 200 francs, which was probably a reduced price), Gauguin no doubt had motivations other than financial ones for taking it on; the sittings provided him with the opportunity to secure information from his model. Suzanne Bambridge was an Englishwoman who, in addition to speaking the Tahitian dialect fluently, also spoke French.

104

119

67, 53

117 *Mask of Tehura*. 1892 (?). Partially painted *pua* panel, 25 × 20 cm. Musée d'Orsay, Paris

118 *Tahitian Landscape*. 1893. Oil on canvas, 68 × 92 cm. Minneapolis Institute of Arts

119 *Portrait of Suzanne Bambridge*. 1891. Oil on canvas,
70 × 50 cm. Musées Royaux des Beaux-Arts, Brussels

120 *Vahine no te Tiare—Woman with a Flower*. 1891. Oil on canvas, 70 × 46 cm. Ny Carlsberg Glyptotek, Copenhagen

She was among the best-received Europeans in Tahitian society, and had married a native dignitary called Taaroa, chief of the Leeward Islands (Iles Sous le Vent). Miss Bambridge had participated in the organization of festivals and official receptions given by King Pomare V. Her intervention resulted in the quelling of the 1897 revolt of the Leeward Islands. Gauguin must have been fascinated by someone who could provide so much information about Tahitian society and customs.

Nevertheless, Miss Bambridge was a European, and what Gauguin wanted was to bring his style closer to his subject-matter. He set out his objectives in *Noa Noa*. This text, which reveals insight into his own method of working, explains the genesis and importance of one of Gauguin's most famous paintings, 120 *Vahine no te Tiare—Woman with a Flower*:

> To properly initiate myself into the character of a Tahitian face, into all the charm of a Maori smile, I had long wished to do a portrait of a woman who lived nearby and was of true Tahitian descent. One day, when she had summoned up the courage to come into my hut and look at some photographs of paintings, I asked her. She was particularly interested in a photograph of Manet's *Olympia*. With the few words I had learned in her language (I had not spoken a word of French in two months), I questioned her. She told me that this Olympia was very beautiful: I smiled at her reflection, and was moved by it. She had a sense of what is beautiful (the Ecole des Beaux-Arts considers it horrible). Suddenly she said, breaking the silence that presides over a thought: "Is it your wife?" "Yes," I lied. Me! the *tane* of Olympia! While she examined, with great interest, some religious paintings by the Italian Primitives, I tried to sketch some of her features, especially that enigmatic smile. I asked her if I could do her portrait. She made a face. "Aita" (no), she retorted in a tone almost of rage, and left.

> I was very depressed about her refusal. An hour later she returned, wearing a beautiful dress. Was it an inner struggle, or capriciousness (a most Maori trait) or simply an impulse of coquetry that only surrenders after resistance? Caprice, desire for the forbidden fruit. She smelled good, she was adorned. I realized that in my painter's scrutiny there was a tacit demand for complete surrender, a clear-sighted searching of what was within. [She was] not very pretty according to European standards, but, in fact, beautiful. All her features had a Raphaelesque harmony in the meeting of the curves, the mouth modelled by a sculptor who spoke all the tongues of language and of kisses, of joy and suffering; that melancholy of bitterness that mingles with pleasure, of passivity residing in domination. A consuming fear of the unknown.
>
> I worked quickly, fearing that her decision was ephemeral. Portrait of a woman: *Vahine no te Tiare*. I worked quickly, passionately. It was a portrait of what my eyes, veiled by my heart, were seeing. I believe that it resembled her interior [being]. That strong fire of a contained force. She had a flower behind her ear that was listening to her fragrance. And her forehead, in its majesty, reminded me, with its raised lines, of Poe's phrase: "There is no perfect beauty without a certain singularity in the proportions."

Vahine no te Tiare constitutes an interesting study of forms, and perhaps of the Maori character, but the composition remains traditional; it is a ceremonial portrait, rather than one set in natural surroundings. Gauguin was keenly aware that as long as he stayed in Papeete he would make no headway towards a genuine understanding of the Maori culture.

121 *Nafea faa ipoipo—When Will You Marry?* 1892. Oil on canvas, 101 × 77 cm. Private Collection, Basel

122 *The Man with the Axe*. 1891. Oil on canvas, 92 × 70 cm. Private Collection, Switzerland

123   *E Haere oe i hia—Where Are You Going?* 1892. Oil on canvas,
96 × 69 cm. Staatsgalerie, Stuttgart

He could barely speak the language yet, and very few Tahitians spoke French. His decision to move to Paea, and, finally Mataiea, some fifty kilometres from the capital, was ostensibly aimed at finding a cheaper lifestyle and removing himself from the official social world, where his increasingly troublesome relations were turning him into somewhat of an outcast. But the fundamental reason was clear: in Papeete he had found neither crafts, nor religion, nor traditional ways of life. By moving away from the capital and immersing himself in indigenous culture, he hoped to find traces of those distinctly Tahitian qualities. We now know he was deluding himself; but none the less, Gauguin painted pictures whose image of Tahitian civilization ultimately imposed itself on the entire Western world.

The interpretation of these paintings has gone through several distinct phases. At first, because of Gauguin's own insistence and the detailed commentary with which he accompanied a few of the works, the paintings were taken to be precise illustrations of a forgotten folklore to which Gauguin alone had access, through painstaking study and observation. Then a period of scepticism set in. Not only did the public become increasingly distrustful of literary commentary in general, but at the same time it came to light that most of Gauguin's information about mythical themes, as described in *Ancien Culte mahorie* and *Noa Noa*, was not based on his own observation, but on previously existing books, in particular one, mentioned previously, by J. A. Moerenhout. Moerenhout was a Belgian tradesman who, after spending several years in Oceania, where he kept a journal and detailed notes of interviews with old natives, compiled his data in the form of a large book with a detailed and cumbersome title: *Voyage aux îles du grand océan, contenant des documents nouveaux sur la géographie physique et politique, la langue, la littérature, la religion, les mœurs, les usages et les coutumes de leurs habitants et des considérations générales sur leur commerce, leur histoire et leur gouvernement, depuis les temps les plus reculés jusqu'à nos jours* ('Voyage to the Islands of the Great Ocean, Containing New Documents on the Physical and Political Geography, Language, Literature, Religion, Mores, Ways and Customs of their Inhabitants, as well as General Discussions of their Commerce, History and Government, from Ancient Times Until Today', Paris, 1837).

This book, rich in first-hand information, had come to Gauguin from a colonist living in Tahiti. Gauguin made good use of it, transcribing or summarizing entire passages in the manuscript of *Ancien Culte mahorie* (now conserved in the Louvre), which he illustrated with piquant watercolours. Recently, meticulous researchers have carefully reconstituted Tahitian life during Gauguin's time, as well as the artist's own movements. The latest works on the subject have, at least partially, reinstated the credibility of an ethnographic interpretation of Gauguin's work.

The fact that Gauguin, when bringing back to life lost deities, sometimes drew inspiration more from his own imagination than from the confidences of his *vahines* (mistresses) merely adds to the interest of his images. During Poussin's time, no one believed in the existence of Apollo, nor in that of Flora or Arcadia, except as symbols of eternal truths. Historians would be delighted to have as detailed records of the discussions of Roman artists in the taverns of the Via Margutta as those documenting Gauguin's disputes with the governor and the gendarme. But would they tell us much about the paintings of Poussin, or of Simon Vouet? Moerenhout and contemporary writers of geographic brochures were for Gauguin what Torquato Tasso had been for Poussin.

Judging from the date inscribed on the canvas (1891), and from a passage from *Noa Noa*, *The Man with the Axe* is generally considered to be one of the first paintings truly characteristic of Gauguin's first stay in Tahiti. However, the extremely linear style and strongly delineated areas of uniform colour bounded by rigid outlines could suggest a much later date. Gauguin himself discussed the origin and, indirectly, the significance of this image: 'Near my hut there was another hut (*Fare amu*, eating place). Near that was a pirogue. An ailing coconut tree looked like a huge parrot letting down its golden tail feathers, holding in its claws a huge bunch of coconuts. A nearly naked man was raising, with both arms, a heavy axe that left, at the top of each stroke, a blue imprint on the silver sky, and, at the bottom, an incision on the dead tree that would then relive a moment of flames, age-old heat accumulated day after day. On the purple ground [there were] long, snake-like, metallic yellow leaves, parts of an Oriental vocabulary, letters (it seemed to me) of some unknown, mysterious language. I thought I saw this word of Oceanic origin: *Atua*—God ... A woman was putting away nets in the pirogue and the horizon of blue sea was often broken by the green of the waves breaking over the coral reefs' (*Noa Noa*).

The chopped wood (Gauguin did not depict the tree itself), whose force is released through burning, is a direct reference to ancient myths linking fire with life, both birth and death. The incision reinforces the allusion to the wound from which the sap of life flows. In his exegesis, Gauguin went on to describe a mysterious inscription which he had placed on the ground but was unable to decipher. In this way, he became a medium, transmitting a message he could not even decode.

The swirls to which Gauguin attributed a symbolic—or, perhaps, symbolist—significance are a somewhat stylized representation of vegetal fibres strewn about the beach, the kind customarily gathered by Tahitian women and used for weaving. These fibres were represented more realistically in several paintings, in particular *Two Tahitian Women* 114 *on the Beach*. In others the motif becomes more stylized. An entirely different interpretation of these cabalistic interlacings proposes the following idea: 'They present a strange signature, in turn leaves, waves, roots. But they also beam forth in the vignettes of Lemmen or Van de Velde, in the tapestry cartoons of Ranson, the embroideries of Obrist, and even in the obsessive furrows of Toorop or the margins and false frames of Munch's paintings and prints.'[1] Yet another interpretation of this painting sees Gauguin himself in the figure of the woodcutter,

severing his link with civilization, symbolized by the old tree. When this painting was shown in Paris, Alfred Jarry dedicated a poem to Gauguin in which he likened the artist to an antique hero, 'like a Caesar on his chariot'.[2]

These interpretations share a common trait: they do not view the Tahitian element as of primary importance. The narrative details of this painting mark it as a transposition of an essentially European scene. Gauguin's prototype could have been Millet, whom he admired. Millet's *Woodcutter* and *Sower* possess, in their execution of a humble vocational act, the same dignity as Gauguin's woodcutter.

The text from *Noa Noa* can be read in yet another light: 'Parrot ... with its golden tail feathers ... blue imprint on the silver sky ... flames ... purple ground ... metallic yellow snake-like leaves ... the horizon of the blue sea was often broken by the green of the waves breaking against the coral reefs.' Few written texts by painters contain so many precise notes of forms and colours in so few lines. Perhaps this painting was inspired at the outset by the artist's straightforward desire to depict a natural spectacle.

According to Gauguin, the famous *Manao* 124 *Tupapau* was inspired by a moment of pagan rapture experienced by Tehura, his young *vahine*. He made a print of the same subject, which he depicted in the background of a self-portrait. On 8 December 1892, 147 Gauguin wrote his wife a long letter, which he hoped would subsequently be published, about the significance of this scene:

'Of course, many of [these] paintings will be inscrutable and you'll have a good time with them. So that you can understand something and appear knowledgeable to the others, I am going to explain the most difficult one, and the one that I wish to keep, or, perhaps sell for the highest price: the *Manao Tupapau*. I painted a young girl in the nude. In this position, the slightest detail can make it indecent. But I wanted her that way, the lines and the movement interested me. I gave her face a slightly frightened look. This fear must be

124 *Manao Tupapau—Spirit of the Dead Watching*. 1892. Oil on
canvas, 73 × 92 cm. Albright-Knox Art Gallery, Buffalo (A. Conger
Goodyear Collection, 1965)

125 *Te Burao—The Burao Tree*. 1892. Oil on canvas, 67 × 89 cm.
Art Institute of Chicago (Joseph Winterbotham)

understood, or else explained, in the context of the Tahitian character. These people have a strong tradition of fearing the spirits of the dead. A young European girl would be embarrassed to be surprised in such a position; this girl, not at all. I had to express this fear with a minimum of literary means, as in olden times. So I did this: a harmony largely sombre, sad, disquieting, reverberating in the eye like a death knell; violet, dark blue, orange-yellow. I made the bedclothes greenish yellow, first because the linens of these savages are different from our own (they are made of beaten bark); secondly, because it suggests artificial light (Tahitian women never go to bed in the dark), yet I did not want the effect of lamplight (too common); and thirdly because the yellow linking the orange-yellow and the blue completes the musical harmony. There are a few flowers in the background, but they should not be realistic, for they are imagined, so I made them like sparks of light. For the Polynesians, the phosphorescences of the night are like the spirits of the dead. They believe in them, and fear them. Finally, I made the ghost quite simply like a little old lady; because the girl, not knowing French theatrical images of spirits, can only imagine death linked with the dead person, a human being like herself. This little text will make you knowledgeable when the critics bombard you with their malicious questions. To sum up, it is necessary to make very simple paintings, with primitive, childlike themes.'

In this commentary, Gauguin mixed references to formal elements, such as line and colour, with discussion of their expressive importance, identifying descriptive markers and providing indications of the images' religious significance. He came back to this painting, which was very important to him, in *Cahier pour Aline*, where he stressed the function of the formal elements as supporting the symbolic meaning. Rarely did he come so close to a Baudelairian—or

126 *Hope* by Pierre Puvis de Chavannes. 1872. Oil on canvas, 70 × 82 cm. Musée d'Orsay, Paris

Symbolist—aesthetic approach: 'In summary— musical aspect: undulating horizontal lines; harmony between orange and blue, linked by yellows and violets; their derivatives, lightened by greenish touches. Literary aspect: The spirit of a living person linked to the spirit of the dead. Night and Day ... This genesis is written for those who always wish to know the whys and wherefores ... Otherwise, it is simply a study of a nude Tahitian.'

It was thus Gauguin himself who paved the way for the variety of different interpretations of this painting, though his emphasis is clearly on the symbolic significance of the scene, which he also stressed in a note in *Noa Noa*.

Despite the fact that *Noa Noa* was extensively rewritten by Charles Morice, the interpretation of this picture as the illustration of an authentic experience is doubtless Gauguin's own. Tehura is seized by terror; she does not see the spirit lurking behind her, yet she is aware of its presence. The light is produced only by the glow of a strip of burning *tapa* (bark). Gauguin opted against representing a lamp or a candle, for the presence of artificial light would have driven the spirit away. This phosphorescence symbolizes *Aa*, light, which has under its domination *Po*, shadow. The *tupapau* is personified by a hooded creature resembling a fifteenth-century statue of a weeping mourner. The hand is placed on the edge of the bed in an ambiguous way, either as a threat, or a gesture of possession. Jehanne Teilhet-Fisk, who has done a detailed analysis of the Tahitian sources of this painting, has argued that the *tupapau* cannot be perceived as a simple, inoffensive old woman. It is a creature of undetermined sex with the terrifying face of a *tiki* (a carved representation of an ancestor) from the Marquesas Islands. Gauguin would have found neither the term *tupapau* nor details of such nocturnal fantasies in Moerenhout's book, which indicates that he must have gleaned the information from other texts, as well as from his exchanges with the Tahitians themselves.

Even though there were no surviving Polynesian cults during Gauguin's time, with the possible exception of the Areois sect, habits and superstitions remained steadfast, and stories and popular adages continued to circulate. The fact that Gauguin appropriated passages from Moerenhout's book for his own *Ancien Culte mahorie* does not exclude his use of sources. His curiosity and intuition allowed him to collect, group, interpret and use at will the various accounts and scattered traces of a folklore that was still very much alive. Contrary to what Teilhet-Fisk has suggested, Gauguin had never been preoccupied with this sort of detail before, neither in Brittany nor in Martinique. It would not be legitimate 50 to consider *Vision after the Sermon* as the transcription of a Breton superstition; rather, it illustrates, in a stylized interpretation, an important biblical theme that had already inspired one of Delacroix's most admired masterpieces.

In the case of certain paintings, the search for a Western equivalent could easily lead to a misinterpretation. This is true for *Vairaoumati Tei Oa—Her Name is Vairaoumati* (Hermitage, Leningrad). A nude woman is seated on a sumptuous *pareo* (loincloth) while a man standing behind watches her, expressionless. In front of her is some fruit placed on a table. In the background there are two silhouettes of statues and a small house. There are few stylistic references: the woman's body, with its mixture of full-face and profile facial traits, recalls the principles of Egyptian art, but also brings to mind a painting by Puvis de Chavannes, *Hope*. The poses, and the 126 accessories—especially the cigarette—suggest the transposition of a flirtatious conversation in a classical park, with a statue of Pan in the background, or, perhaps, of a vulgar streetwalker. But the title insists on a sacred meaning, whose explanation is set out in *Ancien Culte mahorie*. It concerns the legendary 151 origins of the Areois sect, according to which the god Oro admired from afar the beauty of Vairaoumati and sent his two sisters, Teouri and Oaara, to ask her to marry him. She accepted. When they asked her her name, she replied that it was Vairaoumati. She then prepared a table of fruit and a bed in honour of Oro. They had a son, the father of the Areois.

A second version, or rather a second painting on the same theme, is even more allusive (Private Collection, New York). Only the title, hand-inscribed by Gauguin, is explicit: *Te Aa No Areois—The Race of the Areois* or 'The Seed of the Areois'. In this picture, the god Oro is not represented; Vairaoumati holds a flower in her hand, a symbol of their future descendants. Here the resemblance to Puvis de Chavannes's *Hope*—which Gauguin admired and possessed a photograph of—is even more remarkable. This painting is more distilled and less narrative than *Vairaoumati Tei Oa*; it does not claim to be a precise representation of Tahitian mythology, but, rather, the depiction of a sacred character for whom it is difficult to find a parallel in Graeco-Roman mythology. Whether or not the memory of this deity was still alive during Gauguin's time is of little importance. In these two paintings, the impression of gravity, silence and solemnity is created by techniques typical of Western art—a compact composition, with verticals and horizontals and immobile figures—yet the subject-matter is Tahitian.

127 *The Sacred Mountain*. 1892. Watercolour, 18,5 × 22.9 cm.
Fogg Art Museum, Harvard University, Cambridge, Massachusetts
(Bequest of Marian M. Phinney)

128   *Parahi te Marae—The Sacred Mountain*. 1892. Oil on canvas,
68 × 91 cm. Philadelphia Museum of Art, Pennsylvania (Gift of
Mrs Rodolphe Meyer de Schauensee)

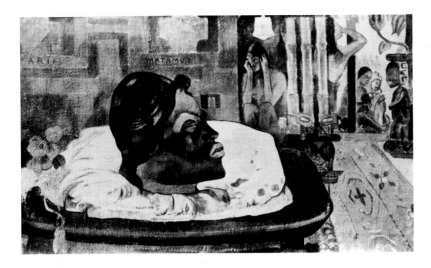

129 *Arii Matamoe—Death of Royalty*. 1892. Oil on canvas, 45 × 75 cm. The whereabouts of this painting is unknown (Formerly the Lerolle Collection)

128 *Parahi te Marae—The Sacred Mountain* is also a religious scene. The unusual, 'terraced' composition consists of four distinct, clearly-outlined sections. In the foreground, a clump of multi-coloured vegetation is cut off by the lower edge of the canvas, partially hiding a fence topped with skulls or masks, the spatial location of which is confused by the fact that its upper crosspieces have no visible supports. Teilhet-Fisk has observed that the design of this fence was inspired by a type of ear-ring, sculpted from ancestral bones, characteristic of the Marquesas Islands. It also resembles the gates of Chinese temples. This fence runs along the bottom of a golden-yellow hill whose dazzling presence occupies nearly a third of the surface of the canvas; the hill is surmounted by a statue. In the background there are outlines of mountains, curiously similar in shape to Mont Sainte-Victoire, in the Midi.

This painting represents a *marae*, or sacred enclosure, rather than an actual temple. The statue, which is vaguely anthropomorphic and gigantic in size and features, is not Tahitian; it is inspired by a *tiki* from the Marquesas Islands, and resembles the representation of Hina, on the back of the idol with a pearl, as well as in *Hina Maruru—Thanks to Hina* (Private Collection, USA). However, Teilhet-Fisk's scholarly interpretation argues that the statue in

Parahi Te Marae is not of Hina. This is the only one of Gauguin's paintings in which he has represented a solitary god, without companions or worshippers. Gauguin clarified the meaning of this painting in a letter to his wife, dated 8 December 1892: 'Marae: temple, or place reserved for the cult of the gods and for human sacrifices' and he mentioned the fairly steep price of 700 francs for the picture.

In Gauguin's time, the practices of human sacrifice and cannibalism had disappeared from the Pacific islands. Perhaps the solitude of the statue symbolizes the passing of this sanguinary cult. The composition's two cultural elements—the statue and the fence—disappear behind the vegetation, symbol of life. Once again, Gauguin expressed this meaning through the devices of his artistic medium.

Amid this solemn world with its Arcadian serenity, one macabre painting stands out: *Arii Matamoe—* 129 *Death of Royalty*. It represents a severed head placed on a Tahitian stool. In a letter dated June 1892, Gauguin himself confided in Daniel de Monfreid that the origin of this painting was fortuitous: 'I think that it is a rather nice bit of painting. It is not altogether mine; I stole it from a piece of pine. Don't let on, but, after all, you do what you can, and when a block of marble or wood draws a head for you, it's jolly tempting to snatch it up.' Apparently he had perceived the shape of a severed head in the veins of a board and had taken up the motif, in the manner of Chinese artists who sign scenes of fantastic cities based on the quirks of a particular block of marble. Whether or not chance was at the origin of the work, Gauguin turned it to his advantage. In the same letter he wrote: 'I have just finished a severed Tahitian head, nicely arranged on a white cushion in an imaginary palace, guarded by imaginary women.'

This insistence on the imaginary elements is both a rationalization for his 'borrowing' and an affirmation of his responsibility for the image.

130 *Mata Mua—Former Times*. 1892. Oil on canvas, 93 × 72 cm. Thyssen-Bornemisza Collection, Lugano

131 *Tahitian*. n.d. Pastel on paper, 39 × 30.2 cm. Metropolitan Museum of Art, New York (Bequest of Miss Adelaide Milton de Groot, 1967)

132 *Vahine no te Vi—Woman with Mango*. 1892. Oil on canvas, 72.7 × 44.5 cm. Museum of Art, Baltimore (Dr Claribel Cone and Miss Etta Cone Collection)

133 *Te Ra'au Rahi—The Big Tree*. 1891. Oil on canvas,
74 × 92.8 cm. Cleveland Museum of Art (Joint ownership of
Cleveland Museum of Art and anonymous collector)

134   *The Tahitians*. 1894 (?) Pencil and charcoal on paper mounted
on cardboard, 85.5 × 102 cm. Tate Gallery, London

135 *La Siesta*. 1894. Oil on canvas, 87 × 116 cm. From the Private
Collection of Mr and Mrs Walter Annenberg

According to Teilhet-Fisk, this head presents a number of specific details characteristic of heads mummified by the indigenous peoples of New Zealand, a practice which was unknown in Tahiti. Gauguin may, however, have seen this type of head in Papeete, where they were sought after as curiosities. The artist's own interpretation of this painting is clearly expressed in the title. Painted shortly after the death of Pomare V, it refers to the demise of Tahitian royalty and, with it, the disappearance of the indigenous culture. The setting, a product of Gauguin's imagination, reinforces the royalty theme. There is also a motif 'borrowed' from Gauguin's earlier work, a rare 'expressive portrait' of a woman seated in a despairing position, her head resting on her hands. This pose is perhaps inspired by that of Peruvian mummies, and it recurs in other works: a print as well as in several paintings, most notably in *Human Misery*, already from the Arles period, and in *Life and Death*. The same pitiful figure appears in a painting which dates from his final stay in Brittany, *Village Scene* (The Art Institute of Chicago). In the background of *Arii Matamoe* there is a man raising an axe—is it a headsman? There is also a statue of a *tiki*, and the wall is decorated with a geometric design from the Marquesas Islands which Gauguin had also used in *Parahi te Marae*. The dead king is thus surrounded by several religious symbols. To interpret this painting—as Teilhet-Fisk does—as a symbolic representation of the end of traditional Tahitian culture seems to be a reasonable suggestion.

128

But it is also clearly the transposition of a Western theme—that of Orpheus, or of Saint John the Baptist. This image of the head of a young man, exposed on a platter and surrounded by lamenting women, belongs to an ancient tradition which experienced a curious revival during Gauguin's youth. Gustave Moreau's *Orpheus* entered the Musée du Luxembourg in 1867; and after 1870, Moreau painted numerous variations on the theme of Salome with the head of St John the Baptist. This image received a sort of literary consecration with Huysmans's *A rebours* (1884), in which the hero, Des Esseintes,

hangs a copy of the picture in his personal museum. Even more closely related to Gauguin's painting is Andrea Solario's *Head of St John the Baptist*, whose entry into the Louvre in 1868 had attracted considerable attention.[3] Odilon Redon drew a copy of it shortly afterward, and used the image quite openly on more than one occasion; Mallarmé's *Hérodiade* was published in 1887; and Jean Delville's *Orphée* appeared in 1893. Such connections in no way undermine a Tahitian interpretation of this painting. On the contrary, they shed light on the way Gauguin transposed Western models.

By Gauguin's own admission, many paintings from his first stay in Tahiti have no precise theme. Their titles were chosen after they had been painted and were sometimes inscribed on the canvases by Daniel de Monfreid in France. But Gauguin was attached to the Tahitian titles for their almost incantatory value. With regard to his own translations of them, he wrote to his wife on 8 December 1892: 'This translation is only for you, so that you can give it to those who ask. But in the catalogue I want the titles exactly as they are on the paintings. This language is bizarre and carries multiple meanings.' This same letter to Mette contained a list beginning with a series of explicitly religious titles; then, as if he were establishing some kind of hierarchy in his output, he continued with four secular, quite general titles: *The Big Tree*, *Beneath the Pandanus*, *The Maori Hut*, *Woman with a Flower*.

133

120

In addition to these, there were about twenty scenes of local life, without precise narrative elements, which probably constituted illustrations of those travel books of which *Le Mariage de Loti* was the best known. We should keep in mind that his expressed demand, as recorded above, for an official mission to Tahiti was to execute 'a series of paintings of the country whose objective will be to capture its character and light'.

About a dozen paintings share similar pictorial elements: small figures set within their natural surroundings, usually consisting of trees and flowers; animals seen in profile, like heraldic silhouettes;

136   *Eaha oe feii—What, Are You Jealous?* 1892. Oil on canvas,
66 × 89 cm. Pushkin Museum, Moscow

137 *Pape Moe—Mysterious Water*. 1893. Oil on canvas, 99 × 75 cm. Private Collection, Switzerland

138 *Hina Tefatou—The Moon and the Earth*. 1893. Oil on canvas, 114.3 × 62.6 cm. Museum of Modern Art, New York (Lillie P. Bliss Collection)

139 *Be mysterious*. 1890. Painted linden panel, 73 × 95 cm. Musée
d'Orsay, Paris

140 *Fatata te Miti—By the Sea*. 1892. Oil on canvas, 67.9 × 91.5 cm. National Gallery of Art, Washington, D.C. (Chester Dale Collection)

a wall of a house, parallel to the picture plane; very little sky. In these pictures, the centring of the image, the reduced size of the figures compared to the natural elements, straightforward, balanced composition, emphasis on verticals, and even the size of the canvases themselves recall scenes painted in Brittany and in Arles. But the French paintings always show peasants working; in Gauguin's eyes, only the children had the right to play there: little girls danced, boys wrestled. In Tahiti, men and women can be seen sitting, chatting or playing a musical instrument, bathing or braiding pandanus fibres, an activity which Gauguin probably recognized as being both utilitarian and artistic: 'A significant number of the decorative motifs painted on *tapas* (cloth made of pounded bark) were inspired by designs created by the interlacing fibres of a braid of pandanus.'[4] These strands of pandanus could often be seen scattered on the ground, and we have already seen how Gauguin used them to represent cryptographic symbols in 122 *The Man with the Axe*.

Did Gauguin really find a kind of Arcadia in Tahiti? The idleness of his characters, whose principal occupations appear to be music, conversation and strolling; the beauty of the natural surroundings, which even bestowed free food on the inhabitants; and the absence of violent natural elements such as wind, storms and harsh contrasts of light, would suggest that he did. But this idyllic vision was not exactly true to life, and, in particular, it contrasted sharply with Gauguin's own financial hardship. His vision was selective, and his imagination filled in the gaps, constructing a coherent universe that conformed to his desires. Many other painters did the same. We hardly believe, for example, that the paintings of Le Nain constitute documentary evidence of peasant conditions in the seventeenth century. Rather, they corresponded to the image that the Parisian bourgeoisie, who hung them in their sumptuous homes, wished to see.

In this idyllic world that Gauguin depicted, some canvases suggest a deep relationship between man 137 and nature. In *Pape Moe—Mysterious Water*, amidst

141   *The Bathers* by Jean-Honoré Fragonard (1732-1806). Oil on canvas, 64 × 80 cm. Musée du Louvre, Paris

lush vegetation, a man leans towards a waterfall to drink. It matters little that this scene was inspired by an old photograph; what matters is that, from among the many motifs presented to him, Gauguin chose to render that particular one. He also did a watercolour and a monotype of the same scene, both treated in the same fairly naturalistic way. Only the title of the painting suggests—somewhat gratuitously—another meaning. In another painting, *Hina Tefatou—The* 138 *Moon and the Earth*, the same motif appears with a much clearer symbolism: here the drinker is a woman, and the waterfall becomes the bust of a male figure, perhaps a statue. Water appears to flow from the figure's chest. This picture is stiffer and more 'synthetist', as if, in moving from a real to an imaginary scene, Gauguin moved to a higher level of stylization. But the title still surpasses the image itself in symbolic content. This figure has a thematic ancestor in another painting in the Louvre by Poussin, the passer-by in *Diogenes*.

142   *Te Nave Nave Fenua—Fragrant Earth*. 1892. Oil on canvas, 91 × 72 cm. Ohara Museum of Art, Kurashiki

This same type of communion with natural elements is evident in *Fatata te Miti—By the Sea*: two women are running towards the water, their arms raised in wave- or branch-like movements, similar to Fragonard's *Bathers*. This work is exceptional for its dynamism, as well as for its subject-matter. Gauguin, who had been a sailor for more than ten years and had spent nearly his entire life by the sea, almost never painted seascapes.

This pantheistic feeling of admiration before such splendid and colourful natural surroundings animates most of the works from this period. In a *Still-Life*, bananas and lemons, products of nature's bounty, are set forth like votive fruit in a still-life by Zurbaran. In *Ia Orana Maria*, or in *Te Nave Nave Fenua*, the vegetation is treated like a precious, richly coloured tapestry. The title of this painting supports a paradisiacal interpretation. In fact, this picture, one of the most successful of its type, has been justifiably compared to earlier paintings that explicitly represent Eve. Gauguin was partial to this natural, graceful pose. It appears again in a print and a watercolour (Musée des Beaux-Arts, Grenoble), one of the rare paintings in which Gauguin gave himself over to the Neo-Impressionist technique of little dots.

The meaning of certain symbols in this painting is less clear. The two red birds, whose forms are almost heraldic, and the black lizard hidden in the vegetation might be interpreted in a variety of ways; the same is true of the peacock feather the woman seems to be picking up. She is alone, entirely nude, in a garden of delights, standing on a globe that dominates the world, not unlike certain Renaissance virgins.

We are well informed, thanks to Gauguin's correspondence, *Noa Noa* and a few notes remaining in local archives, of the many difficulties Gauguin encountered in Tahiti. The most important one was

143 *Tahitian Women Bathing.* 1892. Oil on canvas, 109.9 × 98.5 cm. Metropolitan Museum of Art, New York (Robert Lehman Collection, 1975)

his lack of money, which caused him to devote himself increasingly to sculpture, having no means to buy canvas. His initial resources were quickly exhausted, and the income he managed to come by on the spot was negligible; in addition, he was continually disappointed by the modest sums of money sent to him from home. These financial difficulties finally induced him to request repatriation, which, according to official regulations, he could obtain free of charge within one year of his arrival. On 12 June 1892 he wrote to the new Director of Fine Arts, Henry Roujon, who had taken office on 20 October 1891. (Some Gauguin biographers have confused the ministerial Office of Fine Arts with the Académie des Beaux-Arts, which is a part of the Institut de France and had nothing to do with Gauguin's missions.) The letter read as follows:

Tahiti. 12 June 1892
Monsieur le Directeur des Beaux-Arts,
You were kind enough, at my request, to grant me an official mission to Tahiti, in order to study the customs and landscape of this country.
I hope that upon my return my work will be judged favourably by you. As frugal as one tries to be, life in Tahiti is very dear, and travelling is expensive.
I therefore have the honour to request that I be repatriated. I am counting on your good will to facilitate my return to France.
Respectfully yours,
Paul Gauguin

It would seem, from reading certain biographical accounts, that this first Tahitian period consisted of little more than a long series of problems, ranging from general disillusionment and financial difficulties to misadventures with the authorities and the white population. However, if we ignore those 'superficial' aspects of the sojourn and concentrate exclusively on the works produced during that time, the overall impression is very different. At least forty paintings are fundamentally successful, demonstrating both

full technical mastery and a wealth of themes and subject-matter. These works reflect no nostalgia for Europe; rather, they attest to an intense fascination for this equatorial paradise, with its colours, its exuberance, and its vast repertoire of myths and legends, ideal raw material for Gauguin's intensely imaginative and poetic art.

A comparison with Poussin can serve as a point of reference: his first years in Rome were difficult, marked by hardship due to illness and difficulty in obtaining commissions. The few documents that have survived show him involved in a scuffle with pontifical guards, called as a witness in the trial of a swindler and taking Easter communion in a different parish every year. At the same time, he was painting magnificent religious and secular scenes which derive less from his experiences as part of the bohemian artistic scene in Rome in 1630 than from his hard work, his cultural background and his fertile imagination.

In Gauguin's case, the abundance of information has tended to cover up the essential fact that his output during those eighteen months adds up to a brilliant achievement, and it seems clear that he was fully aware of that fact. But it took time to acquire that certainty; in November 1891 he wrote to Sérusier: 'I am now seriously down to work ... no paintings yet but a mass of research which could prove fruitful, and many documents which will be of use to me for a long time, I hope, in France.' In March 1892 he again wrote to Sérusier: 'Thanks to Morice's desertion I am at the end of the line and must return home. Why? I have no more money. However, I wish I could stay, for I have not finished my work. I have only just started, and I feel that I am on the way to something good.' To Mette he wrote, without false modesty: 'I am an artist and you are right—I am a great artist, and I know it.' Here we can discern echoes of another

great loner affirming: 'There is only one Cézanne.'

A few months later, the tone of his letters was already changing. In the summer of 1892 he wrote to Mette: 'I am quite pleased with my latest work, and I feel that I am beginning to assimilate the Oceanic character. I am sure that what I am doing here has never been done before, and is totally unknown in France.' In fact, he might have tried to find new sources of income there, but the sense that he had achieved what he set out to do motivated him to return home. The scant news he got of the Parisian artistic scene could only confirm his intentions. On 1 April 1892, a long article by Albert Aurier on the Symbolists appeared in *La Revue encyclopédique*. While Aurier's interpretation of Gauguin's work may not have coincided with the artist's own, he none the less gave homage to Gauguin by attributing to him the position of group leader: 'The incontestable initiator of this artistic movement—perhaps one day we shall refer to it as a renaissance—was Paul Gauguin.'

Gauguin felt that the moment was right for him to take up his place in the highest ranks of the Parisian artistic milieu. The Impressionists, despite their various transformations, were, for him, history; Seurat was dead and Cézanne's work remained confidential. Gauguin felt sure that young painters were now looking to him for inspiration. Had it not been for his ambition to take his well-earned place as artistic leader, which he hoped would result in both material and moral rewards, he probably would not have decided to return to France.

Gauguin was granted free passage home. Although Henry Roujon had old-fashioned taste in art, he was friends with Mallarmé and probably solicited the writer's opinion. Unfortunately, because of Governor Lacascade's lack of good will, Gauguin's departure was delayed by several months, and he missed the exhibition organized in Copenhagen by his friend Theodor Philipsen. Philipsen, a Danish painter, had managed to have him invited to participate in a 'Free Exhibition of Modern Art', a sort of independent Salon, which, thanks to the cooperation of Theo Van

144 *Te Faaturuma—The Brooding Woman*. 1891. Oil on canvas, 91.2 × 68.7 cm. Worcester Art Museum

Gogh's wife, also contained a large room consecrated to paintings by Vincent. Gauguin had met Philipsen in Copenhagen in 1884; he saw him again in Paris during the 1889 Exposition Universelle, and again in Copenhagen during his brief visit in April 1891. In 1892 Philipsen bought from Mette Gauguin the *Nude* that had so attracted Huysmans in 1880. Two other Danish painters who were in contact with Gauguin in Paris, Mogens Ballin and Jens Ferdinand Willumsen, subsequently became involved with the Nabi group.

The two organizers of the Copenhagen exhibition, Philipsen and Johan Rohde, asked Mette to lend them the works she already had, and to have more forwarded from Tahiti. This was Gauguin's moment of revenge. He chose eight works and managed, with a good dose of luck, to send them off to Paris with a French soldier who was being repatriated.[5] From there, Monfreid and Schuffenecker sent them along to Copenhagen, where they arrived just in time for the show on 26 March 1893. Mette wrote to Schuffenecker: 'Thanks to you and Monfreid for all your help. I hope it will have positive results for this great husband of mine. Everyone finds the paintings superb.'[6] Mette gave no personal opinion of these canvases from Tahiti, which she had just seen for the first time. However, despite the fact that she was selling earlier works for less than 200 francs, she wrote of this series '... I do not want to sell the paintings from Tahiti for derisory prices; I shall sell them only if I receive reasonable payment—between five and six hundred francs each.' A total of fifty paintings, drawings and sculptures were assembled in the show. Unfortunately, when Gauguin finally arrived in France, he had considerable difficulty ascertaining which works had been sold and regaining possession of the remaining ones.

Chapter XI   Return to France

Gauguin's subsequent, and final, stay in France lasted only twenty-two months, from 30 August 1893 to 3 July 1895. The first months were devoted more to working out a plan for the future—which he had probably already reflected upon during two inactive months of ocean passage—than to painting. His actions during this time demonstrated, once again, that unique mixture of calculation and hasty improvisation, of cunning and naïvety. He arrived in Paris full of hope and determination. At first things went well with the promise of an exhibition at Durand-Ruel's and an unexpected inheritance. But he subsequently met with a series of personal and professional disappointments that ultimately drove him away again, defeated.

Gauguin's first concerns upon arriving in Paris were to renew his friendships and retrieve his work. He went to visit Maurice Joyant, who, as Theo Van Gogh's successor at the Boussod and Valadon gallery, had previously received him favourably. Unfortunately, Joyant had since left the gallery, placing Gauguin's remaining paintings in the care of Daniel de Monfreid. Other works were being kept by the painter's old friend, Schuffenecker. Another dealer, Alphonse Portier, who had once been interested in Gauguin's work, had by now also given over what paintings he had to Monfreid.

Gauguin took lodgings in the Rue de la Grande Chaumière, near the Académie Colarossi in Montparnasse, where he had lived two years earlier. Upon arriving in Marseilles, he had written to Mette, asking her to meet him in Paris, and pressing her to send

him the paintings she was keeping in Denmark; she shied away from both propositions. After some days of living from hand to mouth, Gauguin received word that his father's brother, Isidore, had died in Orleans. He attended the funeral, where he learned that his uncle's estate, totalling 30,000 francs, was to be divided between himself and his sister, who was living in Colombia. Although the settlement was not immediate, Gauguin's reaction was; he rejoiced in a feeling of financial freedom he had not known for years, borrowing—and spending—with abandon. To Mette's entreaties for a share of the inheritance, he argued that his professional expenses were exorbitant, but that this stroke of fortune provided the perfect occasion for his wife to come to Paris: 'As you have a bit of free time, why not come to Paris with little Paul, it would be a change of pace for you, and I would so enjoy embracing you... I have a studio which is fairly well fitted out, so there would be no money worries, nor expenses. And if you can find the money for the trip, in two months or so it will be reimbursed... there's no point in making all sorts of objections and calculations, just *COME*, and as soon as possible.'

Gauguin had another reason for wanting to see Mette. She had sold a number of his paintings at the Copenhagen exhibition. However, not only was she doggedly hanging on to that revenue, but she was also refusing both to provide details about what was sold and to forward the remaining paintings to Gauguin. He was now very much in need of them, for, several days after arriving in Paris, he had obtained

145 *Cahier pour Aline*. 1893. Watercolour on flyleaf of notebook with a photograph of a painting by Corot, pasted, 22 × 34 cm (double page opened out). Bibliothèque d'Art et d'Archéologie, Paris

146 *Annah the Javanese*. 1893. Oil on canvas, 116 × 81 cm. Private Collection

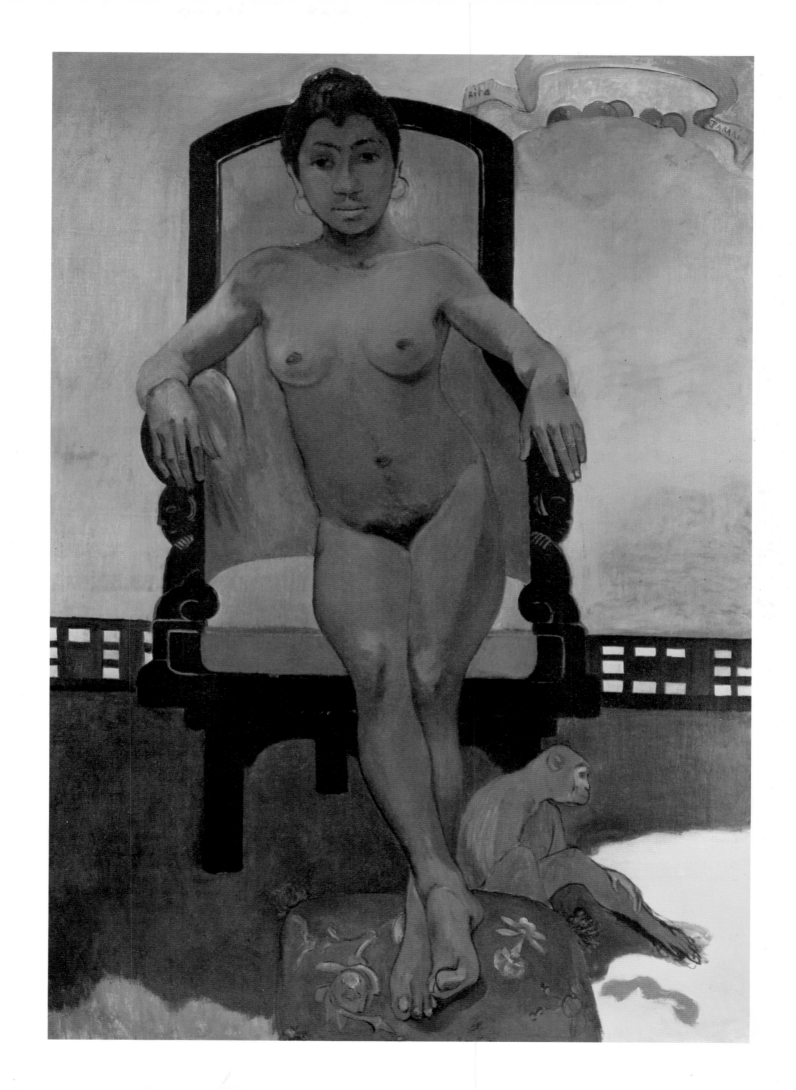

what was, for him, a most cherished prize: an invitation to hold a one-man show at Durand-Ruel's.

During his absence, the artistic climate in Paris had changed considerably. The death of Seurat on 29 March 1891 had had little effect on Gauguin, and he may even have been secretly relieved to note the passing of an artist with such a following among the younger generation. At the same time, certain veteran Impressionists had come into their own. Monet had begun to paint his famous series of works representing changes of light on a single motif: in 1891 he showed his *Haystack* series at Durand-Ruel's, and, in 1892 his *Poplars*, which, in turn, paved the way for the infinite nuances of the *Water-lilies*. Still, the City of Paris refused to commission a mural from him. In 1882 Renoir and Pissarro also had shows at Durand-Ruel's, and it was quite natural that Gauguin's immediate desire was to show his work there as well. Paul Durand-Ruel was finally reaping the benefits of years of persistent efforts to promote the Impressionists. Doubtless he had kept track of the development of an artist who had participated in the final Impressionist exhibitions, and whose showing at the Café Volpini, as well as the auction at the Hôtel Drouot, had been well publicized. Durand-Ruel had already bought a few paintings from Gauguin as early as 1881, and had sold him, in turn, some Impressionist works. But, at the moment when Gauguin returned from Tahiti in 1893, they had had no contact for some years. Perhaps Durand-Ruel had become interested in opening his gallery to a new kind of painting. Or perhaps Degas had advised him to look closely at Gauguin's work. Whatever the reasons, Gauguin was convinced he deserved the opportunity to show his work at the gallery which had finally succeeded in getting recognition for his artistic elders. This was his reward—and his revenge—for those long years of hanging paintings on café walls.

Gauguin immediately set about the task of preparing his show, refusing Mette's entreaties to come to Denmark. On 10 September he wrote: 'In November I intend to strike a tremendous blow, on which my whole future could depend, and, judging from what I've seen so far, I think it will be a great success. But there is not a moment to spare, and you must understand that I cannot leave Paris before the exhibition, that is, end of November.' His first task was to mount and frame his canvases, some of which had probably suffered from the journey. In one letter he wrote that he had 'many canvases to repair, retouch, and fix up for my exhibition'. He may even have painted a few more pictures on Tahitian themes to bolster his collection.

He was probably also concerned, as he had been before the auction at the Hôtel Drouot, to 'prepare' the public for the show by arranging articles in the press. He took up with Charles Morice again, though, not long before, he had hotly accused Morice of being a 'miserable liar and thief' when the latter failed to forward to Tahiti money earned from sales of his paintings. However, when Morice wrote an apologetic letter, Gauguin agreed to see him again. This reversal could be attributed to the fact that Gauguin rarely held a grudge, and that, after all, he admired Morice's intellectual qualities; he may also have been keenly aware that Morice was one of his rare supporters in Parisian literary circles. Indeed, Albert Aurier, who had written sympathetically and intelligently about Gauguin's work, linking him to the Symbolist movement, had died prematurely in October 1892. Gauguin hesitated about contacting Octave Mirbeau.

Besides, he was still counting on Morice to help him with his Tahitian journal, *Noa Noa*. Gauguin was determined to see that book published, and not only for the publicity it would create for his paintings; those short, largely imaginary texts about Tahitian life and folklore were an essential complement to his plastic works. We shall come back to the much-confused story of the writing of *Noa Noa*. As for the other text dating from this period, *Cahier pour Aline*, it was probably written in Tahiti, although this has not been established definitively. In fact, Gauguin pasted into that manuscript reviews of the Durand-Ruel exhibition, sent to him by a press agency.

145

He decided to show forty paintings, mostly from Tahiti, and two pieces of sculpture. Only one picture referred to his Breton period. His objective in limiting his choice from among the more than sixty paintings at his disposal may have been to strengthen the show's impact. Or perhaps he had to limit the number of works shown because of the size of the gallery. The opening, which was originally planned for 4 November, took place five days later. Charles Morice, who wrote the preface for the catalogue, gave this sinister account of the event: 'All his grand projects were ruined, and perhaps the cruellest wound for this proud man was being forced to admit that he had worked things out poorly. Had he not dreamed of being the prophet who, little known to those petty-minded souls who are incapable of bowing down before his genius, moved away temporarily to get some perspective and then returned, even greater in stature? "If my flight was a defeat," he said to himself, "my return will be a victory" ... Yet the return only aggravated the defeat of the departure, and irremediably ... And as soon as he realized that no one was interested in him, that they were not even willing to discuss his work, he affected an unshakable serenity, and, making sure that not a trace of constraint could be detected in his smile, he interrogated his friends about their impressions, and spoke with them openly, gaily, without the slightest bitterness. Towards the end of this ill-fated day, he accompanied Degas, who was expressing his admiration, to the door. All the while he said nothing, but at the moment the old master prepared to take his leave he declared: "Mr Degas, don't forget your cane." And with that he held out a sculpted cane which he had just detached from the wall.'

Though many Gauguin biographers have taken Morice's account as truth, it may in fact be somewhat exaggerated. In fact, Morice's object was to emphasize an image of the artist, pitted against adversity, and himself, the virtuous critic, boldly speaking his mind. This text was written in 1920; Morice thus had five years' distance in which to place himself in the admirable position of defending a hitherto unrecognized genius. In fact, twelve paintings were sold at the show, which constituted more than a quarter of the total number; many painters would have been satisfied with such results. Furthermore, Gauguin had set his prices high, a fact he used, in a letter to Mette, to justify his inability to send her money: 'I put the prices very high: 2 to 3,000 francs on average. At Durand-Ruel's one can hardly do otherwise, taking into account Pissarro, Monet, etc... .'[1] These sales allowed Gauguin to cover his expenses, for Durand-Ruel had lent him the gallery free of charge.

Mallarmé, to whom Gauguin had written to express his intention of attending an upcoming Tuesday gathering in the Rue de Rome, visited the exhibition and remarked: 'It is extraordinary how one can put so much mystery in so much brilliance.' The turn of phrase is pleasant, but the meaning unclear. As we mentioned before, Mallarmé may have influenced his friend Henry Roujon, Director of Fine Arts, to agree to repatriate Gauguin. But he does not appear to have intervened when Gauguin's offer to present a painting, *Ia Orana Maria*, to the Musée du Luxembourg was declined by the then curator, Léonce Bénédicte. In order fully to appreciate the official milieu's persistent lack of understanding of contemporary art, we have only to recall that these events took place on the eve of the Gustave Caillebotte legacy affair.[2] Men for whom an 1874 Monet or Sisley was still an enigma hardly possessed the means to appreciate a Maori *Virgin with Child*.

How did critics react to the show? In general, we tend to remember the spiteful remarks, of which Gauguin received his share: 'To amuse your children, take them to Gauguin's exhibition. They will be distracted by the colourful images of female quadrumanes, reclining on billiard cloth, the whole scene described in the local language';[3] or, again: 'Writing and painting both participate here in the same mockery of good sense, the same affront to reason. To speak of it would be to give importance to this farce... so charitably we indulge the fantasies of a poor, demented brain... however, I have neither the time nor the space to waste on such sweet pity for a

109

147   *Self-Portrait* (on verso, *Portrait of William Molard*). 1893. Oil
on canvas, 45 × 38 cm. Musée d'Orsay, Paris

148   *Mahana no Atua—Day of the Gods*. 1894 (?). (May have been
painted in Paris.) Oil on canvas, 66 × 89 cm. Art Institute of Chicago
(Helen Birch-Bartlett Collection)

poor soul.'[4] Another article was less malicious than unsympathetic, though not lacking in astuteness when it spoke of 'the coquetry that Gauguin uses to violate the most mundane elements of drawing'. This same review evoked the term 'synthesis', much in fashion at the time: 'I can think of nothing more infantile than this affected return to uncertain primitives, emphasizing only their faults, with no attention paid to their naïvety or their desire to please ... There are always unashamed admirers who appear fascinated, using synthesis as a pretext.'[5]

Octave Mirbeau, faithful to the admiration he had expressed for Gauguin's work in 1891, spoke in his review of the process by which Gauguin had arrived at such original work, linking his art to his experiences. Mirbeau's words betray his own aesthetic preference for a realistic style in which observation prevails over imagination: 'He lived exclusively among the natives, and in their manner ... he took part in their games, their pleasures, their traditions. In the evening he attended their meetings, listened to the elder's stories, immersed himself in the sublime poetry of legends and joined in the chorus of improvised chants ... Gauguin mixed his life so totally with that of the Maoris that all this history became as much a part of him as his own. He had only to translate it into his work. And here it is, a body of work bursting with strange beauty, which even Pierre Loti never for a moment suspected.'[6]

Perhaps the most interesting review of the 1893 show was one signed by a certain Fabien Vieillard, a pseudonym for a still mysterious author. Vieillard spoke admiringly, while maintaining a detached tone; he was knowledgeable and perceptive with regard to Gauguin's earlier work. Like Mirbeau, he turned a comparison with Loti to Gauguin's advantage. Vieillard's writing style, precious and carefully worked, recalls that of Mallarmé. Could it be that Mallarmé himself—who had, in the past, used pseudonyms when publishing journalistic commentary—wished to express, through a filter, an admiration for Gauguin's work which, until then, he had only intimated in the briefest, most general terms? This

hypothesis seems unlikely. Yet Vieillard's style is so similar to Mallarmé's that the piece may have been an intentional pastiche, written by Ernest Lajeunesse, a writer who was to make his name the following year with a collection of pastiches,[7] and whose choice of a pseudonym would thus have been a play on the French words *jeunesse* (youth) and *vieillard* (old man). His words are well worth reproducing here, for they are among the most eloquent ever published about Gauguin during his lifetime; this was the article that Gauguin pasted into the manuscript of *Cahier pour Aline*, as mentioned previously:

Paul Gauguin had already shown himself to be a great artist in his earlier works, but one thing is sure: his deep thinking and powerful painting have never been so evident as in the current exhibition at Durand-Ruel's.

The penetrating vision of his earlier works, intuitive as well as knowledgeable, has changed little. But it now reappears with such added brilliance, drenched in that extraordinary light so disconcerting and charming to our unaccustomed eyes, that it can seem quite new. In fact, never before has the sun been painted by an artist who interprets nature so directly, so faithfully, so courageously. Alas! All this is quite incomprehensible for those who swoon over the pretentious, sorry efforts of [artists like] Meissonier and Detaille.

We do not intend, in these lines, to examine the boldness, the robust simplicity, the precision of technique; and there is no need to speak of Gauguin's indisputable decorative skills. What strikes us, at first glance, is the thought, the lofty intellectualism which emanates from these fifty canvases, these rays of sunlight, clustered together, as if by chance, in this exhibition.

In the same way that Gauguin showed us a mystical image of Brittany, with its calm, quietly resigned beings, here he offers us this leaden sky and roughly drawn, nearly incomplete figures, frozen in the hieratic poses of idols, with their limpid, almost automatic look that frightens and disconcerts us.

All these figures become one with their surroundings; one could not tear them away, and it is thus that we must understand them, growing from the very earth, like the harsh flora that clasps them.

Here is a solid conception, truly mystical, accessible to only a very few; indeed, we are far from the irritating preciousness of a Loti, [or] faded decorations in bourgeois sitting rooms. This is an entire, unknown world, an obscure part of humanity that Gauguin reveals to us so simply, yet powerfully, with neither faintness nor flattery.

It is always unpleasant for an artist to read mocking or malicious reviews of his work. But the praise of this exhibition was both more prominent and more plentiful than the criticism. If we compare the reviews with, for example, those of the first Impressionist exhibitions, some ten years earlier, Gauguin could hardly complain; in 1874 the unfavourable, even insulting reviews had been far more numerous. Gauguin was right when, after deploring the exhibition's mediocre financial showing, he wrote to Mette in December 1893: 'Let us think no more of it. The most important thing is that my exhibition was a tremendous artistic success, and even provoked anger and jealousy. The press treated me as they have never treated anyone, that is, reasonably and with praise. At this moment, I am considered by many to be the greatest modern painter.'

Gauguin's words may lack modesty, but they are not devoid of truth. More and more 'disciples' claimed to draw their inspiration from his work. The Nabis, who had been converted to *cloisonnisme* since the *Talisman* period, were now exhibiting at Le Barc de Boutteville. Gauguin's most recent works provided new stimulus for their own research.

Gauguin was quite content to stay in Paris. His inheritance had, at least temporarily, relieved him of financial worries. He moved into more spacious lodgings in the Rue Vercingétorix, also in Montpar-

nasse. The walls were soon covered with his own works, and with reproductions of Renaissance works by Holbein, Cranach and Botticelli, as well as modern paintings by Manet, Puvis de Chavannes and Degas. He enjoyed entertaining, and a number of accounts of his parties have survived. He had a piano on which one of his neighbours, the composer William Molard, played Wagner. Someone invariably took photographs. (Gauguin owned photographic equipment as early as 1891.) The guests included Meyer de Haan, Schuffenecker, Sérusier, the sculptor Paco Durrio and, of course, Charles Morice and Julien Leclercq. It seems that he did not often manage to entertain his true 'disciples', the Nabis, for their somewhat bourgeois lifestyle was incompatible with his self-styled, rather bohemian image.

In February 1894 Gauguin travelled to Brussels for the opening of the Salon de la Libre Esthétique, the group that had succeeded the XX, and was also headed by Octave Maus. Gauguin had responded to the invitation by sending five paintings, including *Manao Tupapau*. We have seen how, in 1891, when 124 invited to show in Brussels, he was unable to go for lack of funds. This time he took advantage of the opportunity to continue on to Bruges to see paintings by Memling. Upon his return, he published a review of the Brussels show in *Essais d'art libre*, a small magazine run by his friend Napoléon Roinard. With the exception of Odilon Redon, he had little praise for the exhibitors. However, he was attracted by the work of Jan Toorop, sensing that artist's Oriental roots.

Despite the fact that he maintained a bitter-sweet correspondence with his wife, and continued to speak of a reunion, Gauguin had a number of love affairs, one of which inspired the most important painting of this Parisian period. Ambroise Vollard 146 boasted of having introduced Gauguin to a young Asian girl called Annah, known as 'the Javanese'. At that time Vollard was just making his name on the Parisian art market, profiting from that astonishing flair that would make him one of the greatest dealers of the first half of the twentieth century. Vollard was interested in Gauguin, Cézanne and Rousseau, all of whom were still relatively unknown. However, Vollard's accounts of that period often corresponded more to his imagination than to the actual facts. Whatever the circumstances of their meeting, Annah became Gauguin's regular companion, revealing herself to be vivacious, capricious and, later, dishonest. But she doubtless reminded Gauguin of Polynesia, and of his gentle *vahines*.

In Gauguin's painting Annah is entirely nude, seated majestically in a wooden chair whose arm-rests are decorated with sculpted Polynesian divinities. Her feet are resting on a floral cushion, next to which is seated a little monkey that Gauguin had bought her. This combination of an animal and a nude recalls the presence of the black cat in Manet's *Olympia*. The skirting-board is decorated with black and white motifs which are more evocative of the Wiener Werkstätte than of the Far East. In the upper right-hand portion of the background there is a suggestion of some fruit and of a second figure with a Maori inscription, all of which are partially erased. The model's stately pose, the absence of narrative elements—the monkey could be seen as a sort of mascot posted at the foot of the throne—and the use of large, flat areas of colour combine to give the painting a solemn simplicity. In addition, Gauguin has pushed formal simplification to a high level of virtuosity through the manipulation of colours: sometimes he places similar tones side by side, such as the indigo of the chair and the light mauve of the wall; and sometimes he introduces sharp contrasts as in the red ribbon against the yellow floor. There seems to be a touch of irony in the emphatic mode used here to treat derisory subject-matter. Perhaps Gauguin simply intended the picture as an homage to the beauty of a woman of whom he was sincerely enamoured. Or he may have wished to let his friends know that from then on only an exotic Venus could inspire him. This painting is exceptional in the context of the period, and in Gauguin's work as a whole. Annah lived with Gauguin for several months but did not appear in any other painting.

Another, somewhat less original painting from this period is the portrait of Gauguin's neighbour, William Molard. This picture has the particularity of being painted on the back of a self-portrait in which Gauguin represents himself, thin-faced and wearing a hat, in his studio in the Rue Vercingétorix. In the background of the self-portrait is a reproduction of *Manao Tupapau*, but because there is nothing to provide scale, it is impossible to know whether he was depicting the painting itself, or a sketch, or even a photograph of it. One interesting feature is that the painting is depicted in reverse, which indicates that Gauguin was working in front of a mirror.

Did Gauguin's output during this nine-month period in Paris (from August 1893 to March 1894) consist only of *Annah the Javanese* and a half-dozen minor pictures? Even if we suppose that some works from that time were lost or destroyed, this is a scanty showing, and for a long time it was suspected that Gauguin completed some 'Tahitian' canvases in Paris. This hypothesis has been confirmed in the case of the 'stained-glass windows' in his Parisian studio. There are also three paintings on Tahitian themes which are clearly dated 1894, the year Gauguin spent in France. However, this is not altogether convincing evidence, for he could have postdated works completed earlier, and these three works present no distinguishing features with regard to those unquestionably painted in Tahiti. Like his Tahitian works, they are largely imaginary compositions, making use of a combination of elements from Nature. In a letter to Daniel de Monfreid dated March 1892, Gauguin noted: 'I am working more and more, but it is mostly studies and documents which are accumulating... .' In the end, it is difficult to establish which works were actually painted in Tahiti and which may have been done in France. Whatever the case, few works have come down to us from this Parisian period. But even if Gauguin painted little during that time, he was writing.

Gauguin had got into the habit early on of setting down his thoughts on paper, and of taking notes at lectures. Even his first letters to Pissarro and to

147

124

NAVE NAVE MOE

149   *Nave Nave Moe—Fragrant Mystery.* 1894 (?). (May have been painted in Paris.) Hermitage, Leningrad

Schuffenecker were not limited to practical or friendly messages; he took the opportunity to theorize and formulate his opinions. He began an article called 'Synthetic Notes' about 1886-8, but left it as a draft. In 1889 he published a number of articles—on the Exposition Universelle, the Centenary of French art, steel architecture and other contemporary subjects—in whatever small reviews were willing to take them. In February 1891, at the time of his sale at the Hôtel Drouot, he was interviewed by Jules Huret for *L'Echo de Paris*. Such practices, which are now customary, were altogether exceptional at the time. While many nineteenth-century artists kept journals, or used correspondence to develop their ideas on art, examples of artists publishing texts on aesthetic topics (Delacroix and Fromentin excepted) were rare. Gauguin was thus an innovator in that field, and it was only subsequently that Signac, Denis and many others began publishing widely. In fact, Gauguin encouraged Denis to write; in 1895 he congratulated him on a text he had written on Armand Séguin: 'I am writing to you because it gives me great pleasure to see painters managing their own affairs ... for some time now, I have realized the necessity for you, young painters, to write sensibly about Art.'

Gauguin had come back from Tahiti with a certain number of manuscripts and notebooks—some of which may not have survived—that he intended to use for future publications. One notebook, which he called *Ancien Culte mahorie*, was fifty-six pages long and contained accounts of Tahitian mythology. Gauguin claimed to have gathered the information first-hand; but it was later discovered, as mentioned earlier, that the greater part of the text had been borrowed from Moerenhout's book, *Voyage aux îles du grand océan*, published in 1837. Gauguin clearly intended this notebook for publication, for it was fastidiously prepared, faultlessly handwritten with title-page and table of contents, and illustrated with numerous gouaches. The notebook was given to the Louvre in 1933 by Etienne Moreau-Nélaton.

Another notebook was made up of separate texts, reconstituted randomly from personal notes. It con-

tained the following inscription: 'This notebook is dedicated to my daughter Aline! Scattered notes, without order, like dreams, like life, made all of pieces!' (In the end, the notebook was too disparate to give to his daughter, and certain passages were inappropriate for her age.) Amidst quotes from Verlaine and Poe, Gauguin injected ideas about politics, the stock exchange and art. He linked Tahiti to his childhood experience, and talked about his paintings. Quoting Wagner, he wrote: 'The idea of the prolific union of all the arts dates back to bygone eras.' Wagner was not alone in advocating the integration of the arts. For some years William Morris (1834-96) had been putting such theory into practice and, in France, the Nabis adopted it early on as an artistic ideal. The general tone of Gauguin's writing is bitter and ironic. On the cover of the notebook he pasted reproductions of Corot's *Woman with a Mandolin* and Delacroix's *Arab on Horseback*; however, there were few original illustrations, apart from a motif based on fish, similar to that of Bracquemond's 'Service Rousseau', a sketch based on *Manao Tupapau* and two watercolours on the back cover. The notebook is dated 1893; it was probably begun in Tahiti and continued in Paris. Press clippings from the exhibition at Durand-Ruel's were pasted on the last pages. This manuscript, entitled *Cahier pour Aline*, is now kept at the Bibliothèque d'Art et d'Archéologie, Paris (Jacques Doucet Foundation). Except for a facsimile edition, which had a limited print run, this text has still not been published in its entirety.

Although Gauguin originally intended to publish *Ancien Culte mahorie* first, he abandoned that project in favour of a larger work, which would integrate into an autobiographical account legends of the ancient cult, as well as descriptions of local ways and customs. This he called *Noa Noa* (a nickname for Tahiti, meaning 'fragrant'). The history of this manuscript, of which for many years the only known version was one that was considerably enlarged and reworked by Charles Morice, has been unravelled bit by bit.

150, 151

145

To recapitulate, when he arrived in France Gauguin was carrying the manuscript of *Ancien Culte mahorie*, and a draft of *Noa Noa*, which was discovered only in 1955 by Jean Loize; in fact, this text may have been rewritten in Paris from these notes. Daniel de Monfreid later recalled that Gauguin read him entire chapters which had been written before requesting Morice's collaboration.

Charles Morice claimed, unconvincingly, to have initiated the project. According to this claim, it was he, Morice, who in 1893, when Gauguin was at Rue Laffitte, proposed the idea of a literary composition for which Gauguin was to write short accounts of his painting themes that Morice would complement with poems. It was, supposedly, at this point that Gauguin, enthused by this suggestion, set to work on the project and Morice undertook to write the narrative sections in verse. However, it has been established without doubt that Gauguin had written some texts before the Durand-Ruel show; in a letter written in October 1893 (before the opening), he affirmed: 'I am preparing a book on Tahiti which will be very useful for making my painting comprehensible. What a job.' Of course, Morice may have conceived of the idea of writing a book about the artist even before Gauguin mentioned his own text to him. But the initial idea of publishing a book on Tahiti, in conjunction with showing his painting in Paris, was clearly Gauguin's own. Further, his earlier articles attest to his taste, as well as his gift, for writing. And if he brought back notes and written texts from Tahiti, it was not merely for his own personal documentation. *Ancien Culte mahorie* did shed light on the context of his painting, but Gauguin was well aware that it did not constitute enough of a personal testimony to provide support for his artistic position. He probably first intended to write *Noa Noa* himself. Then he accepted, or solicited—in the end, it matters little—Morice's collaboration, probably less for a lack of confidence in his writing skills than for a desire to see the book published speedily. Doubtless he appreciated Morice's talent; he was also clearly flattered by the writer's praise of his work.

Gauguin knew full well with whom he was dealing when he opted to work with Morice on *Noa Noa*, and was apparently willing to let bygones be bygones with respect to the latter's earlier dishonesty when managing the sale of his works. Also, literary collaboration was fashionable at the time: among the most illustrious partnerships were Emile Erckmann and Alexandre Chatrian, Auguste Vacquerie and Paul Meurice, Henri Meilhac and Ludovic Halévy and the Goncourt brothers, not to mention unconfessed alliances and fictitious ones like Flaubert's Bouvard and Pécuchet.

We do not know for sure how the Morice-Gauguin partnership functioned, but several hypotheses have emerged from the study of the documents at hand. These consist of a manuscript, entirely handwritten by Gauguin but edited by Morice; and a book, produced by Morice but bearing Gauguin's name. The complete story of this text has been painstakingly reconstituted—with a measure of conjecture—by Jean Loize, as well as by René Huyghe and Pierre Leprohon. When reading them, one is reminded of the erudite introductions to works by ancient writers that describe the transmission of those texts through medieval manuscripts, many of which did not survive.

It was in the autumn of 1893 that Gauguin gave Morice the manuscript of *Ancien Culte mahorie*, as well as the first manuscript of *Noa Noa*. Gauguin, who loved an audience, also recounted or dictated to Morice certain episodes that do not appear in either of these two original manuscripts; in addition, he may have given Morice complementary notes, or drafts. It is altogether likely that Morice, who was used to working in the library, consulted Moerenhout's book and others. He set to work, rewriting, developing and sometimes toning down Gauguin's writings, as well as composing poems of his own by way of commentary on Gauguin's paintings.

Criticism of Morice's work has been severe. His poetry does not suit modern taste. While Gauguin's first draft has an attractive directness, the edited version has lost much of its flavour and vivacity.

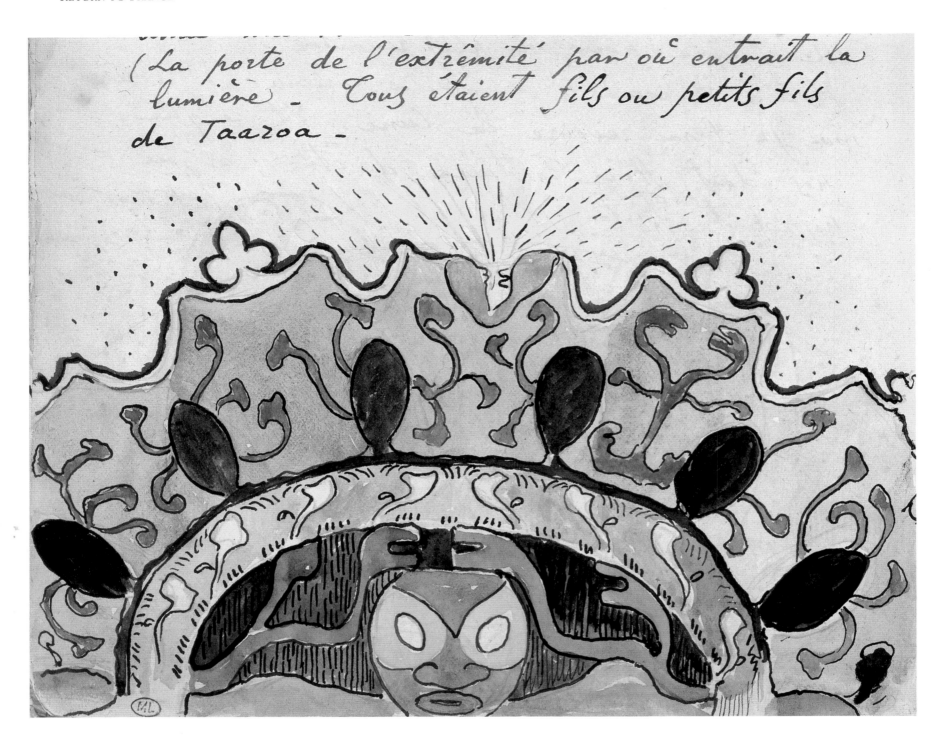

150 *Ancien Culte mahorie*, folio 14, ornamental motif. 1893.
W. 17 cm. Department of Graphic Arts, Musée du Louvre, Paris

dirent qu'elles venaient d'Avanau District

de Bora Bora et qu'elles avaient un

151   *Ancien Culte mahorie*, folio 24, *The Messengers of Or*. 1893.
W. 17 cm. Department of Graphic Arts, Musée du Louvre, Paris

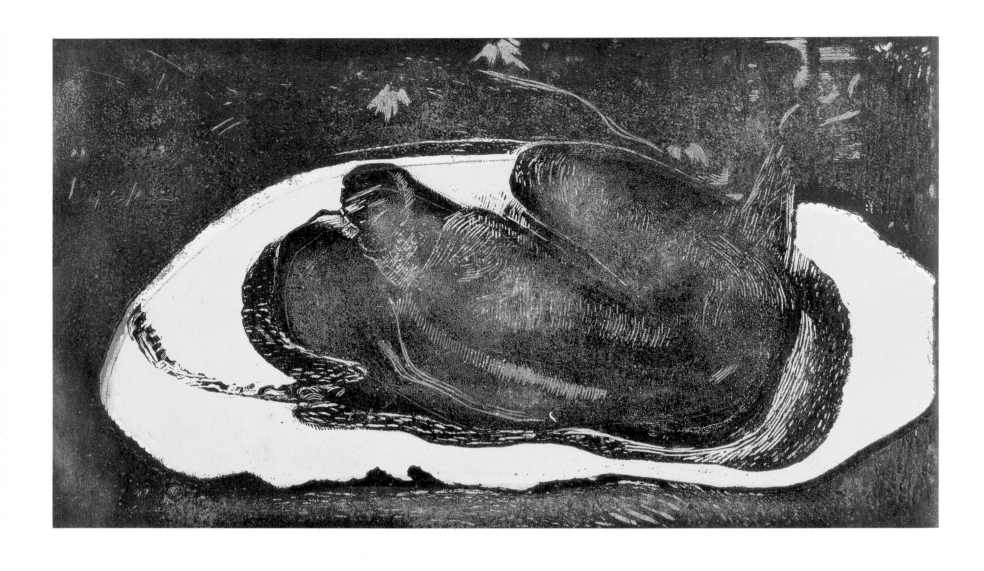

152 *Manao Tupapau—She Thinks of the Return*. 1894-5. Hand-coloured wood engraving 20 × 35 cm. Bibliothèque d'Art et d'Archéologie, Paris

153 *Nave Nave Fenua—Fragrant Earth*. 1894. Hand-coloured wood engraving, trial piece, 34 × 20 cm. Department of Engraving and Photography, Bibliothèque Nationale, Paris

154 *The Moulin David at Pont-Aven.* 1894. Oil on canvas,
73 × 92 cm. Musée d'Orsay, Paris

155 *Breton Peasants*. 1894. Oil on canvas, 66×93 cm. Musée d'Orsay, Paris

Gauguin's original work has the sort of naturalness and simplicity characteristic of works by Alphonse Daudet or by Maupassant, whereas Morice's poems clearly attempt to rival Mallarmé or Leconte de Lisle. Gauguin found this paradox suited his designs, as witnessed by a letter—written much later, in May 1902—to Daniel de Monfreid: 'I had the idea, speaking of uncivilized peoples, to contrast their character with our own, and I found it rather original to write (simply myself) like a savage, side by side with the very civilized style of Morice.' In other words, the same Gauguin who, in his painting, had repudiated realism in favour of intense, deliberate stylization, here reversed his method and wrote like a naturalist, or even a simple transcriber, while leaving the stylization to Morice. This admission disproves an assertion like the following by Bengt Danielsson: 'The aspect [of Gauguin's book] the most open to criticism is not its old-fashioned style, but the constant, deliberate effort evident in the chapters on Tahiti—for which Gauguin alone was responsible—to fool the reader, by presenting life in the 1890s as being utterly idyllic and paradisiacal.'[8]

At a time when even the smallest trifle by the hands of a 'genius' is regarded as sacred, and we scour wastepaper baskets for traces of lost creations, our sensibility is disturbed by the idea of a third party intervening in the very creation of one of those precious gems. It is true that Morice's intervention was lamentable; but we must keep in mind the fact that it was with Gauguin's complete agreement. The facts were as follows: Gauguin arrived in France with a number of texts, some of which were in a near-finished state, others in little more than outline form. He decided to seek publication and, in order to save time, solicited the help of one of the rare critics who had expressed admiration, on more than one occasion, for his work. When Morice had given him a first draft of his own work, Gauguin hand-copied it, leaving blank spaces for the inclusion of both his own illustrations and Morice's poems. It is quite possible that Gauguin foresaw further changes or additions before actually publishing the manuscript, but he was clearly not unhappy with Morice's first efforts. Morice himself was correct in affirming: 'I cannot let it be said that I modified Gauguin's text without his acknowledgment. Every page of *Noa Noa* was read and approved, in manuscript form, by him.' It is not unlikely that certain modifications were either Gauguin's own or resulted from his instructions.

The painstaking job of recopying the manuscript—it totalled 204 pages of meticulous longhand—was probably done in Paris during that winter, rather than in Brittany where, as we shall see, he spent two months in hospital and moved frequently—although the use of the Lezaven studio did allow him a certain measure of isolation. However, it is difficult to know with certainty at what moment Gauguin recopied, with a different ink, additional poems by Morice. Gauguin intended to take the album back with him to Tahiti, where he could continue to work on it, transforming it into a personal journal. But at the moment of his departure, in May 1895, he foresaw an early publication date and, in an interview with the journalist Eugène Tardieu, he stated clearly: 'Before leaving, I am going to publish, with my friend Charles Morice, a book in which I tell the story of my life in Tahiti and my reflections about art. Morice will provide poetic commentary for the works which I brought back. In this way everyone will know why and how I went there. The title of the book? *Noa Noa*, meaning, in Tahitian, fragrant; it will be "that which Tahiti gives forth".'[9]

After Gauguin's departure, Morice set about finding a publisher. In 1897, in a letter of which, unfortunately, only a fragment has survived, Gauguin wrote: 'I shall probably never see the book in print, since my days are numbered'; ironically, at that very moment *La Revue Blanche* was beginning to publish excerpts of *Noa Noa* under the joint signature of Gauguin and Morice. *La Revue Blanche* was one of the periodicals most open to innovative trends. The director and editor-in-chief were the Natanson brothers, who were among Gauguin's, and the Nabis', early admirers (cf. p. 149). Another review, *L'Image*, devoted to the new interest in the graphic arts,

156 *Christmas Night*. 1894 (?). Oil on canvas, 72 × 83 cm. Josefowitz Collection

published in its 15 September 1897 issue Morice's 'explanatory' poems, accompanied by engravings which were vaguely inspired by Gauguin, and probably done by Armand Séguin.

But as time went by Gauguin apparently began to have second thoughts about his collaboration with Morice. A draft letter to an unknown addressee confirmed his dissatisfaction: 'The narrator must not disappear behind the poet ... I understand that everyone is expecting poems from Morice, but if there are too many in this book, all the storyteller's naïvety will vanish and the flavour of *Noa Noa* will be lost.'

Morice later argued that the book did not appear until 1901 because he had been unable to find a publisher before that time, a claim which is not unreasonable. In the end, a publishing house called La Plume took the risk. When Gauguin learned of the book's publication, he wrote to Morice: 'I confess that the publication of *Noa Noa*, at this inappropriate moment, has no interest for me today.' Indeed, for him the publication came too late, being part of a strategy that was now outdated. Yet despite the importance given to the poems, he did not disclaim the work. He even used some passages in the controversial review he was currently publishing in Tahiti, *Les Guêpes*. In his letter to Monfreid of March 1902, Gauguin concluded: 'Morice wanted to bring out the book at the wrong time; in the end, it is not a dishonour for me.'

During the Parisian winter of 1893-4, Gauguin took up engraving again, completing about twenty
152, 153 woodcuts. He was adapting himself to a new medium, boldly exploring its manifold possibilities. At that time—which was just prior to the challenge of photography for illustrating magazines and books— wood engraving was customary for periodicals or inexpensive publications. With the use of finely-grained wood, the art had reached a level of refinement that rivalled etching. Woodcuts for fine books, though, were still rare. Gauguin used slabs of wood, which allowed him to obtain the large, flat areas and simple outlines he desired. His subject-matter was exclusively Tahitian for he intended to use the wood-

cuts to illustrate *Noa Noa*. However, these works are not simple reproductions of his paintings. He reworked the compositions, simplifying and adapting them to the reduced format of the block. Most of the woodcuts have one central figure; Gauguin generally carved the title of the work in Maori directly into the block. Perhaps he was dreaming of producing a luxurious publication, like the one recently published (in 1893) of Gide's *Le Voyage d'Urien*, with illustrations by his young disciple Maurice Denis, or like the sumptuous albums to be issued by the publishing house of Piazza and Floury. He was also familiar with more modest examples of artist's books, such as Vanier's publications of works by Verlaine and the Symbolists. It is altogether in character for Gauguin to be preoccupied with providing the best possible presentation for his images, indispensable as they were to his text. Had his project come to fruition, the result would have been one of the first and most remarkable artist's books ever to have been published; indeed, without knowing exactly what Gauguin's final choice would have been for illustrations, page layout and even typeface, no modern reconstitution could ever embody his original intentions. One single plate, *Manao Tupapau*, 152 appeared in the April-June 1894 number of *Estampe Originale*.

We can thank Gauguin for helping to revive the technique of wood engraving by applying it to book illustration. His influence was indisputable, in the field of illustration—on artists like Auguste Lepère, and of painting proper—on Raoul Dufy and André Derain; and it was precisely because of his contribution that the hitherto strongly enforced distinction between the two fields began to wear down. Ambroise Vollard was among the first to issue reproductions of Gauguin's prints; and they could well have inspired his decision fervently to set about publishing books illustrated with original engravings. Other publishers, such as Daniel-Henry Kahnweiler commissioned illustrations—often in the form of woodcuts—by young artists. Still, artists who, like Rouault, created both text and illustrations, were rare.

In April 1894 Gauguin decided to leave for Brittany. The reasons for this move are not entirely clear. He may have been looking to live more cheaply, as had been the case in the past; or, again, he may have needed a change of scenery—a more stimulating visual environment than that of Paris, which had never much inspired him; or it could be that his near-constant need to move and change was pathological. Brittany could hardly seem exotic to someone

returning from two years in the Tropics; but it did represent a sort of emotional refuge after the partial failure of his Parisian campaign. Pont-Aven was attracting ever-increasing numbers of artists, of every school and every nationality. Only a handful of them were aesthetically akin to Gauguin. One of them, a Polish artist named Ladislav Slewinski who had known Gauguin since 1889 or 1890, invited him to stay with him and even organized a banquet in his honour. Gauguin also renewed his relationship with Charles Filiger, who was increasingly absorbed by esotericism, as well as with Henri Moret, Armand Séguin, Emile Jourdan and the Irish painter, Roderick

157 *Breton Village in the Snow*. 1894 (?). Oil on canvas, 62 × 87 cm. Musée d'Orsay, Paris

158 *Oviri—Savage*. 1895. Partially glazed stoneware, H. 74 cm. Musée d'Orsay, Paris

159 *Still-Life with Engraving* by Delacroix. 1895. Oil on canvas, 40 × 30 cm. Musée d'Art moderne, Strasbourg

O'Conor. He thus managed to surround himself with a much-needed circle of disciples and admirers. On 25 May he was out walking in the port of Concarneau with Annah the Javanese, whom he had imprudently brought with him to Brittany, in the company of Séguin, Jourdan and O'Conor when an argument between the group of artists and some fishermen degenerated into a brawl. Gauguin suffered a bad leg fracture which kept him bedridden for several months and caused him to take strong doses of morphine. Although he won a law suit for damages and interest, the compensation—which was, in fact, too small to cover even hospital expenses—was never issued. Gauguin then attempted to get a court order to reclaim paintings left at Marie Henry's inn at Le Pouldu in 1890, which failed. The result of these two law suits, and the related financial hardship, constituted additional psychological setbacks. To add insult to injury, Annah the Javanese left him, returned to Paris and sacked his studio in the Rue Vercingétorix, making off with everything she deemed saleable. Gauguin was relieved, though perhaps secretly a bit vexed, to learn that she had left his paintings untouched.

Brittany was proving neither more auspicious nor more welcoming than Paris; Gauguin left and, as he explained in a letter of August 1894 to William Molard, resolved to return to Tahiti: 'For two months I have been obliged to take morphine every evening and I am presently quite stupefied. [Also] to avoid insomnia I must drink enough alcohol to allow me to sleep four hours each night. All that exhausts and depresses me. I have to walk with a cane and it is discouraging for me not to be able to go far enough to paint a landscape; still, eight days ago I began taking up my brushes again. All these misfortunes, along with the difficulty of earning a regular living despite my reputation, and with my taste for exoticism, have brought me to an irrevocable decision: in December, I shall return to Paris, where I shall work continuously to sell everything I own, either as a whole, or piece by piece. Once I have the money, I shall leave for Polynesia again, this time with two of my friends

from here, Séguin and an Irishman. Don't bother making any comments. Nothing will stop me from leaving, and, this time, forever. What a senseless existence, this European life.'

It is difficult to ascertain what Gauguin actually produced during those final eight months in Brittany. We cannot judge by subject-matter, for he could have worked from memory. However, even if we take into consideration his stay in hospital, and the immobility due to his injuries, his output during that time seems both scanty and heterogeneous, and the dates traditionally attributed to certain works merit reconsideration.

A few works are painted in the style characteristic of the Tahitian paintings, but with Breton motifs. *The Moulin David at Pont-Aven* has the appearance of a 154 plate, or of a stained-glass window, with its bright colours of like intensity. The horizontal zones are off-set here and there by a vertical axis formed by two poplars.

Breaking with all the traditional rules of perspective, he depicts houses simultaneously from several points of view: the gabled wall is seen from the front, in the extension of the front wall, and the roofs are seen from the diagonal. Only Cézanne, and occasionally Degas, had been so bold, clearly paving the way for Cubism. The figures in *Breton Peasants* 155 (formerly the Kaganovitch Collection) have the same immobile dignity of women in a Tahitian scene, but they are not integrated into the landscape. The girl on the right, whether deliberately or not, bears a striking 117 resemblance to Tehura. *Christmas Night*, with its less 156 uniform style, may have been painted somewhat later. In it the figures are treated with flat areas of colour as in the paintings from earlier years, and the curious silhouettes of cattle—perhaps inspired by Egyptian relief sculpture—have the same appearance of wooden cut-outs as animals in certain Tahitian paintings. However, the snow on the ground and the roofs are treated with longer brushstrokes and thicker paint, giving nuances similar to those in Impressionist landscapes. As in the case of *The Yellow Christ* and *Breton Calvary—Green Christ* of 1889, the sacred 84, 85 figures are not represented directly but in the form of statues. We have observed how Gauguin used both approaches in the Tahitian paintings.

There are other landscapes with snow in which we can observe the characteristic rooftops of the region around Pont-Aven. Still, winter snow scenes do not fit Brittany between April and November, and these landscapes, in which Gauguin recovered a certain rusticity, as well as a sensitivity to impressionistic nuances, were certainly painted from memory. One 157 of them, *Breton Village in the Snow*, was among the rare canvases he took back to Tahiti with him, only to meet a strange destiny. It figured in the sale which took place in Tahiti after Gauguin's death. Victor Ségalen wrote: 'I acquired everything I could come across at the auction. One painting was presented upside-down by the auctioneer, who called it *Niagara Falls*; it was met with general laughter. I bought it for all of seven francs.'[10]

It is also possible that Gauguin created, or at least pulled, a number of xylographies in Brittany, where his example must have stimulated similar work on the part of his disciples, including Maxime Maufra, whose important graphic work is only now emerging from undeserved oblivion, and Séguin, whose handsome illustrations for Aloysius Bertrand's *Gaspard de la Nuit*, published by Vollard in 1904, have since overshadowed all his other work.

Gauguin returned to Paris in November 1894 and remained there until his departure for Tahiti in July of the following year. Once again, little evidence remains of any painting he may have done during those months. It could be that some works were lost, or traditionally attributed to other periods. It is clear that repeated setbacks and the lack of stimulation provided by his visual environment caused him to experience some relatively barren moments.

He took up ceramics again, returning to Ernest Chaplet's studio, where he had worked before. There he sculpted a large female figure in stoneware. The figure, heavy and graceless with a bestial face, presses two small, monstrous creatures to her side. 158 He called her *Oviri*, 'savage', probably wishing to erect an exotic and somewhat frightening idol, while at the same time pitting himself against this difficult medium. Indeed, his lack of technical mastery may well have done him a disservice in that the facial traits were hardened and deformed during firing. He submitted the statue to the official Salon (that of the Société Nationale des Beaux-Arts), where it was, of course, refused; in a letter to the newspaper *Le Soir*, he protested at the mediocrity of the production of the Sèvres factory, citing his own collaboration with Chaplet and his pioneering role: 'At that time (if I may bring up a personal memory) I had seen the possibility of giving a new thrust to ceramic art by creating new, handmade forms... To replace the wheel with intelligent hands that could communicate to the vase the life of a figure while remaining faithful to the character of the material, ... this was my aim.'[11] In another letter, written to Ambroise Vollard on 26 October 1902, just a few months before his death, he stressed his innovative role in the technique of ceramics: *Oviri* is 'not only my best object, but also ... perhaps the only specimen of stoneware sculpture in the style of Chaplet.'[12] He represented the sculpture in a painting of 1898, *Rave Te Hiti Ramu—The Idol*.

Oviri had a special significance for Gauguin; he indicated that he wanted it as his gravestone.[13] Morice suggested that 'perhaps Gauguin left this work of tragic beauty as a fearsome farewell to the civilized world, the ultimate testimony to his contempt and despair'.[14] Gauguin himself added, next to a print representing *Oviri* in *Noa Noa*: 'And the monster, clasping its creature, gave its seed into those generous thighs to engender Seraphitus Seraphita.' This allusion to Balzac's novel is not particularly significant, except in so far as the book, inspired by the ideas of Swedenborg and quite atypical of Balzac's work, was much admired in Symbolist circles. Once more, Gauguin's superimposed verbal commentary on a plastic representation of a simple yet ambiguous theme—an exotic idol—and his words were even further complicated by modern exegetes. However, it could well be that Morice's text was a reflection of conversations with Gauguin. The two men were still seeing each other at that time, and some authors have asserted that it was then that Gauguin recopied the manuscript of *Noa Noa*, rather than before his stay in Brittany.

159   The still-life at the Musée de Strasbourg is less obscure. The bowl of fruit in the foreground recalls, in a discreet homage to Cézanne, the themes and simplified forms typical of Gauguin's still-lifes from 1888-91. On the wall there is an engraving after Delacroix, whom Gauguin greatly admired and whose *Journal* had recently been published (1893-5). The work depicted was *Adam and Eve Driven from Paradise*, which hung in the Bibliothèque de la Chambre des Députés; the theme may have had special significance for Gauguin, who saw himself as an outcast for having tasted the fruit of the tree of knowledge.

The self-portrait dedicated to Charles Morice is generally dated *c.* 1890-1. Goldwater has asserted, not unreasonably, that it may have been executed as late as 1895. The face modelled into hard planes, the near-abstract treatment of the background, and the resemblance to the self-portrait painted on the back of the portrait of William Molard all justify this hypothesis. The physical appearance of the model corresponds exactly to a description by Armand Séguin: '... the astrakhan hat and enormous, dark blue greatcoat held together by delicate clasps revealed to Parisians a magnificent and gigantic Magyar, a Rembrandt of 1635.'[15] In fact, Gauguin used a photograph for the portrait, but its date is no more certain than that of the painting.

During his few remaining months in France, Gauguin's energy was directed towards his imminent departure. He fully realized that life in Paris was not conducive to his work, and resolved to leave forever. For a moment, he hesitated between Tahiti and Samoa, and looked for travelling companions. In November he wrote to Monfreid: 'There I shall be able to end my days freely and peacefully, without worrying about the future and without struggling endlessly against imbeciles. This time I shall not leave alone; an Englishman, O'Conor, and a Frenchman,

Séguin, will accompany me for two or three years; but as for me, I shall stay.' (Gauguin seems to have made little of the difference between English and Irish; in fact, Roderick O'Conor was an Irishman. See p. 227.)

The tireless Morice had organized, for Gauguin's return from Brittany, a banquet in his honour at the Café des Variétés, which served as a pretext for an enthusiastic article: 'His most audacious detractors no longer dared repudiate him yesterday and, ironically, when they declared their lack of understanding of this "genius", it was *this* very word that they were obliged to use when describing *this* very painter.'[16] In December a presentation of engravings and drawings in Gauguin's studio attracted little attention beyond his circle of faithful admirers. In the end, both to make a public appearance and to earn some much-needed funds, he decided to hold a sale at the Hôtel Drouot, a method that had met with reasonable success in 1891. He decided to ask August Strindberg to write the preface for the catalogue. Strindberg, who was Gauguin's contemporary (he was born in 1849), had made his name as a playwright in Paris, and was living there. In 1893, *Miss Julie* was performed at the Théâtre Libre, and Lugné-Poe put on *The Creditors* and *Father* at the Œuvre in 1894. Strindberg was familiar with *La Revue Blanche* and the Nabis, who were among Gauguin's rare admirers. The two men met at Molard's and Strindberg subsequently visited Gauguin's studio on several occasions. He had discovered Impressionism rather early on and painted some small, 'visionary' landscapes, following 'a vague intention'. In 1894 he published an article in French called *Des arts nouveaux! ou le hasard dans la production artistique* ('The new arts, or chance in artistic creation'), wherein he revealed himself to be an astonishing precursor to abstract painting, dripping and automatism. His approach to Impressionist painting was equally striking: 'First, one sees only a riot of colour; then it all takes on an air, and resembles [something], then, no, it resembles nothing. Suddenly a point fixes itself like the nucleus of a cell; it grows, and the colours gather around it, building up; rays form, which grow branches and smaller branches, like ice crystals on windows... and the image presents itself to the spectator, who has witnessed the bringing forth of the painting.'[17] One cannot help but think of Kandinsky's famous text, in which he recounts how, in 1896, when he was unable to decipher the motif of one of Monet's *Haystacks*, he had the first inkling of abstract painting.

The importance that Strindberg gives to chance, to 'nature', and to the beholder's, or listener's, interpretation (most of his examples are in the field of music) contrasts markedly with Gauguin's emphasis on the artist's intention. Still, the example of the painting inspired by the veins in a piece of wood would have interested Strindberg had Gauguin described it to him. If Gauguin chose Strindberg to write his preface, a certain sympathy must already have existed between them.

Strindberg wrote Gauguin a long and thoughtful letter by way of refusal: 'I cannot understand your art and I cannot like it... Sir, you have created a new earth and a new sky, but I am not happy in the world you have created, it is too sunny for a man who comes from chiaroscuro... No, Gauguin was not born of Chavannes's rib, nor from Manet's or Bastien-Lepage's. What is he then? He is Gauguin, the savage who detests a bothersome civilization, something of a Titan who, jealous of the creator, makes his own little creation in his spare time.' Strindberg was disconcerted by not being able to classify Gauguin, and to situate him 'like a link in the chain' that connected him to the Impressionists; Strindberg used as his point of reference Puvis de Chavannes's *The Poor Fisherman*, whose literary character and formal simplicity he admired.

Gauguin avenged Strindberg's refusal with humour by printing the letter at the beginning of his catalogue with the following rebuttal: 'I had the idea of asking you to write this preface when I saw you in my studio the other day, playing the guitar and singing; your blue eye was looking attentively at the paintings hanging on the walls. I sensed a revolt: a collision between your civilization and my barbarism. Civilization from which you suffer. Barbarism which, for me, is a rejuvenating force... This world that neither a Cuvier [Baron Georges, a zoologist] nor a botanist could find, is a Paradise that I will only have sketched... .' And, using a linguistic comparison, Gauguin asserted that it was necessary to use 'savage drawing' to depict 'a savage people and country'. This deep coherence between form and content is an essential key to Gauguin's art. As for Strindberg, a renegade like Gauguin but imprisoned in his rebellion like Munch, he experienced another crisis, which he described in *Inferno*, whereas Gauguin escaped, and built himself a new Eden. Gauguin broke loose from his moorings, and went to the other end of the world to seek a pure and refreshing—and, consequently, positive—barbarism. Strindberg, out of weariness, remained in civilization, but negatively, and nourished his disgust.

Gauguin's auction took place on 18 February. The results were disastrous, especially in comparison with those of the 1891 sale. However, Gauguin was largely responsible for the failure, having set his sights much too high. In 1891 most of the paintings were sold for 260-350 francs, whereas now, in 1895, the majority of his Tahitian works exceeded bids of 400 francs, and Gauguin ended up buying them himself. Were these fictitious bids, or did he consider the real prices unsatisfactory compared with those obtained at Durand-Ruel's? From seventy-four entries, there were only, at the most, twenty-five actual sales, or even less, for several of the buyers mentioned in the minutes may have been figureheads, and many sales concerned drawings and inexpensive works on Breton themes. Purchasers included Degas, who bought two paintings and six drawings; Slewinski and Maufra, who each bought one painting; Degas's friend Daniel Halévy, and a few dealers, including Leclanché, Bernheim and Vollard. Georges de Bellio, the Impressionist collector who had bought a painting in the 1891 auction, attended the sale but bought nothing. The real results are difficult to ascertain, but were doubtless disappoint-

233

ing, and gave rise to a new exchange of bitter letters between Gauguin and Mette. She demanded money; he insisted that he could send her none because he had had to buy back nearly everything. Only a few months earlier, Gauguin had complained about not knowing exactly what paintings Mette had sold. He had discovered that one of his principal Danish buyers, the writer Edvard Brandes, was not buying as a charitable gesture but for speculation.

The disagreement between husband and wife degenerated. On both sides the lack of understanding was total, though there is little reason to take an inventory of their respective faults here. The fact remains that Mette had married a Parisian bourgeois, who possessed not only a brilliant mind but the capacity to earn a comfortable living; after some years, she found herself married to an artist who had no regular income. In addition, her husband's all-powerful need to create led him to travel incessantly, while she herself no longer wished to leave Denmark. To maintain a conventional marriage became an impossibility. Our object is not to condone Gauguin's numerous extra-marital affairs—the latest of which had bequeathed him a case of syphilis from which he never recovered—but to recognize the basic incompatibility between conjugal life accord-ing to the conventions of the time, and the artist's calling experienced as personal destiny. As for his children, he never really lost interest in them—contrary to the example of Jean-Jacques Rousseau, who, a century earlier, was held in reverence by the general public despite the fact that he turned his five children over to the government's care.

One final disappointment came from Emile Bernard. Bernard had left France and travelled widely, finally settling in Egypt. His painting was becoming increasingly academic. At the same time, he published several articles in *Mercure de France* in which he not only claimed his own precedence over Gauguin, but also mentioned Gauguin as figuring among those who 'had no scruples about copying Cézanne', an accusation not altogether unjustified. Gauguin prepared a rejoinder, but either was unable to publish it or decided not to. Instead, Julien Leclercq replied for him in the July number of *Mercure de France*. However, the great Cézanne exhibition at Vollard's, which brought the work of the master from Aix into the public eye for the first time and would have given Gauguin the opportunity to verify both his debt to Cézanne and his profound originality, did not take place until December 1895, some time after Gauguin's departure.

Chapter XII   Where Do We Come From?

The trip to Tahiti via the Mediterranean, the Red Sea and the Indian Ocean provided Gauguin with two more months of forced inactivity and reflection. 'I am travelling—that is, lethargic', he wrote to Molard during a prolonged stop in Auckland, New Zealand. He took advantage of the time there to visit the museum and absorb its fine ethnographic collection. Still, the presence of New Zealand motifs in one of his paintings does not necessarily indicate that it was done after 1895, for he was aware of such motifs before that time. In New Zealand, as in all of Oceania, indigenous cultures, considered to be remnants of barbaric tribes, were becoming extinct.

Tahiti had changed little in the two years since he left. Because he did not have an official mission on this trip, his arrival went unnoticed. However, shortly after disembarking, he met the new governor, Pierre Papinaud, the successor to Lacascade, with whom Gauguin had had strained relations. Papinaud invited him to join an official trip to the neighbouring Leeward Islands. In lieu of carrying out an earlier idea to settle in the more remote Marquesas Islands, he accepted this unexpected opportunity to observe traditional festivals and submerge himself once again in local life. After this short trip he decided to stay in Tahiti, at a distance from Papeete. He bought some land and had a house built, attesting to his intention to settle there permanently.

At first, he lived on the capital brought from Paris and whatever he took in from scanty sales. But, as usual, Gauguin spent recklessly, quickly exhausting his resources; and remittances from France were few and far between. Often obliged to rely on credit, he lived for mail deliveries, with their oft-thwarted promise of money orders, and was forced to do odd jobs to buy food. He lived with a young *vahine*. His health was poor; the leg wound suffered in Brittany continued to torment him. At the age of fifty, Gauguin had become chronically ill, and required frequent hospitalization. In 1897, news of the death of his daughter Aline compounded his depression. The tone of his correspondence became despondent. In addition, the news from France was not encouraging. Few of his works were selling, despite his calculated efforts during the two years he had spent in and around Paris; despite the unfailing help of others, notably the faithful Monfreid, and Chaudet, the dealer; and despite the low prices fixed to his paintings. This lack of commercial success—quite apart from the financial consequences that accompanied it—was psychologically damaging. Gauguin began working irregularly, but intensely, when his health permitted: 'My temperament is such that I must do a picture all at once, and feverishly' (13 July 1896). His poor health and bouts of depression resulted in a much more limited output than that of his first Tahitian period. Furthermore, some of these works are relatively weak compared with earlier ones, and their style lacks dynamism. Gauguin himself was well aware of the malaise. Yet it would be presumptuous to suggest a direct correlation between the economic quality of life and the quality of artistic production. Gauguin did produce a few exceptional works during this time. One self-portrait, inscribed 160 'près de Golgotha' ('nearing Golgotha'), bears a near-blasphemous resemblance to Christ suffering.

160 *Bé Bé—The Nativity*. 1896. Oil on canvas, 66 × 75 cm. Hermitage, Leningrad

161 *Te Tamari No Atua—The Nativity*. 1896. Oil on canvas, 96 × 128 cm. Bayerische Staatsgemäldesammlungen, Neue Pinakothek, Munich

162 *Self-Portrait nearing Golgotha*. 1896. Oil on canvas, 76×64 cm. Museu de Arte, São Paulo

163 *Te Rerioa—The Dream*. Oil on canvas, 95×132 cm. Courtauld Institute Galleries, London

164 *No te aha or riri—Why Are You Angry?* 1896. Oil on canvas,
95.3 × 130.5 cm. Art Institute of Chicago (Mr and Mrs Martin A. Ryer-
son Collection)

This same identification appeared in a self-portrait of 1889 and a ceramic work. The tormented facial expression is in marked contrast to his characters' customary impassivity, and the plain, white tunic is especially significant in the light of Gauguin's predilection for embroidered waistcoats and unusual accessories.

While it is clear that the *Self-Portrait—nearing Golgotha* is an expression of Gauguin's despair and physical suffering, other paintings from this time transcend that sense of desolation. In 1896 the birth of a daughter inspired two nativity scenes, another instance in which Gauguin conferred a sacred dimension on ordinary or personal themes. While these paintings maintain a solemn tone, they are less dramatic than the self-portrait. One of them, *Bé Bé—The* 160 *Nativity*, represents the child being held by a saint, and admired by an angel. The Virgin appears in the background, in a stable which cuts into the perspective in an unusual fashion. In the second version, 161 *Te Tamari No Atua—The Nativity*, this traditional theme is treated in a very particular manner. The Virgin herself has marked Tahitian features (though the haloes leave no doubt as to the painting's Western connotations); she is reclining on a bed. This position, which is rare in Western depictions of the Nativity, fits well with the natural quality that Gauguin wished to confer on this dignified and simple portrayal of a young mother recovering from childbirth. The upper part of the canvas is divided into three segments. In the centre, Gauguin introduces the principal motif of his other Nativity scene: a saint holding the Child on her lap, and an angel; at the left, behind a pole decorated with Maori motifs, there is the suggestion of a nocturnal landscape; at the right, separated from the rest of the composition by a beam supporting the ceiling, there is a French-style stable, treated altogether traditionally. For this painting Gauguin drew inspiration from a work by Octave Tassaert (1800-74). The bed is decorated with the same 146 motif as the skirting-board in *Annah the Javanese*.

In *Te Tamari No Atua*, the principal motif (a young woman reclining), the presence of a character

165 *Ceremony for the Harvest Moon* by Ukiyo-e. Japanese coloured engraving on panel, 26.3 × 36.8 cm. National Museum, Tokyo

in a black headdress in the background, the general layout based on strong verticals and horizontals, and other details are strongly reminiscent of *Manao* 124 *Tupapau*. The Nativity scene offers a Christian response, using Tahitian images, to the pagan terror of *Tupapau*. Another painting, *Nevermore*, from 171 1897, is also an echo of *Manao Tupapau*. This is not the only instance of Gauguin returning to a motif after several years and conferring on it a different, or even opposite, meaning. Another example can be observed in *Te Rerioa—The Dream* and *La Siesta* 163, 135 (1893). Here the elaborate composition is virtually the same in both works. But the bright colours, relaxed poses and sunny landscape of *Te Rerioa* have disappeared in *Siesta*, leaving only a house, its walls covered with grimacing designs, closing up around two troubled beings. Gauguin leaves the painting's interpretation to the viewer; he wrote to Monfreid on 12 March 1897: 'Everything is dream-like in this painting. Is it the child, the mother, the rider on the path or, perhaps, the painter's own dream?' Along with *Te Faaturuma—The Brooding Woman*, these 144 are among the rare works in Gauguin's Polynesian output that depict interiors. They are set inside a hut, which, while Tahitian in origin, clearly resembles the typical interior of Japanese house as presented by 165

241

166 *Tahitian Family with Cat. c.* 1900. Monotype on paper with pencil highlighting and wash, 58 × 43.5 cm. Private Collection, Paris

167 *Nave Nave Mahana—Fragrant Days.* 1896. Oil on canvas, 94 × 130 cm. Musée des Beaux-Arts, Lyons

Ukiyo-e, with pronounced skirting-boards, scant furniture, people seated or kneeling on the mat-covered floor and sliding doors opening directly onto the landscape, linking inside with outside. The allusion to the Japanese model is obviously deliberate: a flattened perspective and the floor tilted upward. However, Gauguin did not go so far as to use parallel lines of perspective; instead, he represented three sides of a cube, using a single vanishing point, in the Western tradition. Certain Japanese print-makers, including Hiroshige, sometimes used Western principles of perspective to represent buildings.

This recurrence of Japanese references, amidst works of an entirely different character (with the exception of their lack of shadows), suggests that Gauguin did not 'adopt' *japonisme* as a complete system of representation, nor was it even a fundamentally important element of his art; instead, it constituted a sort of vocabulary that he employed at will.

In an unpublished note to *Noa Noa*, Gauguin compared Hokusai to Daumier: '... through this false appearance of the grotesque, through similar qualities, the relationship between Hokusai and Daumier exists.' For Gauguin, the Japanese were the inventors of a system of distortion, or, rather, of caricature. They 'found forms'. In a letter of October 1897 to Monfreid he wrote: 'To find forms, what your little sculptor friend from the Midi [young Aristide Maillol] calls distortion. Always have before your eyes the Persians, the Cambodians and a bit of the Egyptian. The big mistake is the Greek [example], as beautiful as it is.' For Gauguin, the choice of exotic models was less important than their exoticism itself: '[one must] find forms that are not Greek'. *Japonisme* satisfied Gauguin's need for exoticism and gave support to his search for an art that was independent of Western tradition. He acknowledged that the Greek exemplar was 'beautiful', but was convinced that the naturalist tradition that derived from it led inevitably to the cardboard nymphs of William Bouguereau and dusty plaster sculptures that filled the halls of the Academy. Japanese prints proved that there were other dynamic traditions, based on different sources.

As with the works of Gauguin's first Tahitian period, historians have endeavoured to trace the sources of these later paintings. Some are obvious: the two versions of *The Poor Fisherman* (Museu de Arte, São Paulo, and Hermitage, Leningrad) are transpositions of a painting of the same name by Puvis de Chavannes that was well known to Gauguin. *Woman with Mangos* is a loose interpretation of Cranach's *Venus*. Photographs of the temple of Borobudur may have provided ideas for poses. But in all these examples Gauguin renounced neither his own style nor his Tahitian subject-matter, while in the previously mentioned *Nativity*, he did literally copy a composition by the realist painter Octave Tassaert, a photograph of which Arosa had given him. He also copied *Joseph with the Wife of Potiphar* (Museu de Arte, São Paulo) from a composition by Prud'hon, also photographed by Arosa. Here the drawing, clothing and decor are Neo-Classical, and only the faces and skin colour evoke Tahiti.

To enumerate such examples might give the impression that Gauguin's work from this period was limited to associating otherwise disparate, borrowed elements. But the works themselves—at least the more successful ones—seem deeply coherent. The importance of this 'borrowing' lies in the way in which he sought to re-use, whether deliberately or not, the general composition of an earlier work to work out new solutions to universal problems of representation. Unlike most of his contemporaries, he did not flinch from the problem of representing several figures; and he evoked the atmosphere of Poussin and of Giotto,[1] not only in his depictions of isolated figures (*No te aha oe riri—Why Are You Angry?*) but also in more complex compositions such as *Nave Nave Mahana—Delightful Days*, so clearly reminiscent of the righthand portion of Poussin's *Rebecca and Eliezer*, in the Louvre. Here, the variety and elegance of the poses; the slow gestures, in harmony with the arabesques of the branches; the strong rhythm created by the verticals; the colour scheme, in which greens and violets create echoes among the reds: all come together to make this one

164

167

168

of Gauguin's most successful paintings. When, in 1912, the great art historian Henri Focillon bought it for the Musée des Beaux-Arts, Lyons, it became the first of Gauguin's works to enter a French museum. Doubtless Focillon had this picture in mind when he spoke of Gauguin's medieval sources: 'The great arrangers of mural figures (of the Middle Ages) assisted Gauguin in erecting, in those carefree islands, with a brilliant, muted harmony, the mysterious statue of ancient man.'[2]

Can this remarkable painting, with its Edenic theme, be attributed to a brighter, though fleeting, moment in Gauguin's existence? It is true that he experienced euphoric moments between bouts of depression. In November 1896 he wrote to Monfreid: 'My studio is very beautiful, and I assure you the time passes quickly. I promise you that from six in the morning until noon I can do a lot of good work. Ah! My dear Daniel, if you knew this Tahitian life, you would no longer wish to live any other way.'

The nudes from Gauguin's first Tahitian period were grand and monumental, and often portrayed from the back. Maillol certainly drew inspiration from them. After 1895 this type of nude became rare in Gauguin's work; bodies became less massive and

168 *Rebecca and Eliezer* by Nicolas Poussin (Detail). 1648. Oil on canvas, 118 × 199 cm. Musée du Louvre, Paris

more elongated, poses more natural. The nude in *Nevermore* is nonchalant and dreamy—a Tahitian 171 odalisque. In a letter to Monfreid of 14 February 1897, Gauguin explained: 'I wanted to suggest, with a simple nude, a certain barbarous splendour of bygone days. The whole picture is bathed in colours that are deliberately sombre and sad; neither silk nor velvet, neither batiste nor gold creates this splendour, but simply paint, made rich by the artist's hand. No tricks... only man's imagination has enriched this dwelling with pure fantasy. For a title, Nevermore; not Edgar Poe's raven, but a bird of the devil that watches and waits. It is poorly painted—I am so nervous and I work in fits and starts—but never mind, I think it is a good picture.'

From Poe's poem, Gauguin retained only the refrain, and the obsessive presence of the bird. He knew the poem well, for Mallarmé had read it at Gauguin's farewell banquet in 1891, in his own translation, published in 1875 with illustrations by Edouard Manet. In the portrait of Mallarmé that Gauguin engraved, he placed a raven behind the poet.

The silhouette of the evil bird reappears in *Vairaoumati*, one of the rare paintings from 1895-7 169, 170 which is directly inspired by the Maori pantheon. The work is more distilled and elusive than earlier 'mythological' paintings. 'She was tall and the sun's fire shone in her golden skin, while all love's mysteries slumbered in the night of her hair' (*Noa Noa*). The face is delicately—and uncharacteristically—modelled,[3] the skin yellow-gold. The figure is seated diagonally, her silhouette standing out against the back of a fabulous throne. The right arm emphasizes the vertical axis of a pyramidal composition. There seems to be no desire to define a coherent space and the bird holding a lizard at the left is treated like a heraldic motif set against an abstract background. In the upper left section of the canvas, two luminous haloes, painted with small, staccato brushstrokes, are reminiscent of certain works from Van Gogh's Impressionist period.

Another work in the same vein is *Poèmes bar-* 173 *bares*, whose title, inscribed by Gauguin, is probably

169 *Vairaomati*. 1897. Oil on canvas, 73 × 94 cm. Musée d'Orsay, Paris

170 *Vairaomati* (Detail of plate 169)

a reference to the work by Leconte de Lisle. At first glance, this painting seems somehow incomplete, doubtless because of the lack of proportion between the two figures. The orange background, which becomes golden around the gnome's head and almost brick red near the top of the canvas, creates a dizzying effect. This luminous background might even suggest the presence of a fire behind the figures. Light seems to radiate from behind the creature's head like a halo, while the face itself is in the shade, with only its bright green, phosphorescent eyes popping from giant sockets like those of a night bird. The bright green appears again above the belt of the loincloth. The unreal quality of the light becomes more evident through an analysis of the shadows, which are totally inconsistent; for example, the inside of the right arm has light thrown on it, as well as the base of the face. The figure seems surrounded by fire.

The contrast between the angel and the beast is striking: in addition to the fact that their appearance and sizes are totally different, one is bathed in light, eyes closed, the other in shadow, wide-eyed. Is the theme here specifically Christian, or does it refer to the universal theme of good and evil? Examples of antithetical pairs of figures are rare in Gauguin's work; one case that comes to mind is the pagan pottery and the figure in *La Belle Angèle*. In Gauguin's work, the simplest interpretation is often the most satisfying. Teilhet-Fisk sees this painting as an evocation of the creation of man according to the Maori world view; in this context the two figures would represent Ta'aroa (the monkey) and Hina (the angel). The creature's head is in fact identical to the one Gauguin gives to Ta'aroa in *Ancien Culte mahorie* (p. 14). But what of the creature's wings? And why are the two figures in such marked contrast to each other? Could this be a representation of St Michael and the demon? The gesture of the right arm raised in front of the chest can often be seen in Gauguin's work. Does it stem from Far Eastern tradition, as illustrated in a bas-relief from Borobudur, of which Gauguin had a photograph? It is true that the pose, the exact meaning of which is unclear, also exists in Western

iconography. As for the painting's title, it contributes little to unravelling the mystery.

During this period, with pictures like *Nevermore*, *Poèmes barbares* and *Vairaoumati*, Gauguin achieved perhaps the best application of his particular approach to colour and form: in *Vairaoumati*, with its pyramidical composition, the solemn reds and golds dominate; in *Poèmes barbares*, there is the orange-red of the flame, and the brown of the earth; *Nevermore* is, as Gauguin himself observed, 'bathed in colours deliberately sombre and sad'. 'Colour! That language so profound, so mysterious, language of dreams', he noted when discussing Delacroix (*Diverses Choses*). On another occasion he wrote: '... there is an impression that results from a certain arrangement of colours, of light, of shadows. One might call it the music of a painting. Even before you know anything about a painting, you enter a cathedral and you find yourself too far from the picture to know what it represents, yet often you are struck by this magical harmony. Herein lies painting's true superiority over other arts, for this emotion addresses the most intimate part of the soul.' These words, found in Gauguin's manuscripts, were, in fact, those of Delacroix. In them Gauguin found the expression of his own deepest convictions, reflected in a letter to Monfreid of August 1901: '... in painting there is, finally, more suggesting than describing, as in music.'

Like many nineteenth-century thinkers, Gauguin subscribed to two distinct, but complementary, theories: that a correspondence exists between the perceptions of the five senses; and that visual perceptions and hearing have layers of meaning. These ideas had been expressed in empirical terms for some time, but only now did they start to be codified, however timidly. Baudelaire's famous lines describe subjective impressions:

Il est des parfums frais comme des chairs d'enfant
Doux comme les hautbois, verts comme les prairies

171   *Nevermore*. 1897. Oil on canvas, 60 × 116 cm. Courtauld Institute Galleries, London

172 *Three Figures. c.* 1898. Monotype on paper, 27.5 × 22 cm. Department of Engraving and Photography, Bibliothèque Nationale, Paris

173 *Poèmes barbares.* 1896. Oil on canvas, 65 × 48 cm. Fogg Art Museum, Harvard University, Cambridge, Massachusetts (Bequest of Maurice Wertheim Collection)

250

178   *Where Do We Come From? What Are We? Where Are We Going?* 1897. Black chalk and coloured crayon on paper, squared, 20 × 37 cm. Musée des Arts africains et océaniens, Paris

255

well, is a rude companion in this place where I am otherwise alone. Music is a great distraction for me.' Later, in the Marquesas Islands, he played the harmonium during sleepless nights.

Even if Gauguin had only amateur musical talent, it was still exceptional in comparison with that of other painters of his generation; though Manet, Fantin-Latour, Renoir, Cézanne and Monet were all knowledgeable music lovers, their relationship to music was entirely passive, and limited to listening to their wives or friends play, or the occasional trip to the Opéra. As far as contemporary writers were concerned, with very few exceptions, music hardly touched their lives. Alphonse Daudet, who was, in fact, one of those rare exceptions, summed up the situation: 'In general, men of letters detest music. We know Gautier's opinion on "the most unpleasant of all noises"; Leconte de Lisle and Banville agreed. Goncourt winced at the sight of a piano being opened. Zola had a vague memory of playing something in his youth, but he couldn't remember what. Flaubert, on the other hand, took himself for a great musician; but it was to please Turgenev who, in fact, never liked the music played at the Viardots.'[5]

It is difficult to say whether Gauguin's failing health, sense of isolation, financial hardship and lack of professional success actually became more acute at this time, or whether they simply felt more intolerable to a man who was old before his years and exhausted from struggling. Despondent over his daughter's death, he began speaking of suicide. It is true that Gauguin had always experienced dramatic mood swings. But now the condition bordered on manic depression. He changed lodgings frequently, each time imagining that the move was permanent.

Near the end of 1897 he took an overdose of arsenic. Afterwards, in February 1898, he wrote to Monfreid: 'Was it that the dose was too strong, or that the vomiting expelled the poison from my system, thus neutralizing its effects... who knows? I had made my decision [to commit suicide] for December, and I wanted, before dying, to paint a large picture that preoccupied me during that whole month; I worked night and day in an extraordinary fever.' On the letter he drew a sketch of the painting he had just finished. 183

Gauguin had long been interested in the particular problems presented by monumental compositions. He often cited examples of works by great mural painters such as Giotto and Raphael, whose works were only familiar to him through photographs. He had seen works by Delacroix, in particular his frescoes at Saint-Sulpice, as well as many paintings which are now in the Louvre but which were, at that time, visible either in Paris or in Versailles. (One notable exception is *Sardanapalus*, which was not exhibited publicly at the time.) The fact that he was personally familiar with works by Delacroix explains why he spoke at length of that artist's use of colour, whereas, in the cases of Giotto and Raphael, he usually referred to the drawing and composition. In *Noa Noa*, he set out a remarkable formal analysis of *The* 176 *School of Athens* with a strange sketch. 177

Gauguin was not the only one to be haunted by the idea of a monumental composition. Other innovative artists, deprived of official commissions, had little opportunity to execute mural paintings, even when the development of their art required it. Among the few monumental paintings of the period were Seurat's *La Grande Jatte* (1884-6) and Renoir's

179 Photograph taken in June 1898 in Gauguin's studio. (Photograph courtesy of Patrick O'Reilly.)

180 *Empire of Flora* by Nicolas Poussin. 1631. Oil on canvas, 131 × 181 cm. Staatliche Kunstsammlungen, Gemäldegalerie, Dresden

Large Bathers (1886); Cézanne's large works were done later, and it was only in 1896 that Monet began his *Waterlilies* series, which, after 1918—and at his own initiative—adorned the walls of the Orangerie. Odilon Redon was lucky enough to have private patrons who commissioned friezes, one of whom was Gustave Fayet, who was also an early collector of Gauguin.

Gauguin's desire to free himself from the circumscription of easel painting was shared by his disciples, the Nabis; he may have been their inspiration for abandoning that practice. In about 1890, Verkade wrote: 'A battle cry rang out from one studio to another. No more easels! Down with unnecessary furniture! Painting must not usurp a liberty that isolates it from other arts ... walls, walls for decorating! Down with perspective! The wall must remain a surface ... There are no paintings, only decorations!'[6]

Such a proclamation sounds more like a manifesto of the Russian avant-garde movement than a passage from the memoirs of a Dutch Nabi who later became a Benedictine monk.

It was thus at the end of 1897 that Gauguin undertook to paint a philosophical and aesthetic testament in the form of a monumental work—the biggest he

ever painted—which he entitled *Where Do We Come From? What Are We? Where Are We Going?*. This painting is intensely satisfying, and Gauguin himself recognized its importance: 'They will say it is careless, unfinished. It is true that one is not a good judge of one's own art, but I do believe that this painting not only surpasses everything I have done until now, but that I shall never do anything better, or even like it.' He prepared himself for the inevitable comparisons with Puvis de Chavannes by insisting in the letter to Monfreid of February 1898 that '... this painting is not done like one by Puvis de Chavannes: studies from Nature, then preparatory cartoon, and the like...' Should we believe Gauguin's assertion that the painting was quickly done? Its numerous visual

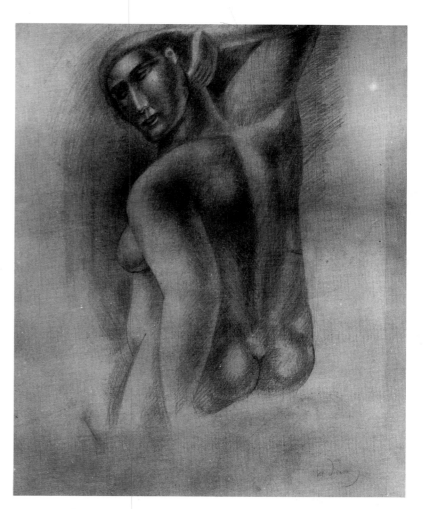

181 Study of one of the principal figures in *Where Do We Come From?* by André Derain. *c.* 1910. Pencil on paper, 57 × 49 cm. Musée d'Art moderne, Troyes (Pierre and Denise Lévy Collection)

258

182 *Where Do We Come From? What Are We? Where Are We Going?* 1897. Museum of Fine Arts, Boston

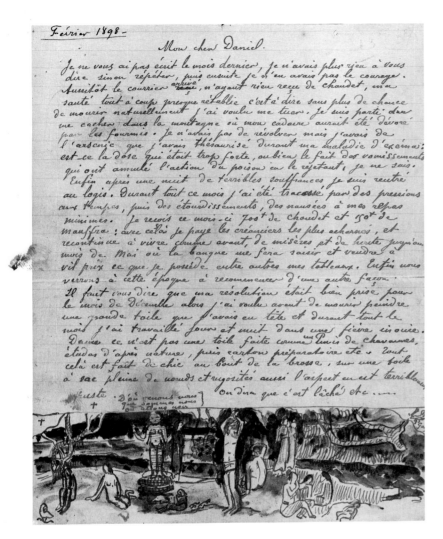

183   Letter from Gauguin to Georges Daniel de Monfreid, February 1898. Wash on paper? Private Collection, Paris

references to earlier works provide no evidence to support that argument; rather, they constitute a sort of recapitulation of earlier themes. It is probable that the squared crayon drawing was a preparatory study for this painting, for its only distinguishing features are a slightly larger picture plane and more sweeping movements. The previously-mentioned sketch on the letter to Monfreid was done after the painting.

The composition of this painting is rigorously architectural. On either side of the slightly off-centre vertical axis formed by the principal figure, two other vertical axes are formed by the idol at the left and by the two women at the right. In the lower area oblique lines dominate, while in the upper part of the

canvas the horizon is clearly marked by the line of the sea. Several triangular elements are too emphatic to be fortuitous. Gauguin spoke of 'enormous mathematical faults' when discussing the painting, a somewhat understated assessment that affirmed his geometric intentions, while, at the same time, suggesting that he was wary of pushing them too far, as disciples like Filiger or Sérusier might have done.

The search for overall harmony can be discerned in the painting's colour scheme. According to Gauguin himself, the dominant colours are 'blue and Veronese green'; yet the light brown of the skin, the bright yellow of the upper corner decorations, and the patches of red or the light pink area at the left do not create a riot of colour. In general, each area of colour is separated from the neighbouring areas, yet delicate nuances soften and modulate the effect, or throw shadows on certain surfaces—for example, the nude bodies, the two figures dressed in pink or the vegetation at the right.

Depth is created not only by the relative sizes of the figures—only the nude figure seen from the back, which was later copied by Derain, is out of proportion—but also by their placement in the surrounding terrain. This latter technique was mastered by Poussin, but had somewhat fallen by the wayside with the fading out of the classical tradition; it was never used by artists of the Barbizon School, for example, nor by Courbet, Manet or Puvis de Chavannes. Another classical technique that Gauguin reintroduces here—either by intuition or from subconscious memory—is that of creating planes by the use of zones of colour: the foreground in brown; middle ground in green; and blue in the background, especially to the left.

In analyzing this picture, it may be appropriate to mention, as Georges Wildenstein has done, Seurat's theory, inspired by the ideas of Humbert de Superville, and published by Jules Christophe (who later became famous, under the pseudonym of Colomb, as the author of *La Famille Fenouillard*). Christophe set down the theory as follows: 'Art is harmony; and harmony is the analogy of opposites (contrasts), and of like elements (shading), both in terms of tone, that is, light and dark; hue, that is, red and its complement, green, orange and blue, yellow and violet; and line, that is, departures from the horizontal axis. These various examples of harmony are brought together in happy or sad colours: gaiety of tone is expressed in luminousness; of hue, in warmth; of line, in upward directions (above the horizontal). Calmness of tone is expressed in the balance of dark and light; of hue, between warm and cool; and of line, between ascending and descending lines. Sadness of tone is expressed in the dominance of darkness; of hue, in the dominance of cool colours; and line, in descending directions.'[7]

Gauguin was vague in his letter to Monfreid concerning the meaning of this painting. Some time later, in July 1901, he expressed himself more clearly in a letter to Charles Morice.

The painting should be 'read' from right to left. The small child represents the beginnings of life, just as the old woman at the left symbolizes the end;

adolescents and adults are scattered throughout the body of the canvas, as are numerous animals, only two of which have a clear meaning: 'A strange white bird, holding a lizard in its claws, represents the futility of vain words.' The cats, goat, dog and remaining bird may have no particular significance. However, there is a striking contrast between the chaos of the right-hand portion of the work, with its disordered mix of vegetation and water, as in Monet's *Waterlilies*, and the well-ordered landscape to the left of the idol. The painting makes an inventory of the entire cosmos: water, rock, vegetation, animals and people. The general impression is one of serenity, or of resignation, rather than of anxiety. Gauguin had neither Munch's nor Van Gogh's gift for dramatization, and this painting is still quite evocative of the classical tradition; the isolated figures, or groups of twos or threes, detached from their surroundings yet carefully placed in an outdoor setting bring to mind Poussin's *Empire of Flora* or Titian's *Vénus du Pardo* 180 (Musée du Louvre, Paris).

Chapter XIII   *Avant et après*

Gauguin's work after 1897 was more scarce and uneven than before. Most of the themes he had been using during the preceding years were abandoned in favour of earlier ones, and only rarely did he explore new territory. Should this stagnation and the weakness of certain paintings from this period be attributed exclusively to his poor health and low morale? When, in 1898, he accepted a job as a draftsman for the public administration, it not only lowered his standing in colonial circles but also deprived him of valuable time for painting. Not one of his paintings is dated 1900. However, as we have already seen, we cannot always establish a causal link between Gauguin's productivity and his material well-being. Even when his correspondence is weighed down with mundane complaints, there are also concerns of an aesthetic or technical nature. In general, periods of discouragement still alternated with periods of renewed ardour.

Gauguin needed to continue to work and break new ground, and he felt sure that the visual environment of Tahiti stimulated him as Paris never had. On 15 March 1898 he wrote to a certain Dr Gouzer, a marine physician who had bought a painting from him on a stopover in Tahiti: 'Each day—my latest important works attest to this—I realize that I have not yet said all there is to say here in Tahiti, that there is still much to say, whereas in France, with the disgust I feel there, my brain would probably be sterile; the cold freezes me both physically and mentally, and everything becomes ugly to my eyes.' Not long afterward, he left Tahiti to seek new inspiration in the Marquesas Islands.

When he sometimes considered returning to Paris, it was with the idea of promoting his career commercially, not of working there. It was thus unfair of Degas to remark (if we are to accept Vollard's account): 'Poor Gauguin! Out there, on his island, he must be thinking of the Rue Laffitte... he needs people with flowers on their heads and rings in their noses.'[1] Or, again: 'One can paint as well at Batignolles as in Tahiti.'[2] This may have been true for Degas, but it was not true for Gauguin, for whom 'everything became ugly' in Paris, and, conversely, everything came to life in Polynesia—the bodies, the faces and the flowers.

Towards the end of 1899, Vollard wrote to Gauguin to commission some pencil and watercolour drawings and paintings of flowers. Gauguin replied in January 1900 with a long, sarcastic letter indicating to Vollard in no uncertain terms that he did not intend to work to order, and that he would send what he liked. (He had learned from Maurice Denis that his work was beginning to attract collectors.) He did accept Vollard's rather mean offer of 200 francs per painting and 30 francs per drawing, but proposed, further, to send Vollard twenty-five canvases per year, in exchange for monthly payments of 300 francs, to be deducted from the total value of his shipments. The works in Monfreid's possession could serve as an advance.[3] Vollard not only accepted Gauguin's proposition, but, eager to secure Gauguin's entire output for himself, he soon raised his buying price to 250 francs per painting, and increased the monthly payments to the artist to 350 francs.

185 *The Smile*. 1899. Detail of frontispiece. Musée Gauguin, Papeete

Vollard has been much criticized for his rapacious, insensitive attitude towards Gauguin, as well as towards other artists. He certainly sensed that he had much to gain from an exclusive contract with Gauguin. At the time, few people believed in Gauguin's commercial future; even those dealers familiar with his work lacked Vollard's intuition and daring. Moreover, if Gauguin's monthly remittances arrived with irregularity—he complained bitterly of this in his letters—it was not only due to Vollard's negligence, but also to the slowness of communications

184 *Self-Portrait. c.* 1900. Black pencil on grey-pink paper, 36 × 26 cm. Private Collection, Paris. This self-portrait, like many others by Gauguin, is in profile; he frequently executed these pictures from photographs

between France and Polynesia. Vollard also knew that, because of Gauguin's spendthrift tendencies, it was better to space out his payments. In the end, Gauguin was able to subsist decently during his last years thanks, mostly, to Vollard and Monfreid.

Historically, Gauguin—a Tahitian by adoption— has often been portrayed as a defender of the indigenous population with regard to the Europeans. This traditional viewpoint, propagated by Ségalen, has been taken up by most of Gauguin's biographers. It was supported, too, by Gauguin's own writing—in particular, by *Noa Noa*—and by his correspondence with Daniel de Monfreid, as well as by reports addressed to the governor of Tahiti. His quarrels with the chief justice of Papeete, and then with the church and colonial authorities of the Marquesas Islands have been recounted repeatedly. These incidents were not due solely to the authoritarian and arbitrary character of the colonial administration, but also to

265

186   *The Idol*. 1897 (?). Wood and various materials, H. 25 cm.
Musée d'Orsay, Paris

187   *Faa Iheihe—Tahitian Pastoral*. 1898. Oil on canvas, 54 × 169 cm. Tate Gallery, London

Gauguin's touchy and quibbling temperament, as well as his interest in what remained of the indigenous culture. But research by Patrick O'Reilly and by Bengt Danielsson has led them to evaluate Gauguin's role of cultural defender as more complex than is usually portrayed. First of all, among the white population in Tahiti, there was strong opposition between the colonial authorities, who, with few exceptions, never stayed longer than two or three years, and the local shopkeepers and landowners who were permanent residents of the island and resented the authoritarianism of the governor and his entourage. In addition, the colonists were divided between Catholics and Protestants, although their religious loyalties had more to do with tradition than with strong personal convictions. Gauguin exemplified this in *Avant et après* when he wrote: 'An election in Tahiti is synonymous with Picpus [the name of the principal Catholic congregation] opposing the Bernese bear [several clergymen were of Swiss extraction]. Here I am (who would ever have guessed?), becoming Picpus, so as not to be Swiss. On the one hand, stupid churchgoers, on the other, vile sectarians. Calvinist, never… never in my life, even when I took my first communion, I was never so Catholic, and I was right.'

Gauguin did, indeed, become a polemicist, and an energetic one, but less in defence of the Polynesians than out of personal vindictiveness towards the judge and the governor. He aired his grievances in a magazine he created, called *Le Sourire*, and then in a monthly journal called *Les Guêpes*, founded in 1899 by Cardella, the mayor of Papeete at that time. Gauguin soon became the editor-in-chief of that journal, and shut down *Le Sourire*. He retained the position until August 1901, when he decided to leave for the Marquesas Islands, where he hoped that Vollard's monthly pension would be sufficient to live on. Deprived of Gauguin's venom, *Les Guêpes* folded.

Most of the articles signed by Gauguin or justifiably attributed to him have little to do with the indigenous population; Danielsson and O'Reilly, who were the first to study this topic in depth, con-

cluded without benevolence that 'Gauguin, from beginning to end, exclusively and with the utmost loyalty, served the most explicit interests of his employers. The fact that he probably did not always believe in what he said and wrote does not render his behaviour more sympathetic. His real motives [were] his thirst for vengeance and his need for money.'[4]

This indictment does not take into consideration either Gauguin's other convictions, or the extreme poverty with which he was struggling. He was not the only artist of his time to accept odd jobs to survive, as long as they did not conflict with personal beliefs. Mallarmé, too, took jobs on the side, calling them his 'basic jobs'. Gauguin had already expressed his personal feelings about colonialism and its consequences before writing in Tahitian journals: in January 1897, the seizure of the Leeward Islands by the colonial administration was the subject of a long letter to Morice, who included it in his reworked edition of *Noa Noa* (which was published in *La Revue Blanche* of 1 November 1897). In the Marquesas, Gauguin was called upon to commit himself personally to the defence of the islanders.

The increase in Vollard's monthly cheques was doubtless the direct cause—or, rather, the enabling factor—leading to Gauguin's decision to move to the Marquesas Islands. Always restless, Gauguin dreamed of moving on. The Marquesas archipelago, which, like Tahiti, was part of the French settlements of Oceania, had been under French sovereignty since 1842. It was no longer virgin territory; whalers and merchants of all nationalities had introduced the local population to alcohol and opium, as well as contagious diseases, bringing it close to extinction. Herman Melville went there in 1842, and recounted his stay in *Typee*. Pierre Loti had also been there; in his book *Rarehu*, he contrasted Hiva-Oa with Tahiti which, according to him, was impregnated with 'our stupid colonial civilization'. In 1888, Robert Louis Stevenson sojourned there. He recounted his journey in *In the South Seas*, in which he demonstrates a particular sensitivity to the beauty of the light and landscapes: 'As the reflux drew down, marvels of colour and design streamed between my feet; which I would grasp at, miss, or seize: now to find what they promised, shells to grace a cabinet or be set in gold upon a lady's finger; now to catch only *maya* of coloured sand, pounded fragments and pebbles, that, as soon as they were dry, became as dull and homely as the flints upon a garden path.'[5] In Gauguin's writing, such notations are rare. Stevenson, who sought to obtain as much information about the island as possible, mentions in his journal the presence of one white man who had settled there permanently and was attempting to start a plantation. Gauguin expressed his own motives for going there in a letter of June 1901 to Monfreid: 'I think that in the Marquesas, where it is easier to find models [in Tahiti it was increasingly difficult], and where there are landscapes still exposed—in short, altogether new and uncivilized elements—I shall do beautiful things. Here my imagination is beginning to cool, and besides, the public has got too used to Tahiti. People are so stupid that when we show them pictures containing new and terrible images, Tahiti will become comprehensible and charming. My paintings from Brittany seemed like rose-water after Tahiti; Tahiti will seem like cologne after the Marquesas Islands.'

Tahiti and the Marquesas Islands are dissimilar. For one thing, the people are of different physical types; the Marquesans tend to be taller and thinner, and most of the men have tattoos. (P. Loti had already published reproductions of Marquesan tattoos.) As for the physical aspect of the islands themselves, they are less colourful and more bushy than Tahiti. But for Gauguin, perhaps the most important difference was that, because of its remoteness, the Marquesas archipelago had been subjected to less 'Westernization'; apart from a few missionaries and police, there were very few whites living there. Gauguin managed to have disputes with the few who were there, largely of his own provocation. One example was a bas-relief plaque he made for the doorway of his hut, on which he inscribed 'Maison du Jouir' (House of Pleasure). At the doorway he placed two statues, caricatures of the island's bishop and his housekeeper.

Gauguin's move to the Marquesas Islands did not change his art significantly. The real break had been in 1897-8, culminating in *Where Do We Come From?* 182 After that, he reworked existing motifs, but rarely innovated.

He attempted another frieze, *Faa Iheihe—Tahitian* 187 *Pastoral*; this picture is only half the size of *Where Do We Come From?* but its proportions are the same. From the monumental Boston painting, Gauguin retained the peaceful motif of a slow, somewhat clumsy procession of Virgilian figures moving through lush vegetation. However, in the smaller frieze, the composition is less successful, and the various sections fit together poorly. In the right-hand part of the background there is a horseman seen in profile. This constituted a new addition to Gauguin's bestiary; before that time, horses made only rare appearances in his work, whereas after 1897 they appeared in a dozen different paintings. It is difficult to know whether to attach any special significance to this new motif. In *Avant et après*, written after 1900, Gauguin wrote: 'Sometimes I withdrew very far, beyond the horses of the Parthenon... back to the gee-gee of my childhood, the faithful hobbyhorse.' In these lines, the horse takes on a cultural significance. Paradoxically, at a time when he challenged the symbol of the horse in Greek sculpture, he used that very motif in two or three paintings. We know that he possessed photographs of the Parthenon frieze; one of them probably served as inspiration for *The White Horse*. 189

Some paintings from this period are of unusual sizes, either larger or narrower than was his custom. The two versions of *Maternity* are examples of these 188 unusual dimensions. Two other works, *The Call* and 204 *The White Horse*, seem, because of their tall, narrow formats, to be meant as sections of a diptych. Gauguin began *The White Horse* after not painting for several months. In it, he used multiple vantage points: the ground and the river are seen from above, while the three horses are seen straight on—or, rather, their silhouettes are foreshortened against the ground and the water. The branches and leaves form

188 *Maternity*. 1899. Oil on canvas, 94 × 72 cm. Hermitage, Leningrad

189 *The White Horse*. 1898. Oil on canvas, 140 × 91 cm. Musée d'Orsay, Paris

a sort of foreground, while the varying sizes of the horses suggest depth. This picture is one of the most ambitious and innovative of Gauguin's final years. The original colour scheme was particularly bold for its lack of realism; however, the colours have aged badly, and the horse, which was never truly white—in the truest Impressionist tradition, Gauguin had given it greenish overtones because of its partially shady setting—has taken on an earthy tone with time. This painting, which was commissioned by Ambroise Millaud, a rich pharmacist from Papeete who had taken a liking to Gauguin, eventually came into the hands of Daniel de Monfreid, who bequeathed it to the Louvre. When, in 1927, it was presented to the Board of Curators, it was strongly endorsed by Robert Rey and Paul Jamot, while the archeological representatives, headed by Salomon Reinach, were violently opposed to its acquisition.

In his bursts of creative activity, Gauguin was not averse to taking up traditional themes, such as that of a still-life with a strongly decentred figure, exemplified by *Sunflowers in an Armchair* (Hermitage, Leningrad). Perhaps the subject-matter of this painting constitutes a tribute to Van Gogh. Two other *Still-Lifes*, one in the Goulandris Collection, the other in the Buehrle Collection, with their airy compositions and rich colours, are reminiscent of Cézanne's still-lifes of 1895.

191, 192 Over the years, the vegetation in Gauguin's paintings had become increasingly intrusive. Openings through which the sky or sea could be seen became rarer, and the horizon was gradually obliterated. After 1895 the combination of vegetation and fresh water dominated the entire surface of many canvases. This profusion of wild growth in which man seems submerged contrasts sharply with the orderly arrangements of trees and gardens and peaceful rivers of Impressionist paintings. There is a striking correlation between these late works by Gauguin and Monet's *Waterlilies*, which were begun at about the same time. But Gauguin never eliminated the human element, and in his work the water's surface is opaque; whereas Monet's monumental paintings

contain no human presence and the water is, to use Paul Claudel's penetrating description, 'transparence, iridescence and reflection'. There is, however, in the work of both masters, a pantheistic character, a kind of celebration of Nature. In an article by Achille Delaroche which Gauguin copied into the manuscript of *Avant et après*, the critic spoke of 'the riches of this Tropical vegetation, where an Edenic and free existence idles beneath lucky stars'. This use of abundant vegetation as a decorative motif, with neither sky nor apparent depth, seems to have been pervasive at the time; we are reminded of Rousseau's 190 jungle paintings, Cézanne's views of *Bibémus*, Klimt's landscapes or Giacometti's unusual still-lifes, not to 193 mention the floral abundance of the Modern Style. Rousseau's first paintings of the jungle date from about 1891, but he did not begin using the theme widely until after 1904, at a time when he could have become familiar with the work of Gauguin. Odilon Redon, in his decoration of the Abbey of Fontfroide (1909-10), linked sumptuous vegetation with mythical figures; the fact that there may have been an iconographic connection between this work and Gauguin's Polynesian scenes, and that it was commissioned by Gustave Fayet, a great admirer and collector of Gauguin's work, in no way diminishes Redon's originality.

As with the works from preceding periods, historians have sought to discover Gauguin's sources during this time. For example, the link between Degas's *Racehorses at Longchamp* and Gauguin's 194 *Riders on the Beach* was pointed out long ago. In *Un* 195, 196 *Beau Ténébreux*, Julien Gracq wrote of 'Gauguin's solemn line of riders, riding bareback with long, noble gestures'.[6] In fact, Gauguin's riders possess a dignity and presence that Degas's do not. In *Avant et après*, Gauguin observed: 'Racehorses and jockeys in Degas's landscapes. Very often nags being ridden by monkeys. In all of that, there is no motif, only lines, lines and more lines. His style is him.' Does this mean that subject-matter counts less than style?

More than Cézanne, Degas remained Gauguin's principal point of reference to the very end. In a pho-

197 tograph of Tohotaua, a lovely young Marquesan woman, taken in Gauguin's studio, there is a
198 reproduction of *Dancers and Harlequin* on the wall which has been tentatively identified as Degas's painting of this title. Alongside it there is a reproduction
126 of Puvis de Chavannes's *Hope* and Hans Holbein's
199 *Mrs Holbein and her Children*. Gauguin wrote, in *Avant et après*: 'Before me [is] a photograph of a

190 *The Waterfall* by Henri Rousseau. 1910. Oil on canvas, 116 × 150 cm. Art Institute of Chicago (Helen Birch Bartlett Collection)

painting by Degas. The lines on the floor lead to a point on the horizon, very far, [placed] very high, intersected by a line of dancers, with their careful, rhythmic, affected steps. Their studied gaze is fixed on the male figure in the lower left-hand corner: a harlequin, one hand on his hip, the other holding a mask. He is watching, too. What is the symbol? Is it eternal love, those traditional antics we call coquettry? Nothing like it ... it is choreography.' As with the racehorses, Gauguin suggests a thematic analysis, only to throw it over in favour of a formal analysis. Choreography is taken as a first level of stylization.

273

191   *The Bathers*. 1898. Oil on canvas, 60.4 × 93.4 cm. National Gallery of Art, Washington, D.C

192   *The Horse on the Path*. 1899. Oil on canvas, 94 × 73 cm. Pushkin Museum, Moscow

274

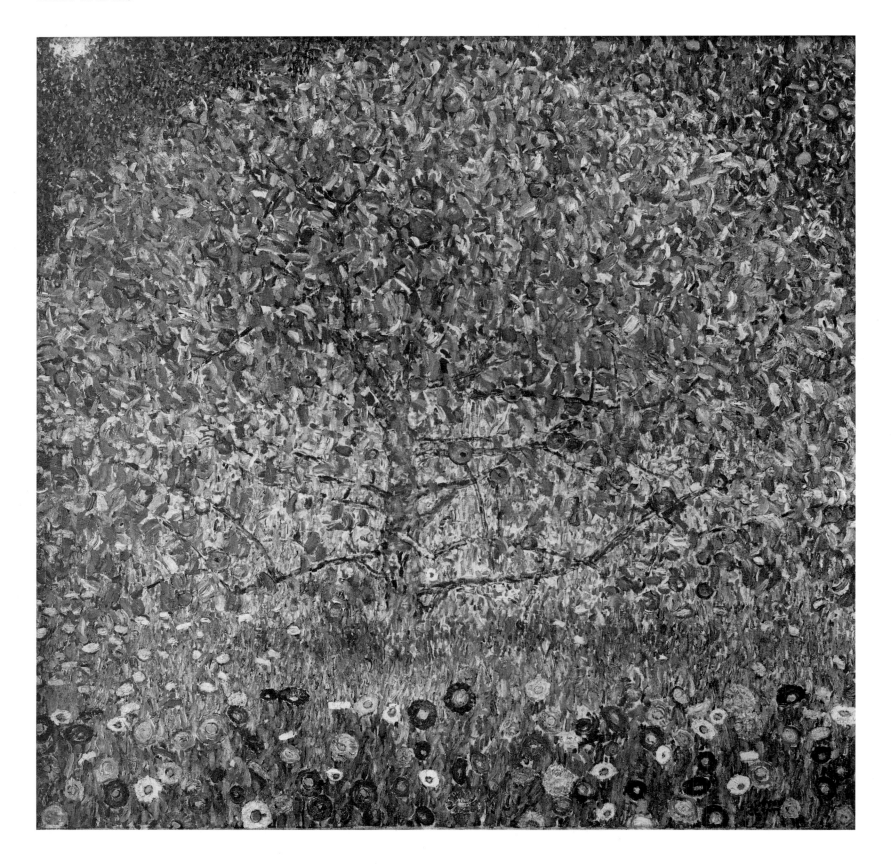

193   *Apples* by Gustav Klimt. 1912. Oil on canvas, 109 × 110 cm.
Museum Moderner Kunst, Vienna

'Beneath it, a portrait by Holbein.' Gauguin makes reference, in the same passage, to another picture 197 also visible in the photograph. This picture of *Mrs* 199 *Holbein and her Children* served on at least two occasions to inspire his own painting. The main theme is reflected in a portrait of a mother with two children (Art Institute of Chicago); and the unusual, leaning pose of Mrs Holbein reappears in a portrait of 201 Tohotaua, *Girl with a Fan*. Gauguin had already used the same pose, though inverted, in *When Will You* 121 *Marry?* (Private Collection, Basel). It could be that the Basel collector who bought this picture was unconsciously drawn to a motif recalling one of the most famous paintings in his city's art museum. A similar conjecture can be made with respect to the ownership of another Gauguin painting, *Portrait of a Young Girl*. The Barnes Foundation, Philadelphia, to which it belongs, has a considerable number of works by Matisse, and certain parallels between the two artists are apparent in this painting.

The traditional culture in the Marquesas was more alive and less debased than that of Tahiti. However, Gauguin did not concern himself with transcribing legends and local customs, as he had during his first stay in Tahiti, though he did allude to them in some of his works.

The Sorcerer of Hiva-Oa (also entitled *The* 202 *Enchanter*) portrays a man, dressed in a blue tunic and a huge, red cape, walking towards the viewer. Bengt Danielsson has identified the man as Haapuani, a remarkable Marquesan who was supposedly destined at birth to become a *tau'a*, sorcerer. The red cape is the sorcerers' insignia. Haapuani befriended Gauguin and introduced him to the customs and legends of the island. In the background of the painting are a river and two women. (Gauguin often portrayed women in twos.) In the lower part of the canvas, a dog and a bird are treated as heraldic figures, as in several other paintings of this period. Jehanne Teilhet-Fisk has carried the analysis of this picture

194 *Racehorses at Longchamp* by Edgar Degas. *c*. 1875. Oil on canvas, 34.1 × 41.8 cm. Museum of Fine Arts, Boston (S.A. Denio Collection; purchased by Sylvanus Adams Denio Fund, 1903)

195   *Riders on the Beach*. 1902. Oil on canvas, 73 × 92 cm. Private
Collection

196 *Riders on the Beach*. 1902. Oil on canvas, 66 × 76 cm.
Museum Folkwang, Essen

197 Photograph of Tohotaua taken in Gauguin's house 'Maison du Jouir'. On the wall hang reproductions of paintings by Hans Holbein the Younger, *Mrs Holbein and her Children*; Edgar Degas, *Dancers and Harlequin*; and Pierre Puvis de Chavannes, *Hope*

somewhat further, proposing that the two women dressed in shrouds represent harbingers of death. However, we would prefer to leave vague the presence of the enigmatic, somehow supernatural sorcerer, whose elegant silhouette and choreographic pose are exceptional in Gauguin's work. There may 200 be a reference to Watteau's *Indifference*, described by Claudel as 'half fawn, half bird'; it was exhibited in the La Caze rooms at the Louvre, which Gauguin knew well.

In another painting from 1902, *Contes barbares*, 203 the symbolic significance is more obvious. In the centre of the picture is an androgynous creature of exceptional beauty, seated in the lotus position; to its right, a kneeling woman, her long, red hair adorned with a delicate crown of flowers. Danielsson suggests that the woman represents Tohotaua, the wife of Haapuani, the sorcerer. To the left of these two magnificent figures is a grotesque creature with a contorted human face and clawed animal paws, to whom Gauguin has kindly attributed the facial traits of his old friend and rival from Pont-Aven, Meyer de Haan. It seems unlikely that Gauguin used this picture to settle an old argument. An almost identical portrayal of de Haan appeared in a painting from 1889, where 101 the symbolic significance was fairly explicit: de Haan, who was passionately interested in occultism, is portrayed seated at a table on which are placed two books: Carlyle's *Sartor Resartus* and Milton's *Paradise Lost*. Perhaps the two figures in the 1902 painting could be seen as incarnations of those two books, symbolizing the replacement of Western wisdom—represented by Carlyle—by Oriental wisdom—represented by the figure in lotus position, and of the biblical Eve—portrayed in Milton—by a Maori one.

198 *Dancers and Harlequin* by Edgar Degas. *c.* 1890. Pastel on paper, 51 × 64 cm. Private Collection

182, 202   As in *Where Do We Come From?* and *The Sorcerer*, a pair of feminine figures constitutes the principal

204   motif of *The Call*. One of the women, her arm and index finger raised, beckons to someone, or something, beyond the picture plane. The other woman appears indifferent. There are strange irregularities in the representation: the vegetation and a third figure, seen from behind, are painted with care and precision, while the women's faces demonstrate a relative clumsiness of technique that is, unfortunately, prevalent in Gauguin's late work. The later paintings tend to make use of freer, more supple brushwork, with paint often applied in streaks. But stylistically they show scant traces of development. In the end, the Marquesas brought little that was new to Gauguin's work, apart from the slight distinctions of body type and vegetation already mentioned. By 1901, Gauguin

200   *Indifference* by Antoine Watteau. *c.* 1717. Oil on canvas, 25 × 19 cm. Musée du Louvre, Paris

199   *Mrs Holbein and her Children* by Hans Holbein the Younger. 1528. Distemper on paper mounted on panel, 77 × 64 cm. Kunstmuseum, Basel

was worn out; though he was still able to produce a few successful paintings.

If we consider only Gauguin's painting and sculpture during the last years, we are left with a painful impression that certain biographers have not hesitated to dramatize: the image of the tortured Parisian artist fleeing to a lost island, only to endure the persecution of church and colonial authorities; and when he was just coming into the public eye in Paris, being so physically diminished that he could barely hold his brush. Such pathos provided ideal material for literature, stage and screen and, indeed, it was by means of this extensive dramatization that Gauguin's name and story entered the annals of popular culture.

281

201 *Young Girl with Fan*. 1902. Oil on canvas, 92 × 73 cm.
Museum Folkwang, Essen. The expression is the same as in the photograph shown in plate 197

202 *The Sorcerer of Hiva-Oa*. 1902. Oil on canvas, 92 × 73 cm.
Musée d'Art moderne, Liège

203 *Contes barbares*. 1902. Oil on canvas, 130 × 89 cm. Museum
Folkwang, Essen

204 *The Call*. 1902. Oil on canvas, 130 × 90 cm. Cleveland
Museum of Art (Gift of the Hanna Fund)

藤原
實方

205 Series from *Noa Noa*, two studies of work by Eugène Delacroix, with a Japanese print and *Jesus Meeting Saint Veronica* by Lucas van Leyden (sixteenth century). 1902 (?). Watercolour on paper, 31.5 × 23 cm. Department of Graphic Arts, Musée du Louvre, Paris

206 *A Marquesan Family*. 1902. Wood engraving and monotype, 46.5 × 27.5 cm. Musée d'Arts africains et océaniens, Paris

In fact, during his last years Gauguin remained an active, prolific writer, a facet of his creativity little known to the general public. It is true that most of his texts are largely unavailable; either they exist exclusively in private editions, or are only partially published; some have even remained unpublished. We have already discussed his three most important early works, *Ancien Culte mahorie*, *Noa Noa*, and *Cahier pour Aline*, as well as his work for two Tahitian reviews, *Le Sourire* and *Les Guêpes*. From the time he returned to Polynesia, in 1895, until his death, he wrote the rest of *Noa Noa*, *Diverses Choses*, *Racontars de Rapin*, *Avant et après*, *L'Eglise Catholique et les Temps Modernes*, and its sequel, *L'Esprit Moderne et le Catholicisme*. In addition, he kept up regular correspondence with Daniel de Monfreid, André Fontainas and Ambroise Vollard.

All this amounts to more than a thousand carefully hand-written pages, many of which are decorated 205 with drawings, engravings or photographs pasted in. Reproductions of works by Dürer, Lucas van Leyden and Giotto appear side by side with ones by Daumier and Forain. It seems quite clear that, in his last years, Gauguin spent more time at his writing table than before his easel.

No detailed examination of all these manuscripts has yet been undertaken, and, unfortunately, the present study is not an appropriate forum for such an analysis; for one thing, it would require a massive effort to find and reassemble the original sources from which Gauguin, in the manner of the time, copied freely. He rarely cited references, or even used quotation marks, an omission which accounts for the fact that he was long given credit for a lovely phrase about the 'music of a painting' that was, in fact, copied from Delacroix (cf. p. 248). In addition, while his choice of quoted passages was certainly far from arbitrary, he did not necessarily agree wholeheartedly with the statement. In this regard, we have already seen how much of the basis for *Ancien Culte mahorie* was taken from the book by Moerenhout, and that quotes from Wagner, Poe, Verlaine and others mingled in the pages of *Cahier pour Aline*.

Some of Gauguin's manuscripts have a highly organized presentation, as if Gauguin fully expected them to be published. We have already noted how he brought back to Tahiti the hand-copied text of *Noa Noa*, already somewhat reworked by Morice. He subsequently added watercolours and engravings, and pasted photographs into the spaces left for Morice's own poems. In the same notebook, on the pages following the conclusion of *Noa Noa*, he added a miscellany of texts of a more personal nature, to which he gave the following introduction: 'Diverses choses 1896-7. Scattered notes, without order, like dreams, like life, all made up of pieces, and consequently the work of several people; a love of beautiful things seen in a neighbour's house (with a drawing pasted in) by the dear, departed Vincent Van Gogh. My God, there are so many childish things to be found in these pages, written with such personal abandonment, such a setting down of beloved—if a bit outlandish—ideas, in defiance of faulty memory, and so many rays to the vital centre of my art. Of course, if the work of art were a chance creation, all these notes would be virtually useless.'

The 'beautiful things seen in a neighbour's house' written down 'in defiance of faulty memory' refer to the fragments of works cited in his texts. *Diverses Choses* has not been published in its entirety.[7] Certain ideas were taken up and further developed in *Avant et après*. In addition, he inserted into the manuscript of *Noa Noa* a small folder containing a text entitled *L'Eglise Catholique et les Temps Modernes*, the last page of which carries the mention 'end of volume January 1898'. This note is doubtless related to his suicide attempt, as well as to the completion of his monumental testament, *Where Do We* 182 *Come From?* After 1898, he took up the notebook again, continuing to add disparate notes and engravings clipped from *Le Sourire*. But *Noa Noa* was, by this time, a thing of the past for him; he had resigned himself to a partial publication by Morice. Now he concentrated on writing other texts, largely with the objective of sending them to Europe as a sort of defence of his painting, and of his ideas.

207 *Women and a White Horse*. 1903. Oil on canvas, 72.5 × 91.5 cm. Museum of Fine Arts, Boston (Bequest of John T. Spaulding)

Gauguin sent *Racontars de Rapin* to André Fontainas for publication in *Mercure de France*, a magazine he received and read regularly until his death. The piece's sarcastic title (meaning 'Stories of a Dauber') hides a bitter text. Unfortunately, Fontainas was unable to have the text published. However, without even waiting for a reply, Gauguin sent Fontainas a second, much longer manuscript, illustrated with several drawings. The cover decoration consisted of an ornamental composition of Capetian fleurs-de-lis intertwined with Polynesian motifs, and the following inscription appeared:

AVANT et après

P. Gauguin

in the Marquesas Islands

To Cry		To Laugh
To Suffer	1903	To Live
To Die		To Enjoy

In secula Secularum

On the endpapers, Gauguin pasted one of his own engravings, as well as two Japanese prints; on the back cover, a reproduction of Dürer's *Knight, Death and the Devil*.

Gauguin was probably dreaming of making of this text a *Livre d'artiste*, a genre which was blossoming at the time. In *Avant et après*, whose title probably alludes to his attempted suicide, he brings together childhood memories, accounts of life in Tahiti and the Marquesas, remarks on aesthetics, and general commentary, peppering the whole with a good dose of lively anecdotes. He reveals himself to be both a gifted story-teller and a brilliant polemicist.

In *Avant et après*, as well as in *Diverses Choses* and *Racontars de Rapin*, the most interesting sections are those devoted to reflections on his own art, the use of colour, the importance of the decorative arts (one of Gauguin's favourite tenets) and the links between the visual arts and music. Contrary to his image, Gauguin was not, in fact, an instinctual painter, but a man who reflected on his art and who carried out specific artistic intentions. In his earliest years as an artist, he practised the techniques of

Impressionism almost methodically, then abruptly abandoned them. His 'primitivism' was in no way a return to an artistic state of nature. He used Polynesian motifs while drawing inspiration from Giotto, Raphael, Poussin and Delacroix.

Another conclusion is obvious from reading Gauguin's texts: however strong were his moments of doubt and discouragement, he did acquire, over the years, a keen sense of his worth as an artist. He spoke lucidly of his artistic contribution, and of the influence his work would surely have on future generations. Certain written works, in particular *Racontars de Rapin*, formulate a veritable moral doctrine of artistic life. He often quotes Wagner's famous words,[8] which Sérusier transcribed on a wall of the inn at Le Pouldu: 'I believe in a last judgement where all those of this world who dared trade illicitly in art, so sublime and chaste, all those who have soiled and degraded it by the vulgarity of their sentiments and the vain quest for material pleasure would be condemned to terrible sentences. I think that, on the contrary, those faithful disciples of great Art will be glorified and, enveloped in a celestial gown of rays, perfumes and melodious chords, they will be released for eternity into the bosom of the divine source of all harmony.'

Gauguin denounced the carelessness and obscurantism of the public authorities with regard to art. His pet hate was Henry Roujon, the Director of Fine Arts, not only because Roujon had personally rejected both him and his work, but also because he held Roujon responsible for keeping the truly creative artists apart from the official art world, and for preventing the Musée du Luxembourg from evolving with the times. Surprisingly, Gauguin made no allusion to the Caillebotte legacy case, which was the talk of Paris during his final stay there in 1894-5 (see Chapter XI, p. 202, note 2). Nor did he call for the

208 *Nativity* (with self-portrait in upper left section). 1902. Monotype on paper, 31.8 × 19.2 cm. Saint Louis Art Museum (Gift of Vincent Price, Beverly Hills, in memory of his parents, Marguerite and Vincent L. Price)

abolition of official institutions, but, rather, for their opening up to new ideas and approaches. He knew very well that behind men like Roujon there was a whole body of academic artists, exemplified, for Gauguin as for Cézanne, by Bouguereau. In our own times, when academic art has come back into fashion, we tend to forget that its advocates attempted to smother the efforts of contemporary artists whose work reached out in new directions.

Gauguin often discusses topics ostensibly unrelated to art, including education, patriotism, money and the condition of women. Two of his last written pieces concern religious questions. He affirmed: 'my soul is not irreligious, [and] I do not speak lightly while ignoring holy things' (*Diverses Choses*). His thorough knowledge of both the Old and New Testaments was certainly more the result of extensive reading in his adult life than of the Catholic education of his youth. He shared the much-espoused opinion, widely disseminated by Renan, that the Catholic Church, as a human institution, had distorted and misrepresented the teachings of Jesus, some of whose precepts he embraced, especially the commandment to love thy neighbour as thyself, and God above everything. For Gauguin that meant the goodness, justice, beauty and truth He represents were the cardinal values in life. He gave free rein to his bitterness towards missionaries, and if he sympathized in his last months with the minister of Atuana, it was because he was the only white man with whom he could talk, not because he was attracted by Protestant doctrine. He rejected the idea of joining the Freemasons: 'I have never thought of becoming a Freemason, not wishing to join any group on account of my free spirit and lack of sociability' (*Avant et après*).

In *L'Esprit Moderne et le Catholicisme*, he renewed his violent attacks on the Church, but his ideas had evolved somewhat. For one thing, he had fallen upon a book by Gerald Massey, translated under the title of *Jésus Historique*, in which Jesus is treated purely as a mythical figure. In this book, Gauguin's style is less natural, and more sententious. It may well be that certain passages are either transcriptions or clumsy translations of texts by other authors. He rejected all formal religions. He had studied Buddhism and the Gospel alike, finding in them 'satisfaction, not because I found there the unfathomable mystery solved, but [because] its marvellous, supernatural form was pleasing to my artist's imagination ... and I admit that just as I thought I understood them, I always found wisdom, and a higher, more noble level of thinking. I loved God without knowing him, without defining, or understanding' (*Diverses Choses*). Like a man in search of himself, he contradicts himself from one text to another. His deepest conviction seems to centre on a kind of syncretism, or, rather, pantheism, a belief that was shared by Claude Monet towards the end of his life.

Gauguin's and Monet's religious beliefs have caused their names to be associated, on occasion, with that of the twentieth-century Jesuit paleontologist Pierre Teilhard de Chardin. Teilhard's ideas, which were always deeply rooted in his Christian faith, posited a sacralizing vision of creation that he called the biosphere, and his theoretical writings were an attempt to give a theological description to his scientific findings. That Post-Impressionist artists are linked with him is not surprising given their tendency to perceive a sacred force in Nature.

In 1875, for the Impressionists, Nature was still limited to country gardens. After 1890 painters began to give it a more cosmic dimension: Cézanne carried on a solitary dialogue with his holy mountain; Monet meditated before his flowered pond and discovered the world's secrets. Gauguin reinvented a terrestrial paradise from the defiled vestiges of nature that he found in the Tropics, and imposed his image on subsequent generations. 'The public, and the critics, bellowed before my paintings ... Did they want me to present a Tahiti that resembled the suburbs of Paris, all raked and planted in rows? What came ... from logical deduction originating in my deepest self, rather than from materialist theories invented by Parisian bourgeois, became for them a grave fault, that of not joining in with the crowd' (*Diverses Choses*).

Chapter XIV   In the Annals of Art

Once, when he consented to express himself with a minimum of polemic, Emile Bernard summed up quite aptly what he referred to as Gauguin's influence: 'Through his numerous disciples, and through his work, Paul Gauguin was an influential person. Gifted with an exotic decorative sense, his works, in which form tends towards the realistic rather than the geometric, ensured his success. Using a particular scientific method, he orchestrated the strange harmonies of his Tahitian or Martiniquan scenes, often recalling, in his Breton paintings as well, the discoveries of his friends. Although he was ill read, Gauguin possessed the keen mind of enlightened men; his intuition and taste guided him along paths of varying difficulty. His work met with appalling injustice. He possessed gifts that he could not always exploit to the full because of his late entry into the world of painting. He was a student, in turn, of Pissarro, Renoir and Cézanne; and nothing in his work before 1888 suggested that he would one day become a Symbolist. This transformation he owed to a series of fortunate circumstances, and, at Pont-Aven, he was the self-appointed apostle of these new acquisitions. Until his death, he remained faithful to his principles, attempting in vain to impose theory onto the synthesis he practised, in which distortion marred otherwise successful compositions. His works reveal a marvellous sense of colour; for all that, [he remains] a great barbarian artist.'[1]

The most important artistic figures of the late nineteenth century did not actively seek disciples. Cézanne is a prime example. He exerted an influence on all his contemporaries, and his successors unanimously recognized him as probably the most influential figure, both on their personal development and on the history of art in general. Many of them, including Gauguin, Pissarro, Monet, Degas, Signac, Denis, Matisse and Picasso, sought to own works by him; others, such as Gleizes, Kandinsky and Malevitch, commented on his art. But, ironically, Cézanne always remained suspicious of his admirers and irritated at being the centre of attention of other painters. Degas, Monet and Renoir may have been pleased by the eventual success of Impressionism, but were disappointed to see it watered down and made commonplace. Degas remarked bitterly: 'They shoot us, but they empty our pockets.' Seurat trusted only a few of his numerous disciples and imitators, and Van Gogh did not live to see the impact of his revolutionary work.

Gauguin's attitude was totally different. From the time he first became interested in the Impressionist group, he helped organize exhibitions and choose participants. He had an obliging audience in his faithful friend, Schuffenecker; then, at Pont-Aven, in the midst of a colony of largely uninspired artists, he held court with a small group. He planned to take Schuffenecker with him to Martinique, but then ended up leaving with Charles Laval. During his second stay in Brittany, he became the acknowledged leader of a new group of artists. Without reopening the controversy over whether he or Bernard was first in their ground-breaking artistic research, it is clear that, starting in 1888, a number of young artists looked to

Gauguin for questions of technique, subject-matter and the basic principles of a kind of Symbolist painting whose object was to express an idea rather than to represent an image of reality. Maurice Denis expressed the dictum thus: 'Remember that a painting, before being a battlefield, a nude woman or a story of any sort, is a flat surface covered with colours assembled in a specific way.' This was an entirely new concept, and Gauguin's art was instrumental in its emergence.

From 1888 on, the core of artists gathered around Gauguin became known as the School of Pont-Aven. Gauguin's forceful personality, verbal eloquence, and personal example together with the originality of his art led many artists, some of whom were far from *débutants*, to adopt his 'formula' so completely that some of their paintings were presented as authentic 209 Gauguins. The story surrounding *The Talisman* exemplifies Gauguin's consecration as schoolmaster. Maurice Denis wrote: 'It was in September of 1888 that Gauguin's name was introduced to us by Sérusier, who had just returned from Pont-Aven. He showed us, with something of an air of mystery, a lid of a cigar box on which one could barely make out a landscape that was all misshapen, built up in the Synthetist manner with spots of violet, vermilion, Veronese green and other colours, applied straight from the tube, with practically no admixture of white. "How does that tree look to you?" asked Gauguin, standing by a corner of the Bois d'Amour. "Is it green? Then take some green, the most beautiful green you have on your palette. And this shadow, it's blue, isn't it? Don't be afraid to make it as blue as you can" ... This was the beginning of a movement ... We [Henri-Gabriel Ibels, Pierre Bonnard, Paul Ranson and Maurice Denis] began to frequent places unknown to our boss, Jules Lefebvre: the mezzanine of the Maison Goupil in the Boulevard Montmartre where Van Gogh, the brother of the painter, showed us not only Gauguins from Martinique, but pictures by Van Gogh, Monet and Degas; and the boutique of Père Tanguy in the Rue Clauzel, where we discovered ... the work of Paul Cézanne ...'[2]

It is easy to forget that this text is an isolated, indirect and late account of the events, and it may well be that, over the years, the paradoxical character of Gauguin's words has been somewhat exaggerated. Although history has retained only the episode, with its initiatory overtones, Gauguin surely did not transmit his ideas to Sérusier exclusively through *The Talisman*; he must have shown him paintings as well. It may not even be unreasonable to suppose that Gauguin took the brush from Sérusier's hand and painted the panel himself; in fact, a recent cleaning has restored a brightness to the colours that was closer to Gauguin's own palette than to Sérusier's. Moreover, this would not have been the only example of Gauguin intervening in a work by one of his disciples: in an effort to lighten up *The Portrait of Marie Jade* by Séguin, the master took his friend's 211 brush and painted the little landscape in the background. In any case, the religious metaphor continues: Sérusier, having received the 'revelation' of the new truth, was 'converted'; he brought the precious 'talisman' to Paris, where he showed it to a small group of 'initiates', who called themselves 'prophets' (Nabis) and formed a 'chapel'.

Gauguin's feelings about art motivated him to acquire disciples; he was convinced that he was exploring uncharted territory that would be as important for others as for himself (in contrast to Cézanne's entirely individualistic approach). There were also the obvious psychological motivations: a quest for power, a need to impose his ideas, and, perhaps, to fill the emotional gap left by the separation from his wife and children. This might also account for his overbearing attitude towards Van Gogh.

The members of the Parisian group (Bonnard, Vuillard, Roussel, Denis, Ballin, Lacombe, Ranson and others) were more interested in getting to know Gauguin's work than in becoming acquainted with the painter himself; some considered him not the sort of person they wished to associate with.[3] From Gauguin's work they borrowed *cloisonnisme*, the use of matt colours, and the rejection of perspective.

However, they took little interest in his exotic subject-matter; most preferred to stick to the cosy, somewhat confined world of the Parisian middle class, while others, like Georges Lacombe, invented their own repertoire of symbols. They admired Gauguin as a painter, not as an inventor of images. None of them took up the call of the sea.[4] In fact, after some years, the Nabi group survived largely through bonds of friendship; receptive to outside influences, each one developed according to his individual temperament. But they always acknowledged, and even defended, their debt to Gauguin. Maurice Denis referred to it on numerous occasions in his written texts: 'We understood [thanks to Gauguin] that every work of art is a transposition, a caricature, the impassioned equivalent of a felt sensation.'[5] Denis wrote this in 1903; his 'we' was no longer an exclusive reference to the Nabi group, but, indirectly, to the burgeoning Art Nouveau movement, which was also based on the stylization of forms. Denis also sensed the potential of Gauguin's teaching for future generations of artists.

Matisse exemplified the ways a strong personality could assimilate his predecessor: in 1895, while he was still in his formative years he made a 'pilgrimage' to Pont-Aven. In 1899 he bought a portrait of a young boy from Vollard, and in 1905, when he left for the Midi in early spring, he met Maillol, who had been an admirer of Gauguin. Together they went to Daniel de Monfreid's estate in the Pyrenees, where many of Gauguin's paintings were kept. They may also have visited Gustave Fayet and Maurice Fabre, two collectors of Gauguin's work who lived in that region. We can see a shift in Matisse's work during that time if we compare a painting such as *La Pastorale* (Musée d'Art Moderne de la Ville, Paris), done in a style still influenced by Impressionism and by Van Gogh, with *Joie de Vivre* (Barnes Foundation, Philadelphia) which, though painted only a few months later, is marked by a monumental, linear style with prominent outlines. This monumentality was to become one of the keynotes of Matisse's mature style.

It may have been Gauguin's influence that led Matisse to take up the ancient myth of the Golden Age, the poetic imagery of the joy of living, and the representation of a harmonious humanity. Picasso, too, may have borrowed from Gauguin the flattened, carefully outlined forms of his blue and rose periods. Only a few years earlier, those same Gauguins had inspired Denis to create an entire seraphic universe. Each of these artists found something uniquely his own in Gauguin's work; and it is interesting, and surprising, to note that the same paintings helped generate three such remarkably different moods. Clearly, the notion of influence deserves further consideration.

In 1903 a small group of Gauguin's works was included in the Autumn Salon. In no time, photographs, publications, prints and paintings were circulating. In about 1904-5 Gauguin's work became widely known throughout France, as well as in Germany, especially among the younger generation of painters. His example helped to bring the Fauve and Die Brücke groups into their own. In 1906 with the collaboration of Vollard, Daniel de Monfreid organized the largest assembling of Gauguin's works to date, again at the Autumn Salon. There were 277 items. Gauguin's renown spread from Paris, to Munich and Berlin, and soon to Moscow, as a principal precursor of avant-garde art. Maurice Denis had written: 'He freed us of all the shackles that the notion of copying imposed on our painters' instincts.'[6] In 1908 Emil Nolde, one of the principals of the Die Brücke group, expressed the same conviction, with heightened imagery: 'Cézanne, Gauguin and Van Gogh were the ice-breakers. The French threw out all the old ways of working and this is the only way of creating a new art, which will take its place alongside the greatest forms of ancient art.'[7] For the Germans, the interest in Gauguin's style was enhanced by a fascination with things 'primitive'; they were discovering Black art at the same time. In fact, Gauguin's example may have stimulated Pechstein to travel to Palau, in the Pacific islands. In 1909 Marius-Ari Leblond noted that the Germans were

great admirers of Gauguin, 'being less subservient to the conventions of studios.'[8] In short, well before the First World War, there was sufficient information circulating that, in avant-garde circles, everyone knew of the revolutionary painter whose deliberate departure for the far ends of the earth had already been elevated to the status of artistic legend.

However, Gauguin's prestige among the following generations of painters, surpassed only by that of Cézanne, did not set the general tone. Apart from a few good critical reviews, principally induced by Vollard, most articles were either reticent or down-right hostile, despite the fact that Gauguin, during his many sojourns in Paris, mingled with the literati. His Nabi admirers and disciples were also involved with Parisian writers, as well as theatre people, such as Lugné-Poe. The studio in the Rue Pigalle which was rented communally by Bonnard, Vuillard and Denis—and where Lugné-Poe was a regular visitor—was a meeting place for painters, writers, critics and collectors alike; Gauguin had visited there, and was generally admired.[9] But few written accounts of these meetings have survived.

We have already spoken of Mallarmé's cautious praise of Gauguin's work. André Gide, a painting enthusiast who maintained a lasting friendship with Maurice Denis, noted his 1889 meeting with Gauguin in Le Pouldu, but gave neither an account of their long conversation, nor any commentary on the painter's work. Alfred Jarry was more enthusiastic. In 1894 exercising his talent for art criticism, the author of *Ubu Roi* produced perceptive commentaries on the work of the Nabis and Henri Rousseau. When Gauguin exhibited at Durand-Ruel's in 1895, three paintings from Tahiti inspired poems by Jarry which were a tribute to the poet's verbal inventiveness, but contributed little to Gauguin's fame.[10]

Ségalen's efforts were more successful in securing Gauguin's reputation for posterity. He already knew

210 Pont-Aven, entrance to the Bois d'Amour. Postcard

of Gauguin when, by coincidence, his career as marine physician took him to the Marquesas Islands on 10 August 1903, some three months after the painter's death. He arrived in time to gather personal accounts of Gauguin's life on the island, as well as to discover his manuscripts. At the auction of Gauguin's work which took place on 2 September 1903, he bought twenty items, including books, manuscripts, woodcut blocks, the remnants of the 'Maison du Jouir' and seven paintings, including a self-portrait and the famous *Breton Village in the Snow*. All of 157 Gauguin's remaining work was dispersed through that sale.

Ségalen also propagated a greater understanding of Gauguin's artistic intentions, which he shared to a certain extent. As early as April 1902, in an article which appeared in the *Mercure de France* (and was probably read by Gauguin), as well as in his medical thesis, Ségalen studied the relationship between colour and hearing and, on a more general plane, the relationship between the arts, which, as we have seen, also interested Gauguin. Ségalen was an admirer of Rimbaud, whose rejection of naturalism and urgent flight from the Old World inspired him; but it was Gauguin who truly opened his eyes. In a letter of 29 November 1903, he confessed to Daniel de Monfreid: 'I can say that I saw nothing of the country or of the Maoris before seeing, and virtually

209 *The Talisman* by Paul Sérusier. 1888. Oil on canvas, 27 × 22 cm. Musée d'Orsay, Paris

experiencing, Gauguin's sketches.' Ségalen believed in 'the power of the imagination, the visionary element of all poetry.'[11] When he was preparing *Les Immémoriaux* (1905), his novel based on the demise of the Maori civilization, and also his later books on China, he researched the subject scrupulously before writing; nevertheless, for him, as for Gauguin, the artist's intuition is often more penetrating than the ethnologist's study.

211 *Portrait of Marie Jade* by Armand Séguin. 1893. Oil on canvas, 88 × 150 cm. Musée d'Orsay, Paris

212 *Two Tahitian Women.* 1889. Oil on canvas, 94 × 72.4 cm. Metropolitan Museum of Art, New York (Gift of William Church Osborn, 1949)

The admiration of artists and the clear-sightedness of a few collectors should not conceal the fact that, in general, the Western world was slow to accept Gauguin's 'savage' art. As in Cézanne's case, an abundance of misguided criticism and general misunderstanding accompanied Gauguin for much of the way on his slow rise to celebrity. It was only after World War I, when Cubism and Black art were becoming known to intellectual circles, that public opinion began warming to Gauguin's art. André Michel, curator of the department of sculpture at the Musée du Louvre and an eminent medievalist and author of a monumental survey of art history which was for years considered authoritative, wrote a thoroughly documented article tracing the evolution of public acceptance of Gauguin's work.[12] The study—whether consciously or not—also traced the path of author's own conversion. The article, which appeared in two instalments in *Journal des Débats*, began with a commentary on Gauguin's letters to Daniel de Monfreid. The author's tone is mocking when he discusses Gauguin's marital problems, his sentimental escapades, his illnesses and his financial difficulties ('scrounging for tuppence'), all of which inspire him with little pity. Van Gogh is described as 'foreign and crazy', and therefore hardly in a position

214 *Isis* by Georges Lacombe. *c.* 1894. Painted wood sculpture, H. 111 cm. Musée d'Orsay, Paris

213 *Landscape of Pouldu* by Charles Filiger. Gouache, 26 × 38 cm. Musée des Beaux-Arts, Quimper

to be proclaimed one of the 'prophets of the French art of the future'. As for Maurice Denis, Michel respected him but was wary of his taste; he declared that 'Denis claimed to be indebted [to Gauguin] for a *law*, a body of *knowledge*, a *method* (enough!). And it is striking how in the calls for rules and discipline

215   *Landscape near Pont-Aven* by Maxime Maufra. *c.* 1890. Oil on canvas, 150 × 300 cm. Musée des Beaux-Arts, Quimper

that rose up more and more frequently from the depths of anarchy ... Paul Gauguin's name was heard again and again.' The article ended on the same sarcastic note, while announcing the publication, in the next number of the journal, of a sequel, this time to be centred on an analysis of Gauguin's ideas.

The second article begins in the same mocking tone, describing Gauguin's tardy conversion to a career in painting and illustrating the account with a curious anecdote, given by René Piot: one day, irritated by the verbose theories of the pupils at the Académie Jullian, Gauguin 'became furious. Dipping a finger into the inkwell, to the great despair of the waiter, he drew a circle on the clean white table-cloth and, pointing to a bowl of apples, exclaimed, "but that is not an apple, it's a circle!".

Gradually, the tone of the article changes; Michel acknowledges Gauguin's place in a changing histori-

cal picture, while at the same time admitting one of the reasons for his suspicion, at a time when national boundaries were still strong in the world of art. 'It seems to me that it is not impossible [...] to place this nostalgic half-breed, part Peruvian, part French, whose perennial restlessness urged him on from Brittany to Tahiti to the Marquesas, in the context of the history of French painting in the last two decades of the nineteenth century.' Michel then proceeds to analyze and to justify, with considerable perspicacity, Gauguin's rejection of both academicism and naturalism. Gauguin maintained 'a fierce hatred of academic calligraphy and of ideals reduced to formulas ... like those produced by Bouguereau's hopelessly impeccable hand. He had no less antipathy for the kind of naturalism professed by certain highly placed doctors.' Here we have the clear vindication of Gauguin's search for 'efficient distortions'. André Michel did not hesitate, either, to link him to Puvis de Chavannes, and also to compare, without fear of sacrilege, Chassériau's *Two Sisters* and Gauguin's *Two Tahitian Women.*

216 *Te Ra'au Rahi—The Big Tree*. 1891. Oil on canvas, 73 × 91.5 cm. Art Institute of Chicago (Gift of Kate L. Brewster)

217 *Te Ra'au Rahi*. Detail of plate 216

At last Gauguin was being taken seriously. Michel's choice of references added further credibility to his article. In quoting one of Gauguin's letters ('just when the strongest sentiments are in fusion in the deepest part of one's being, just when they explode, there is a sort of hatching of the newly created work') Michel likens it to Delacroix's *Journal*. And, on the subject of the monumental *Where Do We Come From?* he declares: 'Here is where Gauguin began thinking like Poussin, while the landscape, in which crudely drawn figures sometimes appear... (but we are soon on his side!), ... has a Poussinesque rhythm, opulence and harmony.' If we keep in mind that Delacroix and Poussin were then at the very top of the scale of values for men of André Michel's generation and standing, this was a very important endorsement of Gauguin.

182

At the same time (on 13 December 1919 in fact), by some significant coincidence, Paul Claudel, then French ambassador to Denmark, visited the Hansen Collection which was rich in works by Gauguin. (Gauguin may have crossed paths with Claudel in Paris during the 1890s.) Claudel had not previously had occasion to see an ensemble of Gauguin's works; he reacted energetically in his journal: 'The only painter descended from Impressionism having such grandeur of composition and style. Instead of scattering colour, he distributes it in solid, homogeneous patches, carefully delimited, creating balance not only with hue, but with expansiveness and form. The character and meaning of each form is assigned in advance to each colour. It was truly the Tropics that he needed, a land with large forms and spacious, clearly defined areas, not the blurred flickering of European climates, so well portrayed by our landscape artists.'

This entry is brief, its style concise. But the essence is there. Just after the First World War, an art historian and poet had recognized Gauguin's importance. Glory, and popularity, would come still later.

Chronology

June 1848 – November 1873

Eugène Henri Paul Gauguin is born on 7 June 1848 in Paris, Rue Notre-Dame de Lorette. His father, Clovis Gauguin, originally from Loiret, is a Republican, and editor of the newspaper *Le National*. Paul's mother, Aline Marie Chazal, is the daughter of a painter and lithographer, André-François Chazal, and a writer and active socialist, Flora Tristan, whose mother was French and whose father, Don Mariano Tristan y Moscoso, was Spanish. Paul has one sister, Marie, born in 1846.

Le National actively criticizes the candidacy of Louis Napoleon Bonaparte for the presidency of the Republic. On 10 December 1848 Bonaparte carries the election. Fearing reprisals, Clovis Gauguin decides to take his family to Peru, where his wife has relatives. They embark on 8 August 1849, but Clovis dies on the way, at Port Famine in the Magellan Strait. Aline and the two children are greeted in Lima by her great-uncle, Don Pio Tristan y Moscoso. The Gauguin family remains in Peru for five years.

Early in 1855 Aline and her children return to France and settle in Orleans. Paul begins his school years, of which we know little. He apparently began as a day student at a school in Orleans, then became a boarder for three or four years at the Petit Séminaire de la Chapelle Saint-Mesmin. In 1862 he rejoins his mother, who by then has moved to Paris and is working as a seamstress. He begins preparations to enter the Naval Academy at the Loriol Institute. However, in 1865, he is over the age limit for entering the Naval Academy. Like Manet in 1848, he opts for a career in the merchant marine, and embarks as officier-in-training on the *Luzitano*, a vessel on which he makes two crossings to Rio de Janeiro (7 December 1865-March 1866 and 3 May 1866-August 1866). Later, he serves as second lieutenant on the *Chili*, departing on 29 October 1866 for a thirteen-month trip around the world.

On 14 December 1867 Paul returns to France and learns that his mother died on 7 July of that year. She designated Gustave Arosa, financier, photographer and art collector (and godfather of Claude Debussy) as her children's legal guardian. In March 1868, under obligation to serve the French government like all registered sailors, Gauguin leaves from Cherbourg on the *Jérôme-Napoléon*. He travels the seas around Europe, all the way to the polar circle, and serves in the Franco-Prussian war. Finally, he obtains leave and is discharged at Toulon on 23 April 1871. On his return to Paris, he lives with his sister in the Rue La Bruyère, near the Arosas. Thanks to Arosa, he finds a job at Bertin's, a stockbrokers' office, where he meets Schuffenecker. He paints during his spare time. On 22 November 1873 he marries a young Danish girl, Mette Sofie Gad. The couple settles at 28 Place Saint-Georges.

November 1873 – end of 1883

A relatively uneventful decade. The Gauguins' first child, Emile, is born on 31 August 1874. Four others follow in rapid succession: Aline, on 24 December 1877; Clovis, on 19 May 1879; Jean René, on 12 April 1881; and Pola, on 6 December 1883. In January 1875 the family moves to the Rue de Chaillot. In that same year, Paul's sister Marie marries a young Colombian merchant, Juan Urube.

In late 1876 or early 1877 Gauguin quits his job at Bertin's. By this time he is an experienced broker; he takes a less taxing job as clerk for an unofficial broker. It may be that, following the acceptance at the Salon of 1876 of one of his paintings, *Undergrowth at Viroflay*, he then decided to devote more time to painting. In 1877 he and his family move to 74 Rue des Fourneaux, today known as the Rue Falguière. At number 74 of this street begins a cul-de-sac called Frémin, which has since become famous as the Cité Falguière, where, some forty years later, many of the painters and sculptors of the School of Paris, including Modigliani, Brancusi, Kisling and Soutine, lived and worked. Gauguin's circle of friends changes; his neighbour, a sculptor named Bouillot, introduces him to the profession, as well as to another sculptor named Aubé.

In 1879 he works for André Bourdon. In 1880 he takes a job with the Agence Thoméreau, specializing in insurance transactions. He leads an affluent existence, buys paintings and tries to get his stockbroker friends to buy pictures by Pissarro.

Also in 1879 at the invitation of Pissarro and Degas, he participates in the fourth Impressionist Exhibition, lending his own Pissarros for the show. He participates in all the subsequent Impressionist shows: in 1880, 1881, 1882 and 1886.

In 1880 the Gauguins move to the Rue Carcel, next to the Eglise Saint-Lambert de Vaugirard, in a house belonging to the painter Jobbé-Duval who, though of Breton origin, is now a municipal official of the city of Paris. During that summer, Gauguin visits Pissarro at Pontoise; then, in 1883, he again joins Pissarro, this time painting with him at Osny. In August 1883 Gauguin travels to the south of France (Montpellier and Cerbère) to lend assistance to Spanish Republicans.

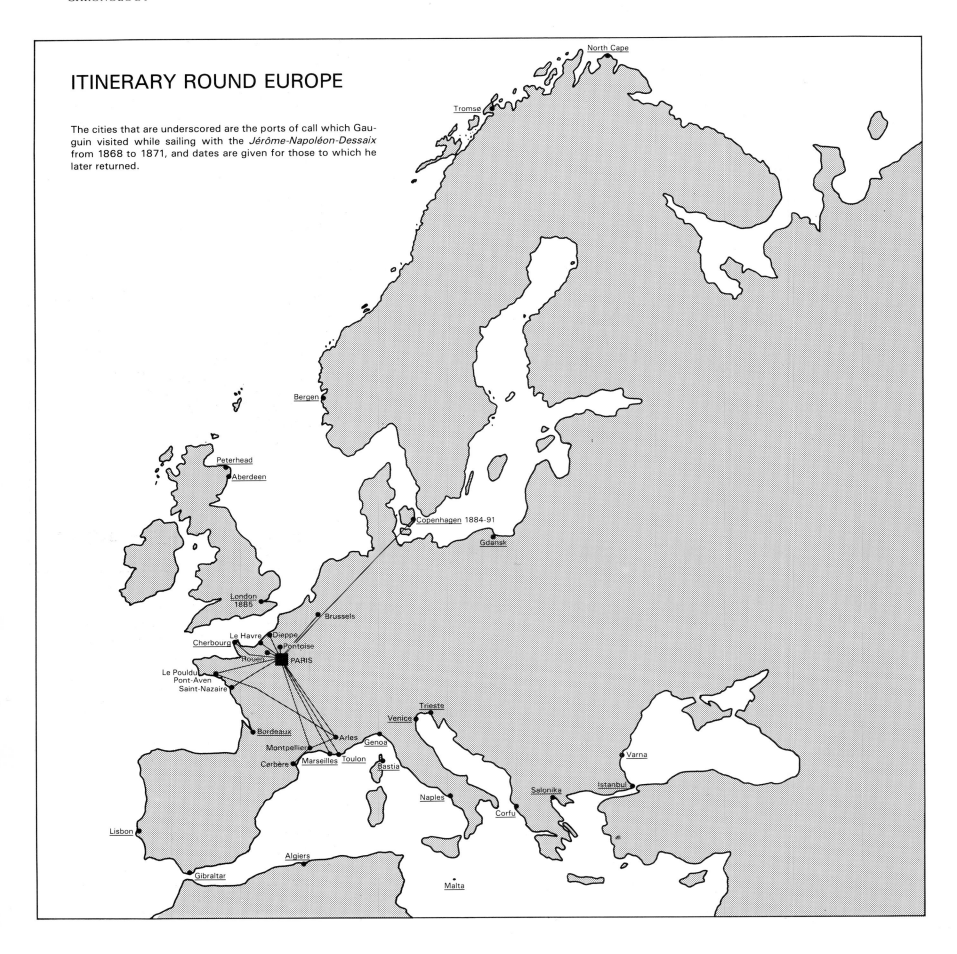

ITINERARY ROUND EUROPE

The cities that are underscored are the ports of call which Gauguin visited while sailing with the *Jérôme-Napoléon-Dessaix* from 1868 to 1871, and dates are given for those to which he later returned.

North Cape

Tromsø

Bergen

Peterhead
Aberdeen

Copenhagen 1884-91
Gdansk

London
1885

Brussels

Le Havre   Dieppe
Cherbourg   Pontoise
Rouen   PARIS
Le Pouldu
Pont-Aven
Saint-Nazaire

Trieste
Venice
Bordeaux   Arles
Montpellier   Genoa
Cerbère   Marseilles Toulon   Varna
Bastia
Istanbul
Salonika
Naples
Corfu
Lisbon

Algiers

Gibraltar   Malta

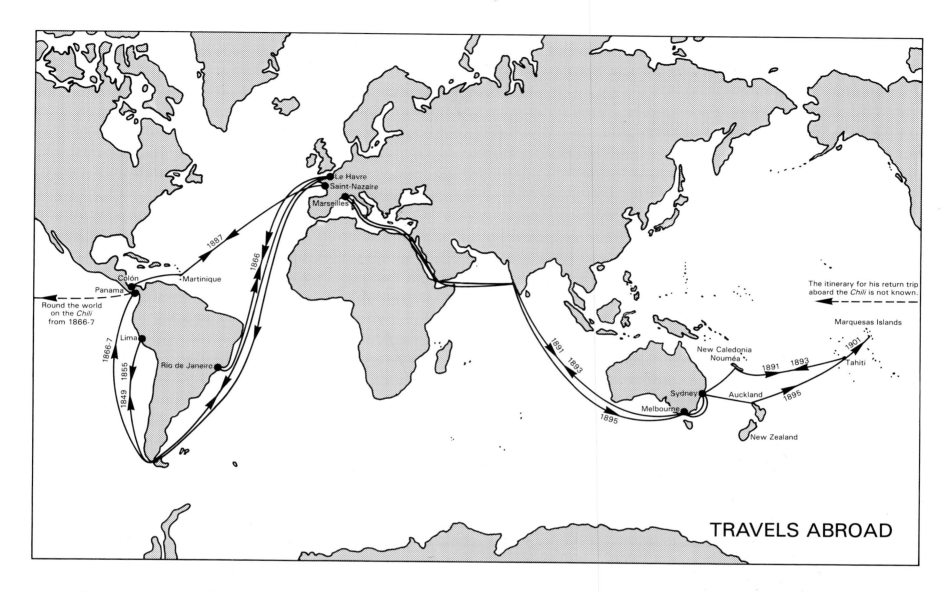

Colón
Martinique
Panama
Round the world
on the Chili
from 1866-7
1887
1866
Le Havre
Saint-Nazaire
Marseilles
Lima
Rio de Janeiro
1866-7
1855
1849
The itinerary for his return trip
aboard the *Chili* is not known.
Marquesas Islands
1891
1893
New Caledonia
Nouméa
1891
1893
Tahiti
1901
Sydney
Auckland
1895
Melbourne
1895
1895
New Zealand

TRAVELS ABROAD

But, since the end of January 1882 the stock market crash has affected the Parisian financial world. In October 1883 Gauguin leaves his job. His efforts to find another are in vain, and he decides to earn his living as a painter.

January 1884 – July 1886

Thus begins the search for short-term measures and dreams of inexpensive living that haunt Gauguin for the rest of his life.

On 4 January 1884 he moves his family to Rouen, where he hopes to find a market for his painting. But his hopes are quickly dashed. In addition, Mette has difficulties adjusting to a life of limited means. Through a friend who works for the Dillies Company, manufacturers of canvas, Gauguin obtains a job in the same line in Denmark. He counts on the Gad family to help him settle there. But the canvas sells poorly, his painting is ill received by Danish collectors and the Gad family have nothing but disdain for a son-in-law incapable of earning a living. In May 1885 a short-lived exhibition of his paintings,

which goes virtually unnoticed in the press, does not help matters.

In June 1885, Gauguin returns to Paris with Clovis, leaving Mette and the other children in Copenhagen. He begins to sell the paintings in his collection. He makes a short trip to Dieppe and, at the end of August, spends three weeks in England.

Winter 1885-6 is very hard. Gauguin does not obtain much-needed work as a practician in Bouillot's sculpture studio. Clovis falls ill, and in order to get by Gauguin is forced to take work as a bill-poster.

Through Bracquemond, he meets the ceramist, Chaplet, who has a small stoneware factory in the Rue Blomet and makes pottery.

July – November 1886

Probably on the advice of Jobbé-Duval, Gauguin leaves for Brittany, where he hopes to live cheaply, He takes a room at the Pension Gloanec, at Pont-Aven. There he finds a group of artists, among them Emile Bernard, who are astonished and fascinated by his painting. On 13 November he returns to Paris, takes lodgings at 257 Rue Lecourbe, and continues to sell paintings from his collection.

1887

Gauguin decides to leave for Taboga, a Pacific island located off the coast of Panama, where his brother-in-law has settled. Mette comes to Paris to fetch Clovis, and takes advantage of the occasion to take back with her to Denmark paintings and objects she finds in Gauguin's studio. On 10 April 1887 Gauguin embarks at Saint-Nazaire with Charles Laval, a young painter he had met in Brittany; on 30 April they arrive in Colon, an Atlantic port. After crossing the isthmus, they arrive in Taboga, which disappoints them; they consider going on to Martinique but, instead, return to Colon, where Gauguin takes work (probably as a temporary agent and not a navvy, as he writes to Mette). Towards the end of May Laval contracts yellow fever and Gauguin is laid off, probably due to the construction company's financial and political difficulties. In June the two move on to Saint-Pierre, in Martinique. Gauguin begins painting but falls ill. He writes to Schuffenecker for money, and returns to France on a sailing ship, probably as a passenger—passage on sailing vessels was less expensive than on steam ships—and not as a sailor, as has been suggested.

Before leaving for Taboga, Gauguin had met Vincent and Theo Van Gogh. Theo, who now works for the art dealers Boussod and Valadon, visits Gauguin in his studio in late 1887 and takes some paintings and pottery on consignment.

1888

Gauguin returns to Brittany, where, at the end of January, he once again takes lodgings at the Pension Gloanec. Emile Bernard joins him there. Gauguin paints *Vision after the Sermon*: he counsels Paul Sérusier, who executes the *Talisman* at his dictation, and takes it to Paris to show to his friends, the future Nabi group, at the Atelier Jullian.

Gauguin begins corresponding with Theo and Vincent Van Gogh. Vincent, who has been living at Arles since February, encourages his brother to help Gauguin financially, while urging Gauguin to join him in creating his much-dreamed-of 'studio of the south'. After much hesitation, Gauguin leaves for Arles on 23 October 1888. Together, he and Van Gogh travel to Montpellier, where they visit the Musée Fabre. But, because of their differences of personality and of artistic conception, their relationship soon becomes stormy. Van Gogh suffers a breakdown, during which he becomes violent, allegedly threatening Gauguin's life, and ends by severing his own ear. Gauguin leaves for Paris on 26 December.

January 1889–March 1891

Gauguin spends January and February of 1889 in Paris, at 25 Avenue Montsouris; he leaves for Pont-Aven in March, only to return to Paris in early May for the opening of the Exposition Universelle; on 10 May the *Groupe impressionniste et synthétiste* opens a parallel exhibition at the Café Volpini, in which Gauguin shows 17 works. Gauguin visits the Exposition Universelle, in which an entire section is devoted to presentations of the French Colonial Empire.

He returns to Brittany in June 1889, but is disappointed to find Pont-Aven so full of artists of all sorts; he seeks quiet in the small port of Le Pouldu, at an inn owned by Marie Henry, and until February 1890 travels regularly between the two villages. He begins to dream of establishing, along with fellow painters and admirers Meyer de Haan, Schuffenecker and Bernard, a Studio of the Tropics.

In February 1890 he returns to Paris; at the end of June he is once again in Le Pouldu.

After initially planning to go to Madagascar, and then on to Tonkin, he finally decides to leave for Tahiti. In November 1890 he stores his canvases at Marie Henry's inn and returns to Paris to prepare his trip. He takes lodgings in the Rue Delambre, and then in the Rue de la Grande Chaumière. In order to gather together enough money for the trip, he decides to hold an auction of his work at the Hôtel Drouot, and asks the young Symbolist poet, Charles Morice, to organize the publicity. The sale takes place on 23 February 1891; 29 paintings out of 30 are sold. *Vision after the Sermon* fetches 900 francs.

On 7 March Gauguin travels to Copenhagen to bid his family farewell. He stays one week, lodging in a hotel. On 15 March he submits a written request for an official mission to the Ministry of Education and Fine Arts; thanks to Morice's contacts with Clemenceau and the Director of Fine Arts, Gustave Larroumet, Gauguin's request is honoured.

On 23 March Gauguin's friends organize a farewell banquet at the Café Voltaire. On 31 March he leaves Paris on his own, his colleagues having abandoned the project as the departure date drew near.

April 1891–June 1893

On April 1 Gauguin embarks at Marseilles on the *Océanien*; after a stopover at Sydney, he boards the *Vire* at Noumea, and sails for Papeete. He arrives on 9 June, and on the 16 of that month attends the funeral of Pomare V, the last king of Tahiti.

At first, Gauguin is received in official colonial circles; however, he soon tires of this atmosphere and begins frequenting popular events, which tarnishes his image in the eyes of the colonial authorities. He decides to leave Papeete in search of less 'civilized' places, but falls ill and is obliged to spend time in hospital. In August 1891 he leaves for a trip around the island, following the southern coast. He stops at Paea, and then stays for a time at Mataiea. His lack of money forces him to return to Papeete periodically.

Gauguin's interest in native customs leads him to seek out historical information. A colonist named Goupil lends him a book by Jacques Antoine Moerenhout, published in 1837, called *Voyage aux îles du grand océan*. The book contains accounts of local legend and Maori mythology, given by the last surviving oral historians of the island. Gauguin copies certain passages into a notebook, which is subsequently used by Charles Morice in his edited version of *Noa Noa*. Much later, in 1951, the text is published separately as *Ancien Culte mahorie*. In addition, in 1892-3, Gauguin writes *Cahier pour Aline*.

In June 1892 Gauguin submits a request to Governor Lacascade for a position as Justice of the Peace in the Marquesas Islands. The request is denied, and Gauguin takes a temporary job. He considers returning to France. On 12 June 1892 he writes to Henry Roujon, Dirctor of Fine Arts, to request repatriation.

A few local sales of his work allow him to leave Papeete again for Mataiea, and then for Taravao and Faaone, where he takes a *vahine* (mistress) called Teha'amana (referred to in *Noa Noa* as Tehura).

In late 1892 he learns that a room has been reserved for his and Vincent Van Gogh's work at an exhibition of modern art to be held in spring 1893 in Copenhagen. Two Danish painters, Theodor Philipsen and Johan Rohde, invite him to participate in the show. Thanks to his friend, Lieutenant Jénot, the paintings leave for Europe in time for the show.

Meanwhile, his request for repatriation, transmitted by the Ministry of Education and Fine Arts to the Ministry of Colonial Affairs, is returned to the governor of the French Settlements of Oceania in Tahiti, and then once again to France; no one wants to pay for his trip. Finally, in May 1893, he receives word of his repatriation at the expense of the Ministry of the Interior.

June 1893 – September 1895

On 14 June Gauguin embarks for Noumea on the *Duchaffault*; then on the *Armand Béhic* for Marseilles, via Sydney. He arrives penniless, and is obliged to call upon Sérusier and Monfreid in order to get to Paris. Bad news awaits him. Joyant and Portier, two dealers on whom he had counted, have given back to Monfreid the canvases in their possession. He contacts Durand-Ruel, who agrees in principle to give him a one-man show.

In early September Gauguin learns of the death of his uncle, Isidore, whose estate is to be divided between himself and his sister Marie, who is living in Central America. He begins preparing his exhibition and calls upon Charles Morice, despite the fact that Morice revealed himself to be something of an unscrupulous collaborator during Gauguin's sojourn in Tahiti, to help him publicize the event in the local papers. The opening takes place on 9 November 1893.

Gauguin sets about writing his memoirs, which he plans to submit to Morice, a writer by profession, so that Morice can include some of his own poems. Gauguin is now living with Annah, an Asian girl, at 6 Rue Vercingétorix. He entertains friends every Thursday.

In February 1894 Gauguin receives his inheritance. In the company of Julien Leclercq, co-founder of the review *Mercure de France*, he travels to Belgium, where the group La Libre Esthétique exhibits five of his works. In early May he returns to Brittany (Pont-Aven and Le Pouldu) where he stays with the Polish painter, Slewinski. On 25 May, while visiting Concarneau, he is injured in a brawl with some sailors who are excited by Annah's provocative behaviour. He takes his attacker to court, but obtains only limited damages. In addition, he loses another law suit against Marie Henry, regarding paintings he had left in storage since 1890 at her inn in Le Pouldu. Annah leaves him and, returning to Paris, pillages his studio.

Gauguin decides to return to Tahiti. He organizes another sale of his work at the Hôtel Drouot, once again asking Morice to organize the publicity. Whether because the scenario too closely resembles that of his previous departure, or because of the partial failure of the 1893 show, the sale, which takes place on 18 February 1895, is a commercial failure: of 47 paintings, only 9 are sold, including 2 to Degas.

Morice, who has rewritten the text of *Noa Noa*, has still not completed his own poems for the publication. Gauguin copies the incomplete manuscript. Detained in France for a time because of poor health, he finally sails, on 2 July 1895, on the *Australien*. He travels via Sydney and Auckland, where he visits collections of Maori art at the Museum of Ethnography. On 9 September he arrives in Tahiti on board the *Richmond*.

September 1895 – 8 May 1903

Gauguin's second stay in Tahiti begins well. The new governor, Papinaud, invites him to take part in a trip to the Iles sous le Vent or Leeward Islands. In November 1895 he rents a piece of land at Punaania, 12 kilometres south of Papeete, where he has a house built and takes up residence with a new *vahine*, Pau'ura a Tai (Pahura).

However, despite his entreaties, money is not forthcoming from Paris. In July 1896 his health failing, he spends two weeks in hospital. The death of his landlord obliges him to move. With a cheque from Chaudet, one of his dealers, he buys a piece of land in Punaania and has a house built with a loan from a French bank.

In April 1897 a letter from his wife brings news of the death of his favourite daughter, Aline. He and Mette break off relations. He writes *L'Eglise Catholique et les Temps Modernes*.

In December 1897 the monthly boat delivers the October issue of *La Revue Blanche*, which contains a first instalment of excerpts from *Noa Noa*. Morice has sent no money. Gauguin suffers from eczema, which has plagued him since the unfortunate incident at Concarneau. He paints *Where Do We Come From? What Are We? Where Are We Going?*. Around Christmas 1897 he attempts suicide.

In early 1898 Gauguin, whose financial situation becomes ever more precarious, is forced to accept a low-paying job as draughtsman for the Department of Public Works. He takes lodgings in the western quarter of Papeete, called Paofai, and lives a cramped existence for a year.

In January 1899 Gauguin receives a thousand francs from Monfreid which enables him to quit his job and return to Punaania. Pau'ura has a baby boy, whom they name Emile.

The irregularity and slowness of the Tahitian judicial system make a polemicist of Gauguin. From August 1899 to April 1900 he publishes a monthly journal called *Le Sourire*. In addition, on 15 February 1900, Cardella, the Mayor of Papeete and co-owner of another journal, *Les Guêpes*, offers him a position as editor-in-chief. Until August 1901, Gauguin uses these journals as forums for defending the colonists against the authorities; but shortly thereafter, following the replacement of governor Gallet, the principal target of *Les Guêpes*, that journal folds. Gauguin decides to leave for the Marquesas Islands.

Starting in January 1900, Gauguin enters into a contractual agreement with the Parisian dealer, Ambroise Vollard, which, despite the somewhat aggravating and complicated obstacles of distance and slowness of mail deliveries, promises him the possibility of working in peace. Moreover, several new collectors have shown interest in his work, including Emmanuel Bibesco, a Romanian prince and friend of Marcel Proust, and Gustave Fayet, a wealthy landowner from Béziers. From now on, Gauguin's financial well-being is ensured. He sells his land and house, repays his loan and, on 10 September 1901, sails for Atuona, a small port on the island of Hiva-Oa.

He buys a piece of land from the Catholic mission, has a house built on it (his 'Maison du Jouir') and takes up residence with his new *vahine*, Marie Rose Vaeoho.

But this calm is precarious and Gauguin soon comes into conflict with the head of the Catholic mission, His Grace Martin. He begins to write counter-propaganda against the Catholic school, and writes a petition for the island's local population, who resent the heavy taxes they are forced to pay into the pockets of Tahitian authorities. Gauguin's health declines, and he considers returning to France, but Monfreid discourages him on the pretext that the timing is wrong.

Gauguin writes a new version of his 1897 text on the Catholic Church; it takes the form of two treatises, *L'Esprit Moderne et le Catholicisme*, and *Racontars de Rapin* (1902). He submits the latter text to the critic André Fontainas for publication in *Mercure de France*, but it is refused. In January 1903 a cyclone hits the Marquesas but Gauguin's house is spared. He finishes a final notebook, which he entitles *Avant et après*.

The 'Maison du Jouir' becomes the meeting place for malcontents, and Gauguin is in continual conflict with the local judge and a policeman called Claverie. Reports denouncing his behaviour reach Tahiti, and then France. Wrongfully accused of slandering a police officer, he is condemned to three months in prison and a fine of 500 francs. He attempts to defend himself, but is exhausted, and dies on 8 May 1903.

Notes

Preface

1   Meyer Schapiro, *Style, artiste et société*, Paris (1982), p. 79.

Chapter I

1   Henri Perruchot, *La Vie de Gauguin*, Paris (1961), p. 29.
2   John Rewald, *Paul Gauguin*, Paris (1948), p. 8.
3   Joris-Karl Huysmans, *L'Art moderne*, Paris (1883), pp. 237-42.
4   *Ibid.*

Chapter II

1   Exhibition catalogue, *Gustave Moreau*, Paris, Musée du Louvre (1961), p. 11.
2   In fact, Proust may well have borrowed a name for one of his characters from a repentant Symbolist named Adolphe Retté. Rette, who published some chronicles in *La Plume* under the pseudonym of Harold Swann, served a prison term for 'anarchist activities' and then went into retreat for several months at the Château de Guermantes near Paris.
3   Quoted by Paul Leprohon in *Paul Gauguin*, Paris (1975), p. 177.
4   Gauguin, *Racontars de Rapin*, Paris (1951), p. 68.
5   J.Y. Tadié, *Le Roman d'aventure*, Paris (1982), p. 147.
6   André Fontainas, *Mes Souvenirs du symbolisme*, Paris (1928), p. 17.
7   Quoted by Charles Chassé, *Gauguin et son temps*, Paris (1955), p. 11.
8   Paul Claudel, *Mémoires improvisées*, Paris (1954), p. 73.
9   Michel Decaudin, *La crise des valeurs symbolistes*, Paris (1981), p. 502.
10   Quoted by Denise Delouche, *Peintres de la Bretagne*, Paris (1977), p. 26.
11   *Ibid.*
12   Pierre-Jean David d'Angers, *Carnet*, Paris (1951), vol. 2, notebook 41, p. 171.

Chapter III

1   According to Ralph Shikes and Paul Harper in *Pissarro*, Paris (1981), p. 180, this took place in 1874; however, the authors are uncertain of the date of the first purchase of a painting of Pissarro's by the Arosa brothers.
2   John Rewald, *Gauguin*, Paris (1949), p. 264.
3   Quoted by Shikes and Harper, *op. cit.*, p. 182.
4   Medical term referring to the junction between the nose and the forehead.
5   *La Revue indépendante*, (1888).
6   Jean d'Albis, *Ernest Chaplet, un céramiste art nouveau*, Paris (1976), p. 53.

Chapter IV

1   Quoted by Marc Logé in the preface of *Esquisses martiniquaises*, Paris (1924).
2   Quoted by Marc Logé, *op. cit.*, pp. 5 and 29.
3   'The beautiful girls you will have seen in Nîmes will not, I think, have delighted your mind less than the beautiful columns of the Maison Carrée, in so far as the columns are little more than old copies of the girls' (Nicolas Poussin).
4   Jean de Rotonchamp, *Paul Gauguin*, Weimar (1906) and Paris (1925), pp. 48-9.
5   *The Complete Letters of Vincent van Gogh*, London and New York (1958 ed.), vol. III, p. 440.
6   Eugène Delacroix, extract, n.d., from his *Journal*, Paris (1980), p. 881.
7   *Mercure de France* (1891), vol. 2, p. 165.

Chapter V

1   Charles Chassé, *Gauguin et son temps*, Paris (1955), p. 59.
2   On the importance of these grids, which were numerous in Manet's work, see Michel Hoog, *La Thématique de Manet*, Paris (1982), pp. 22-3.

3 J.P. Bouillon, *Journal de l'Art Nouveau*, Geneva (1985), p. 35.
4 Wayne Anderson, *Gauguin's Paradise Lost*, New York (1974), p. 118 and Edward B. Henning, 'Bulletin of the Museum of Cleveland', November 1984.
5 Emile Bernard, *Souvenirs inédits sur P. Gauguin et ses compagnons*, Lorient (1941), p. 11.
6 *The Complete Letters of Vincent van Gogh*, London and New York (1958 ed.), vol. III, p. 228.
7 *Vincent Van Gogh*, op. cit., p. 43.
8 John Rewald, *Post-Impressionism*, third edition, New York (1978), p. 446.
9 Emile Bernard, *Le Symbolisme pictural*, Brussels (n.d.), p. 57.

Chapter VI

1 John Rewald, *Studies in Post-Impressionism*, London and New York (1986).
2 *The Complete Letters of Vincent van Gogh*, London and New York (1958 ed.), vol. II. p. 589.
3 Bernard Zurcher, *Vincent Van Gogh: Art, Life, and Letters*, New York (1985), pp. 183-5.
4 *Vincent van Gogh*, op. cit., vol. II, p. 581.
5 *Vincent van Gogh*, op. cit., vol. III, pp. 43-4.
6 *Vincent van Gogh*, op. cit., vol. III, p. 66.
7 John Rewald, op. cit., p. 144.
8 Gauguin, *Avant et après*, p. 11.
9 Bernard Zurcher, op. cit., p. 193.
10 *Vincent van Gogh*, op. cit., vol. III, p. 444.
11 *Vincent van Gogh*, op. cit., vol. III, p. 31.
12 *Vincent van Gogh*, op. cit., vol. III, p. 444.
13 *Vincent van Gogh*, op. cit., vol. III, p. 103.
14 *Vincent van Gogh*, op. cit., vol. III, p. 522.
15 Robert Goldwater, *Gauguin*, New York (1957), unpaginated.
16 However, in a letter dated 1889, which was published in the exhibition catalogue of the Museum of Saint-Germain-en-Laye (1985), Gauguin wrote: 'I was meant to stay in the Midi a year to work with a painter friend; unfortunately he went stark raving mad and for one month I lived in fear of a mortal and tragic incident.'

Chapter VII

1 Théodore Duret, *Les Peintres impressionnistes*, Paris (1906), p. 147.
2 See the various autobiographical works of Georges Daniel's son, the great navigator Henri de Monfreid, especially *Le Feu de Saint-Elme* (1973).
3 Félix Fénéon, *La Cravache* (6 July 1889).
4 *Ibid*.
5 John Rewald, *Post-Impressionism*, p. 171.
6 Albert Aurier, *Œuvres Posthumes*, Paris (1893).
7 *Ibid*.
8 Exhibition catalogue, *Vincent Van Gogh*, Tokyo, National Museum of Western Art (1985), pp. 169-77.
9 The same fan often appears in other paintings of the period, notably *Madame Monet* by Renoir (1872, Sterling and Francine Clark Art Institute, Williamstown, Massachusetts), *Nina de Callias* by Manet (1878, Musée d'Orsay, Paris) and *La Japonaise—Camille Monet in Japanese Costume* by Monet (1876, Museum of Fine Arts, Boston).
10 Maurice Denis, *Théories*, p. 246.

Chapter VIII

1 Paul Deschanel, *La Politique française en Océanie à propos du canal de Panama*, Paris (1884), p. 34.
2 M. Tournefond, *Les Missions Catholiques en Océanie*, Paris, n.d. (c. 1880).
3 *The Complete Letters of Vincent van Gogh*, London and New York (1958 ed.), vol. III, p. 430.
4 Pierre Loti, *Correspondance inédite publiée par sa nièce*, Paris (1929), p. 36.
5 Loti, op. cit., p. 66.
6 Loti, op. cit., p. 82.
7 Loti, op. cit., p. 90.
8 Loti, op. cit., p. 133 (19 May 1872).
9 André Antoine, *Mémoires*, p. 261.
10 Philippe Peltier, 'Arts d'Océanie, arrivée et dispersion des objets', unpublished manuscript, courtesy of the author.
11 *Ibid*.
12 *Six jours à l'exposition*, practical guide to the Exposition Universelle of 1889, Paris (1889), p. 61.
13 Pierre Brunel, *L'Echange de Paul Claudel*, Paris (1974).
14 Exhibition catalogue, *Paul Claudel*, Paris, Bibliothèque Nationale (1968), p. 39.
15 Willibrord Verkade O.S.B., *Le Tourment de Dieu*, Paris (1926), p. 69.
16 Thérèse Denimal was born in Brussels in 1837, to a modest family of French extraction. She became the mistress of a certain David Cohen, a businessman from Marseilles, originally from Belgium; on 8 April 1885 they were married. Cohen claimed to be legal guardian to a child born in Brussels to unidentified parents. The boy entered the Military Academy at Saint-Cyr in 1885 under the name of Maxime de Nimal. He later became the celebrated French General Weygand. The identity of the General's parents has always remained shrouded in mystery; his father was probably Leopold II, king of Belgium, and it has been suggested that his mother was the pseudo-Countess of Nimal. We also know that the Cohen-de Nimal had close ties with Maurice Rouvier, deputy of Marseilles and several times a minister. On the Countess of Nimal, see Charles Fouvez, *Le mystère Weygand*, Paris (1967).
17 Exhibition catalogue, *Gauguin*, Paris (1949), pp. 95-6.

Chapter IX

1 *Le Figaro* (18 February 1891).
2 Gauguin, *Lettres à O. Redon*, p. 193.
3 This pose can be seen in a Breton painting of 1886, *The Shepherdess*, in the Laing Art Gallery, Newcastle-upon-Tyne.

Chapter X

1 J.P. Bouillon, *Journal du symbolisme* (1985), p. 41.
2 Alfred Jarry, in a poem published in *Mercure de France* (1895), no. 1024, p. 599.
3 Sylvie Béguin has discussed the interest aroused by the entry of Solario's painting into the Louvre in *Andrea Solario au Louvre: the records of the Département des Peintures*, Paris (1985); on p. 99, she reproduced a little-known drawing by Redon.
4 Jean Guiart, *Découverte de l'art océanien*, Musée des arts africains et océaniens, Paris (1985), p. 3.
5 The eight works cited were: *Manau Tupapau—The Spirit of the Dead Watching*, Albright-Knox Art Gallery, Buffalo; *Parau Parau—Conversation*, Yale University Art Gallery, New Haven; *I Raro te Oviri—Under the Pandanus*, Museum of Art, Dallas; *Te Faaturuma—The Brooding Woman*, Worcester Art Museum; *Eaha oe feii—What, You Are Jealous?*, Pushkin Museum, Moscow; *Te fare Maori—House and Horse*, Private Collection, Switzerland; *Te Ra'au Rahi—The Big Tree*, Art Institute of Chicago; and *Rarahi te Mare—There Resides the Marae*, Philadelphia Art Museum.
6 Quoted by Merete Bodelsen, exhibition catalogue, *Gauguin et Van Gogh à Copenhague en 1893*, Copenhagen (1985), p. 27.

Chapter XI

1 In the edition of Gauguin's correspondence edited by M. Malingue, Manet is mentioned in place of Monet; however this is certainly a typographical error, as Manet's works sold for much higher prices and would not likely be mentioned in this context. Moreover, Monet had recently had several exhibitions at Durand-Ruel's.
2 The artist Gustave Caillebotte (1848-94) exhibited with the Impressionist group. In possession of a certain fortune, he bought many works of his fellow artists which he bequeathed to the Musée de l'Etat, Luxembourg. However, upon his death endless negotiations, which took a disagreeable turn, led to only a small number of works from this superb collection finally coming to the museum. The dispute became known as the Caillebotte legacy affair.
3 Quoted by Henri Perruchot, *La Vie de Gauguin*, Paris (1961), p. 273.
4 Newspaper clippings which Gauguin pasted into the *Cahier pour Aline*.
5 *Ibid.*
6 *L'Echo de Paris* (14 November 1893).
7 *Les nuits, les ennuis et les âmes de nos plus notoires contemporains*, Paris (1896). This is a collection of pastiches or fictitious conversations with Anatole France, Loti, Bourget, Heredia, Coppée, Huysmans and others. In it, Lajeunesse did not include the text on Gauguin, and Mallarmé's name only appears indirectly. The plastic arts receive little attention, though there is one mention of Cézanne in an interview with Zola. Lajeunesse (1874-1917) became known as a caricaturist, journalist and writer of fiction.
8 Bengt Danielsson, *Gauguin in the South Seas*, p. 159.
9 *L'Echo de Paris* (13 May 1895).
10 Victor Ségalen, 'Hommage à Gauguin', introduction to *Lettres de Paul Gauguin à Georges-Daniel de Monfreid*, Paris (1918), p. 68.
11 *Le Soir* (25 April 1895).
12 B. Danielsson, *op. cit.*, p. 302.
13 A replica was installed in 1973 by the Singer-Polignac Foundation.
14 Charles Morice, *Les Hommes d'aujourd'hui*, no. 440, (1886).
15 Armand Séguin, *L'Occident* (March 1903).
16 Charles Morice, *Le Soir* (23 November 1894).
17 Exhibition catalogue, *August Strindberg–Peintures*, Paris, Musée d'Art moderne (1962), unpaginated.

Chapter XII

1 Gauguin pasted a photograph of *The Arrival of the Holy Women in Marseille* (Basilica of St Francis, Assisi) in the manuscript of *Noa Noa*.
2 Henri Focillon, introduction to the exhibition catalogue, *Chefs-d'œuvre de l'art français*, Paris (1937), p. xxi.
3 An X-ray of the painting has revealed considerable changes in the facial appearance.
4 Text published in *Arts*, (8 July 1949), and probably written after 1895.
5 Alphonse Daudet, *Trente Ans de Paris*, Paris (1888), p. 290.
6 Willibrord Verkade O.S.B., *Le Tourment de Dieu*, Paris (1926), p. 94.
7 Jules Christophe, 'Seurat', *Les Hommes d'aujourd'hui*, Paris, (1890), vol. 8, no. 368. There is another, slightly different version of this text in a letter from Seurat to Maurice Beaubourg.

Chapter XIII

1 Ambroise Vollard, *Degas*, Paris (1924), p. 45.
2 Ambroise Vollard, *Souvenirs d'un marchand de tableaux*, Paris (1937).
3 John Rewald, *Studies in Post-Impressionism*, London and New York (1986), pp. 189-92. In a letter to Vollard, which Mr Rewald has translated here, the artist sets out his conditions for supplying this Parisian art dealer with a steady flow of paintings in return for a steady income. This lengthy letter gives insight into Gauguin's personal reflections on the quality of his work in relation to his output. Subject-matter and technical specifications are discussed in terms of artistic imagination; and here Gauguin asserts that constraints in these areas based on market value cannot be imposed on an artist who, like himself, experiments, for if he is inhibited in such a manner, 'the spirit goes out of the work'. Although these lines are full of insight regarding Gauguin's estimation of his artistic activity, the tone of the letter, nevertheless, accentuates his financial woes and how much these concerns plague him. On the one hand he needs to assure his survival as an artist faced with a dealer who claims no one is interested in his work; and on the other he has to plead for means both to paint and to live.
4 Bengt Danielsson and Patrick O'Reilly, *Gauguin journaliste à Tahiti et ses articles des 'Guêpes'*, Paris (1966), p. 19.
5 R.L. Stevenson, *In the South Seas*. Vol. 7 of *The Works of Robert Louis Stevenson*, New York (1906), p. 19.

6 J. Gracq, *Un beau ténébreux*, Paris (1945), p. 36.

7 We have quoted excerpts on several occasions.

8 This phrase is not strictly from Wagner but from Camille Benoît who translated *Richard Wagner—Musiciens, poètes et philosophes*, Paris (1887). This fact about Gauguin's references to the writings of Wagner has come to light in the work of Henri Dorra, 'Le "texte Wagner" de Gauguin', in *Bulletin de la Société de l'histoire de l'art français 1984* (1986), pp. 281-88.

We might add here that Camille Benoît (1851-1923) was himself a music critic with a predilection for Wagner, which was perhaps due to his specialization in the German language and German culture. He was associated with the Musée du Louvre in the department for the conservation of paintings from 1894 until his retirement in 1918. A respected art collector, he willed the Musée du Louvre *The Ship of Fools* by Hieronymus Bosch. It is Camille Benoît who, in fact, figures in a painting by Fantin-Latour, *Round the Piano* (Musée d'Orsay, Paris).

Chapter XIV

1 *Charles Baudelaire, critique d'art*, Brussels (n.d.), p. 52.

2 M. Denis, *L'Occident* (October 1903).

3 'Gauguin was still the master, the uncontested master, whose works we collected, whose contradictions we hawked, and whose talent, volubility, gestures, strength, nastiness, inexhaustible imagination, romantic appearance and resistance to alcohol we admired' (M. Denis, *L'Occident*, October 1903).

4 The call of the sea was a leitmotif of the contemporary sensibility; an example of such adolescent dreams is provided by a poet and painter close to the Nabis. Francis Jammes tells in his *Mémoires* (Paris, 1971, p. 123) how, in 1885, he became friends with Charles Lacoste at the Lycée of Bordeaux: 'After I had told him of my intention to live in an inactive volcano in the middle of the Pacific Ocean, he brought me, on the very next day, a charming wash drawing in which waves mingled with the azure of the crater ... I do not wish to know, even today, whether my watercolour artist was as determined to realize such whims as I was.' For Gauguin, and for Stevenson, they were more than whims.

5 M. Denis, *L'Occident* (October 1903).

6 *Ibid.*

7 Quoted by R. Delevoy, *Dimensions du XXᵉ siècle 1900-1945*, Geneva (1965), p. 77.

8 M. A. Leblond, *Peintres de races*, Paris (1909). The long text on Gauguin, pp. 207-28, is one of the first efforts to summarize his life and work.

9 Geneviève Aitken, Les Peintres et le théâtre à Paris, autour de 1900. Unpublished thesis for the Ecole du Louvre (1978).

10 The most savoury poem, written with the lilting rhythm of a nursery rhyme, was inspired by *Ia Orana Maria*.

> Et la Vierge bonne
> et Jésus aussi
> d'un œil adouci,
> d'un œil qui pardonne,
> voient se tendre nos mains vers leurs couronnes.
> Et la Vierge bonne
> et Jésus aussi.

('And the good Virgin / and Jesus too/ with a gentle eye/ an eye of forgiveness/ see our hands reaching out to their crowns./ And the good Virgin/ and Jesus too.)

11 Henry Bouillier, *Victor Ségalen*, Paris (1986), p. 116.

12 André Michel, 'A propos des thèses de Paul Gauguin', *Journal des Débats* (21 and 28 September 1919).

Bibliography

In *Post-Impressionism—From Van Gogh to Gauguin* (third edition, New York 1978), which is still the most authoritative work on Gauguin and his circle, John Rewald has provided a highly detailed, annotated bibliography. We have mentioned only the most important works published prior to Mr Rewald's book.

Many books have been, and continue to be, written about Gauguin. Despite this apparent abundance, our knowledge of the artist and his life remains incomplete: we would do well to eliminate definitively the undocumented works; to confirm a complete chronology of works; and to establish a complete repertoire of drawings. Some texts remain unpublished and/or inaccessible. Moreover, the interpretation of Gauguin's work is far from unanimous, a problem the artist himself foresaw. In an unpublished sequel to *Noa Noa*, Gauguin imagined a conversation with a 'critic... who was awaiting posterity's sanction before... shouting', and ends the dialogue, not without a note of bitterness, by affirming: 'my paintings probably speak Hebrew, which you do not understand; [it is] therefore useless to continue this conversation.'

For some time historians and critics have attempted to decipher Gauguin's 'Hebrew'; in recent years several important books and exhibitions have brought us closer to its meaning. The meticulous volume of correspondence edited by Victor Merlhes, as well as the biographical research of Bengt Danielsson and Patrick O'Reilly have clarified many previously vague points, and a new interpretation of Gauguin's Polynesian paintings has been set forth by Jehanne Teilhet-Fisk.

I   Written works by Gauguin

These are difficult to find. The most important have been reproduced in facsimile editions, and the ordinary print runs are generally out of print. The principal works are the following:
Ancien Culte mahorie, facsimile edition with commentary by René Huyghe, Paris (1951).
Cahier pour Aline, facsimile edition presented by Suzanne Damiron, Paris (1963).
Noa Noa Gauguin, Paris (1966), includes the reworked text by Charles Morice (see p. 182). The Louvre manuscript was reproduced in facsimile in Berlin (1926) and Stockholm (1947), and republished in an ordinary edition several times.
Noa Noa—Gauguin's Tahiti, edited by Nicholas Wadley, London (1985).
Racontars de Rapin, Paris (1951).
Avant et après, facsimile edition, Leipzig (1918) and Copenhagen (1951); ordinary edition, Paris (1923).

Gauguin's correspondence is the subject of an extremely detailed publication edited by Victor Merlhes: *Correspondance de Paul Gauguin*, Paris (1984). As of today, only the first volume (in French) has been published. Individual publications include:
Lettres de Gauguin à Daniel de Monfreid, presented by Victor Ségalen, Paris (1919); revised and republished by A. Joly-Ségalen, Paris (1950).
Lettres de Gauguin à André Fontainas, introduction by André Fontainas, Paris (1921).
P. Gauguin: Letters to Ambroise Vollard and André Fontainas, edited by John Rewald, San Francisco (1943), reproduced in *Studies in Post-impressionism* by J. Rewald, London (1986).
Lettres de Gauguin à sa femme et à ses amis, edited by Maurice Malingue, Paris (1946) and Paris (1949). Published in an English edition under the title *Paul Gauguin, Letters to his Wife and Friends*, Cleveland and New York (1949).
Lettres de Paul Gauguin à Emile Bernard, 1888-91, with a text by Emile Bernard, Geneva (1954).
Paul Gauguin's Intimate Journals, translated by Van Wyck Brooks, New York (1936).

Additional, otherwise unpublished letters appeared in:
Madeleine Octave-Maus, *Trente années de luttes pour l'art*, Brussels (1926).
Paul Sérusier, *ABC de la peinture*, Paris (1950).
Lettres de Gauguin, Gide, Huysmans, Jammes, Mallarmé. Verhaeren... à Odilon Redon, presented by Ari Redon, texts and notes by Roseline Bacou, Paris (1960).
Michel Hoog, 'Questions sur Gauguin', exhibition catalogue: *Le Chemin de Gauguin*, Musée départemental de Saint-Germain-en-Laye (1985).

In the body of this book, quoted letters have been given with a reference date, which should enable the reader to locate them in the above-mentioned volumes.

Various excerpts from Gauguin's writtings were also published by Daniel Guérin in *Oviri*, Paris (1974).

II   Catalogues of works

A complete catalogue was undertaken by Georges Wildenstein, entitled *Gauguin*; only one volume was published, in Paris, 1964. A revised edition of the catalogue is being prepared. Numerous rectifications have been proposed by Merete Bodelsen in 'The Wildenstein-Cogniat Gauguin Catalogue', *Burlington Magazine*, January 1966, and by Bengt Danielsson in 'Gauguin's Tahitian Titles', *Burlington Magazine*, April 1967. The Wildenstein catalogue has been published in a smaller edition, including remarks and modifications by M. Bodelsen, under the title *Tout l'Œuvre peint de Gauguin*, Paris (1981), in the 'Classiques de l'Art' collection (published in French, English, German, Spanish and Italian editions).

Marcel Guérin published *L'Œuvre gravé de Gauguin*, Paris (1927), in two volumes. A new catalogue of Gauguin's engravings is being prepared by Eberhart Kornfeld.

Also noteworthy are Christopher Gray's *Sculpture and Ceramics of Paul Gauguin*, Baltimore (1963), and Merete Bodelsen's *Gauguin's Ceramics*, London (1964).

Gauguin's monotypes have been catalogued by Richard S. Field under the title *Paul Gauguin: Monotypes*, exhibition catalogue, Philadelphia (1973).

III Monographs

The most important monographs are mentioned chronologically by year of publication, as follows:

Jean de Rotonchamp (pseudonym of Brouillon), *Paul Gauguin*, Weimar (1906) and Paris (1925).

Charles Morice, *Paul Gauguin*, Paris (1920).

Arsène Alexandre, *Paul Gauguin, sa vie et le sens de son œuvre*, Paris (1920).

John Rewald, *Gauguin*, Paris, London, New York (1938).

Maurice Malingue, *Gauguin*, Paris (1948).

Charles Chassé, *Gauguin et son temps*, Paris (1955).

Robert Goldwater, *Gauguin*, New York (1957).

Gauguin, sa vie, son œuvre, studies and documents published under the direction of Georges Wildenstein, special edition of the *Gazette des Beaux-Arts* (January-April 1958) (articles by L.J. Bouge, Jénot, G. Le Bronnec, J. Loze, U.F. Marks-Vandenbroucke, H. Rostrup, Y. Thirion, G. Wildenstein).

Gauguin, collection 'Génies et Réalités', Paris (1960) (texts by Henri Perruchot, Gaston d'Angélis, Bernard Dorival, François Nourissier, Maurice Malingue, Richard Field, Claude Roger-Marx, Maurice Rheims, René Huyghe). New edition, Paris (1986) (supplementary text by Vivian Forrester and Michel Hoog).

Sylvie Béguin, 'Arearea', *Le Revue du Louvre*, Nº 4-5 (1961).

Henri Perruchot, *La Vie de Gauguin*, Paris (1961).

Bengt Danielsson, *Gauguin in the South Seas*, London (1965), New York (1966).

Françoise Cachin, *Gauguin*, Paris (1968).

Pierre Leprohon, *Paul Gauguin*, Paris (1975).

Wojtech Jirat-Wasiutynski, *Paul Gauguin in the Context of Symbolism*, New York and London (1978).

Yann le Pichon, *Sur les traces de Gauguin*, Paris (1986).

IV Works on particular aspects of Gauguin's œuvre

Charles Morice, 'Quelques opinions sur Paul Gauguin', *Mercure de France* (November 1903).

Maurice Denis, 'L'influence de Paul Gauguin', *L'Occident*, October 1903, republished in *Théories 1890-1910*, Paris (1912).

Marius Ary Leblond, *Peintres de race*, Paris (1912).

Robert Rey, *La Renaissance du sentiment classique*, Paris (1931).

Bernard Dorival, 'Sources of the Art of Gauguin from Java, Egypt and Ancient Greece', *Burlington Magazine* (April 1951).

René Huyghe, *Le Carnet de Paul Gauguin*, Paris (1952).

Henri Dorra, 'The First Eves in Gauguin's Eden', *Gazette des Beaux-Arts* (March 1953).

Bernard Dorival, *P. Gauguin—Carnet de Tahiti*, Paris (1954).

René Puig, *Paul Gauguin, G.-D. de Monfreid et leurs amis*, Perpignan (1958).

Charles Chassé, 'Le Sort de Gauguin est lié au krach de 1882', *Connaissance des Arts* (February 1959).

André Chastel, 'Seurat et Gauguin', *Art de France*, Nº 2 (1962).

Merete Bodelsen, 'Gauguin's Cézannes', *Burlington Magazine* (May 1967).

Henri Dorra, 'More on Gauguin's Eves', *Gazette des Beaux-Arts* (February 1967).

Merete Bodelsen, 'Gauguin the Collector', *The Burlington Magazine* (September 1970).

Wladyslawa Jaworska, *Gauguin and the Pont-Aven School*, London (1972), originally published as *Gauguin et l'Ecole de Pont-Aven*, Neuchâtel (1971).

Jean-Pierre Reverseau, 'Pour une étude du thème de la tête coupée', *Gazette des Beaux-Arts* (September 1972).

R.D.J. Collins, 'Paul Gauguin en Nouvelle-Zélande', *Gazette des Beaux-Arts* (November 1977).

Roger Gucchi, *Gauguin à la Martinique*, Vaduz (1979).

D.L. Paul, 'Willumsen and Gauguin in the 1890s', *Apollo*, Nº 215 (1980).

Ralph Shikes and Paula Harper, *Pissarro*, Paris (1981).

Jos Pennec and Sylvain-Christian David, 'Jarry et Gauguin', *L'Etoile-Absinthe* (1982).

Jehanne Teilhet-Fisk, *Paradise Reviewed, an Interpretation of Gauguin's Polynesian Symbolism*, Ann Arbor (1983).

Philippe Peltier, 'From Oceania', and Kirk Varnedoe, 'Gauguin', in *Primitivism in 20th Century Art*, edited by William Rubin, New York (1984).

John Rewald, *Studies in Post-Impressionism*, London and New York (1986).

V Exhibition catalogues

We have already mentioned the exhibitions before 1914 in which works by Gauguin appeared. After that date, individual and collective exhibitions containing Gauguin's works became increasingly numerous, and consequently more widely known to the general public. At the monumental exhibition 'Chefs-d'œuvre de l'art français' (Paris, 1937), Gauguin, along with Cézanne, represented the most contemporary art, presented alongside works dating back to prehistory. From then on, Gauguin was no longer considered a modern painter.

John Rewald (*op. cit.*) gives a list of these exhibitions, some of which were accompanied by important catalogues.

Noteworthy recent catalogues include:

Gauguin og van Gogh i Kobenhavn i 1893, Copenhagen, Ordrupgaard (1984), catalogue: Hanne Finsen, Merete Bodelsen, Kirsten Olesen.

Le Chemin de Gauguin, Saint-Germain-en-Laye, Musée départemental du Prieuré (1985), collective work under the direction of Marie-Amélie Anquetil.

1886-1986 Cent ans—Gauguin à Pont-Aven, Pont-Aven, Musée d'Art (1986).

List of Exhibitions

Individual exhibitions during Gauguin's lifetime

Late 1884	Christiania, Norway, Fine Arts Exhibition. 3 works
1885	Copenhagen, 51 Norregade, private exhibition, closed after five days by order of the Academy.
1888, early November	Paris, Galerie Boussod et Valadon, 19 bd. Montmartre, organized by Theo Van Gogh. Ceramic works and paintings from Brittany and Martinique.
1889, 30 October-11 November	Copenhagen, 'French and Scandinavian Impressionists'.
1891, 23 February	Paris, Hôtel Drouot, exhibition-sale. 30 paintings. Catalogue preface by Octave Mirbeau.
1892, September	Paris, Galerie Goupil. Enters *Vahine No Te Tiare*, one of his first Tahitian works.
1893, 4 November-1 December	Paris, Galerie Durand-Ruel, 'Œuvres récentes de Gauguin'. Catalogue preface by Charles Morice. 49 paintings, 2 sculptures.
1894, December	Paris. Exhibition in Gauguin's studio.
1895, 18 February	Paris, Hôtel Drouot, second sale. Catalogue preceded by a letter from Strindberg, with Gauguin's response. 49 paintings, drawings, prints.

Group exhibitions before 1916 in which Gauguin participated

1876, 1 May	Paris, 'Salon', Palais des Champs Elysées. 1 painting (*Undergrowth at Viroflay [Seine-et-Oise]*)
1879, 10 April-11 May	Paris, 'IVᵉ exposition impressionniste', 28 Avenue de l'Opéra. 1 sculpture.
1880, 1-30 April	Paris, 'Vᵉ exposition impressionniste', 10 Rue des Pyramides. 7 paintings, 1 marble bust.
1881, 2 April-1 May	Paris, 'VIᵉ exposition impressionniste', 35 Bd. des Capucines. 8 paintings, 2 sculptures.
1882, 1 March	Paris, 'VIIᵉ exposition impressionniste', 251 Rue St.-Honoré (Galerie Durand-Ruel). 12 paintings and pastels and 1 bust.
1886, 15 May-15 June	Paris, 'VIIIᵉ exposition impressioniste', 1 Rue Laffitte. 19 paintings.
1886-7, 10 October-15 January	Nantes, 'Exposition des Beaux-Arts', Palais du Cours St-André. 2 works.
1889, March	Brussels, 'Salon des XX'. 12 works, including *Vision after the Sermon*.
1889, June	Paris, Champ de Mars, 'Exposition du groupe impressionniste et synthétiste', Café Volpini. 17 paintings and pastels, and album of lithographs.
1891, February	Brussels, 'Salon des XX'. 2 vases, statuette of enamelled stoneware, several faïences, wood reliefs (including *Be Mysterious*).
1891, 15 May	Paris, 'Société Nationale des Beaux-Arts', Champ-de-Mars. 4 objects.
1892, November	Paris, Galerie Le Barc de Bouteville, group exhibition with 1 work by Gauguin presented without his knowledge.
1893, March-April	Copenhagen, Centre for Free Exhibitions of Modern Art. 50 paintings, sculptures and drawings.
1894	Brussels, 'La libre esthétique'.
1897	Brussels, 'La libre esthétique'. 6 paintings from Tahiti.
1900	Paris, 'Exposition centennale de l'art français de 1800 à 1889', during Exposition Universelle. 1 Breton landscape.
1901	Béziers, Société des Beaux-Arts. Group exhibition organized by Gustave Fayet.
1903, January-February	Vienna, 'Sixteenth Independent Exhibition'. 2 works.
1903, Spring	Berlin, Kantstrasse 12. 'Eighth Independent Exhibition'. 1 work.
1903, 31 October-6 December	Paris, Petit Palais, 'Salon d'Automne', first exhibition. 9 works.
1904, 24 February-29 March	Brussels, 'La libre esthétique', Impressionist painters. 11 works.
1905, November-December	Vienna, 'Twenty-fourth Independent Exhibition'. 1 work.
1906, Spring	Berlin, 'Eleventh Independent Exhibition'. 2 works.
1907, October-November	Prague, Manès Gallery, 'Impressionnistes français'. 3 oil paintings, 3 pastels.
1907, 14-30 November	Paris, Galerie Bernheim-Jeune, 'Fleurs et natures mortes'. 3 works.

1907-8, 16 December-4 January	Paris, Galerie Bernheim-Jeune, 'Portraits d'hommes'. 2 self-portraits.
1908, March-April	Munich, W. Zimmermann Gallery, 'Van Gogh, Gauguin and Others'. 8 works.
1908, 18 April-24 May	Moscow, 'The Golden Fleece'. 3 works.
1908-9, 21 December-16 January	Paris, Galerie Druet, Group exhibition without catalogue.
1909, 11 April-9 May	Bremen, Kunsthalle, 'Exhibition of Paintings, Drawings and Sculptures from Private Collections'. 2 works.
1909, May-October	Vienna, 'Vienna International Exhibition'. 1 work.
1909, 4 August-16 September	Hagen, Museum Volkwang, 'Sonderausstellung'. 9 Breton lithographs, engravings for Germinal, 10 wood engravings, from Pacific period.
1909-10 27 November-9 January	Berlin, Ausstellungshaus, Nineteenth Secession, 'Exhibition of Graphic Arts'. 3 lithographs.
1910, 12 March-17 April	Brussels, 'La libre esthétique—L'évolution du paysage'. 5 works.
1910, 20 April-15 May	Florence, Lyceum Club. 'First Italian Exhibition of Impressionism'. 1 work, 4 photographs from Tahiti.
1910, 17-28 May	Paris, Galerie Bernheim-Jeune, 'Nus'. 2 works.
1910, September	Stockholm, Sveriges Allmänna Konstförening. 'Foreign Modern Graphic Arts', from the Thorsten Laurins collection. 1 self-portrait.
1910, October-November	Leipzig, Kunstverein. 'Exhibition of Eighteenth, Nineteenth and Twentieth-Century French Art'. 1 work.
1910-11, 8 November-15 January	London, Grafton Galleries. 'Manet and the Post-Impressionists'. 46 works, including drawings, pastels and oils.
1910, 19-30 December	Paris, Galerie Bernheim-Jeune. 'La faune'. 4 works.
1911, 26 June-13 July	Paris, Galerie Bernheim-Jeune. 'L'eau'. 3 works.
1911, 20 July-5 August	Paris, Galerie Bernheim-Jeune. 'La montagne'. 1 work.
1911, October	Cologne, Wallraf-Richartz-Museum. 'Contemporary Art in Cologne Private Collection'. 1 work.
1911, November-December	Berlin, 35 Victoriastrasse. 'Twenty-third Secession'. Graphic arts. Suite of 10 lithographs.
1911-	Paris, Galerie E. Blot. Wood sculptures.
early 1912	Saint-Petersburg, French Institute. 'Centenary Exhibition 1812-1912'. 19 paintings, 2 drawings.
1912, 7 April-end of June	Leipzig Verein LIA. 'Annual Leipzig Exhibition'. 2 wood sculptures.
1912, May	Berlin, 'Der Sturm', third exhibition of graphic arts. 4 engravings, 1 drawing.
1912, 25 May-30 September	Cologne, Städtische Ausstellungshalle. 'Sonderbund'. International Exhibition of Art. 25 works, including oils and watercolours.
1912, June-July	Hagen, Museum Volkwang. 'Modern Art: Sculpture, Painting, Engraving'. 7 paintings, 3 engravings.
1912, 18 July-30 September	Frankfurt. Frankfurter Kunstverein. 'Nineteenth-century French Classical Painting'. 6 works.
1912, October	Munich, Hans Goltz Gallery. 'Art Nouveau—first group exhibition'. 8 works.
1912, 1 October-8 November	Paris, Grand Palais. 'Salon d'Automne' (tenth). 3 works.
1912, 6 October-7 November	Amsterdam, Stedelijk Museum. 'Moderne Kunst Kring'. 23 works.
1912, December	Vienna, Arnold Gallery. Exhibition of modern French works. 1 work.
1913	Berlin, Paul Cassirer Gallery, 'Collection Reber' (XV. Jahrgang, III. Ausstellung). 2 works.
1913, January	Budapest. Ernst Muzeum Francia Impresszionistàk. 1 work.
1913-14	Munich, Thannhauser Gallery. 'Hangings'.
1913, February	Vienna, Miethke Gallery. Dr. Oskar Reichel Collection. 1 work.
1913, 27 February-15 March	New York, Armory of the Sixty-ninth Regiment. 'Armory Show'. 13 works.
1913, March-April	Vienna Gallery. 'Collection of Modern French Artists'. 2 works.
1913, 24 March-15 April	Chicago, Art Institute. 'Armory Show'. 14 works, including sculptures, paintings, watercolours, drawings and engravings.
1913, 28 April-18 May	Boston, Copley Hall. Copley Society of Boston. 'Armory Show'. 14 works (same as those shown in Chicago).
1913, May-October	Stuttgart, Königliches Kunstgebäude. 'Grand Exhibition of Art'. 2 works.
1913, August-September	Munich, Hans Goltz Gallery. 'Second General Exhibition'. 1 painting, 1 ceramic work.
1913, Autumn	Budapest. Ernst Museum. 'A XIX Szàdad Nagy Francia Mesterei'. 1 work.
1913-14, 12 October-16 January	London, Dore Galleries. 'Post-Impressionist and Futurist Exhibition'.
1913-14 December-January	Vienna, Miethke Gallery. 'French Masters'. 2 works.
1914, January	Vienna, Arnold Gallery. 'Modern French Masters'. 9 works, including 2 wood sculptures.
1914, 1 February-31 March	Bremen, Kunsthalle. 'International Exhibition'. 2 paintings, 2 watercolours.
1914, 12 April-end September	Berlin, Ausstellunghaus Secession. 'First Independent Exhibition'. 1 work.
1914, Summer	Munich, Neue Kunst, Hans Goltz Gallery. 'Exhibition of Summer, 1914'. 1 ceramic work.
1915, February-June	Rome. 'Third International Independent Exhibition'. 4 works.
1916, July	Berlin. 'Der Sturm', Forty-third Exhibition—Expressionists, Futurists, and Cubists. 1 work. (His work was viewed as a forerunner to these movements.)

Retrospectives, individual exhibitions or exhibitions containing significant numbers of Gauguin's works after his death

1903, 31 October-6 December	Paris, Petit Palais, 'Salon d'Automne' (first) retrospective: 9 works (4 landscapes, 4 studies and a self-portrait belonging to M. Denis).
1903, 4-28 November	Paris, Galerie Vollard, 6, Rue Laffitte, 'Paul Gauguin'. 50 paintings, 27 drawings.
1904	Brussels, 'Les peintres impressionnistes'. 11 paintings.
1906, 6 October-15 November	Paris, Grand Palais, 'Salon d'Automne' (fourth), 'Œuvres de Gauguin' (Retrospective organized by D. de Monfreid). 227 works, catalogue preface by C. Morice.
1907, March-April	Vienna, Miethke Gallery, 'Paul Gauguin and Others'. 6 sculptures, 4 ceramic works, 21 graphic works, 41 paintings.
1907, May	Budapest, Nemzeti Szalon. 'Gauguin, Cézanne and Others'. 65 works, including sculptures, paintings, graphic works.
1909, early May	Paris, Galerie Druet, 20 Rue Royale. 'Tableaux de Paul Gauguin'.
1910	Dresden, Thannhauser Gallery.
1910	Munich, Thannhauser Gallery.
1910	Brussels, 'L'évolution du paysage'.
1911	Paris, Galerie E. Blot. Wood sculptures.
1911, November	London, Stafford Gallery, 'Gauguin and Cézanne'. 14 works.
1912	Cologne, Sonderbund. 25 oils and watercolours.
1917, 7-31 March	Paris, Galeries Nunès et Fiquet, 88-90 Avenue Malakoff, 'Paul Gauguin'. 37 works (paintings, watercolours, drawings, lithographs, wood sculptures, bronze, plaster, ceramics), catalogue preface by Louis Vauxcelles.
1917	Copenhagen.
1919, 10-30 October	Paris, Galerie Barbazanges, 'Paul Gauguin, exposition d'œuvres inconnues'. Catalogue preface by Francis Norgelet.
1923, 16 April-11 May	Paris, Galerie L. Dru, 11 Rue Montaigne, 'Exposition rétrospective de P. Gauguin (1848-1903)'. 68 works (paintings, watercolours, pastels, drawings, engravings, wood sculpture, ceramic works), catalogue preface by D. de Monfreid.
1924	London, Leicester Galleries.
1926	Stockholm, Copenhagen, Oslo, 'Scandinavian Gauguins'.
1926, 17 December	Paris, Association Paris-Amérique Latine, Study by F. Cossio del Pomar. 135 works, catalogue preface by D. de Monfreid.
1926	Moscow, Pushkin Museum, 'Paul Gauguin 1848-1903'.
1927, April-May	Boston, Museum of Fine Arts, exhibition of engravings (Russel Allen and Fuller Collections).
1928, January-February	Paris, Musée du Luxembourg, 'Gauguin sculpteur et graveur'. 107 works. Studies by C. Masson and M. Guérin.
1928, July-August	Basle, Kunsthalle, 'Paul Gauguin 1848-1903'. 254 works. Preface and catalogue by W. Barth.
1928	Venice, Biennial, 'Gauguin Retrospective'. 42 works.
1928, October	Berlin, Thannhauser Gallery. 230 works, preface and catalogue by W. Barth.
1931, 7-28 February	Paris, Galerie Le Portique, 99 bd. Raspail, 'Exposition Gauguin', paintings and sculptures, preface by Robert Rey.
1931, 26 May-14 June	Paris, Galerie de la Pléiade, 'Gauguin, Œuvre gravé'. Introduction and catalogue by Henri Petiet.
1934, February-March	Paris, Galerie des Beaux-Arts, 'Gauguin, ses amis, l'Ecole de Pont-Aven et l'Académie Jullian'. Notice by R. Cogniat, preface by M. Denis.
1936, April	New York, Marie Harriman Gallery, 'Where Do We Come From, What Are We, Where Are We Going?'.
1936, March-April	New York, Wildenstein Gallery.
1936, 1-21 May	Cambridge, Fogg Art Museum.
1936, May-June	Baltimore, Museum of Art. Catalogue preface by Henri Focillon.
1936, 5 September-4 October	San Francisco, Museum of Art, 'Paul Gauguin: Exhibition of Paintings and Prints'. 139 works, preface and catalogue by G.L. McCann Morley.
1936, November	Paris, Galerie des Beaux-Arts. Preface by Henri Focillon, catalogue by R. Cogniat.
1938, 19-31 October	Paris, Galerie Charpentier, 'Exposition Daniel de Monfreid et son ami Paul Gauguin'. Preface by M. Denis.
1942, 15 May-13 June	Paris, Galerie Marcel Guiot, 'Aquarelles, monotypes, dessins', foreword by M. Guiot, catalogue by M. Guérin.
1946, 3 April-4 May	New York, Wildenstein Gallery. 91 works, foreword by G. Wildenstein, preface by S. Maugham.
1947	Washington D.C., National Gallery of Art, 'Gauguin and Edvard Munch'.
1948, May-June	Copenhagen, Ny Carlsberg Glyptotek, 'Retrospective on the Occasion of the Centenary of P. Gauguin's Birth'. 129 works, preface and catalogue by Haavard Rostrup.
1949, February	Paris, Galerie Kléber, 'Gauguin et ses amis'. Preface and catalogue by M. Malingue.
1949, July	Paris, Orangerie des Tuileries, 'Gauguin, exposition du centenaire'. 101 works and 15 documents. Catalogue by J. Leymarie, preface by R. Huyghe.

1949-50, 26 November- 29 January	Basle, Kunstmuseum, 'Paul Gauguin zum 100. Geburtsjahr', catalogue by G. Schmidt.
1950, July-September	Quimper, Musée des Beaux-Arts, 'Gauguin et le groupe de Pont-Aven'. 29 works and documents.
1955, 30 September- 26 October	London, Tate Gallery, 'Gauguin, an Exhibition of Paintings, Engravings and Sculptures'. Texts by Philip James and Douglas Cooper.
1955, 11 November- 1 December	Oslo, Kunstnerforbundet, 'Paul Gauguin'.
1956, April-May	New York, Wildenstein Gallery, 'Gauguin'. Forewords by R. Goldwater and C.O. Schniewind.
1959	Chicago, Art Institute and New York, Metropolitan Museum, 'Gauguin: Paintings, Drawings, Prints, Sculpture'. Preface by T. Rousseau.
1960	Paris, Galerie Charpentier, 'Cent œuvres de Gauguin'. Preface by J. Leymarie.
1961, 1 July- 15 September	Vannes, Musée de Limur, 'Hommage à Gauguin, vision d'outre-mer'.
1963	Prague, Narodni Gallery, 'Paul Gauguin'.
1963, 19 May	Williamstown, Sterling and Francine Clark Art Institute.
1969	Japan, travelling exhibition: 23 Aug.-30 Sept.—Tokyo; 5 Oct.-7 Nov.—Kyoto, Seibu Department Store; 13 Nov.-7 Dec.—Kyoto, Fukuoka Cultural Centre.
1970	Stockholm, Etnografiska Museet, 'Gauguin Sodershavet'.
1973, 23 March- 13 May	Philadelphia, Museum of Art, 'Gauguin—Monotypes'. Catalogue by R. Field. Chicago, Art Institute, 'Paul Gauguin—His Life and Paintings'.
1979-80 17 November- 16 March	London, Royal Academy of the Arts, 'Post-Impressionism'. 14 works.
1981, October- November	Paris, Musée Marmottan, 'Gauguin et les chefs-d'œuvre de l'Ordrupgaard de Copenhague'.
1984-5 12 December- 10 February	Copenhagen, Ordrupgaard, 'Gauguin and van Gogh in Copenhagen in 1893'. 51 works.
1985, 7 October- 31 December	Saint-Germain-en-Laye, Musée du Prieuré, 'Le chemin de Gauguin'.
1986, 28 June- 30 September	Pont-Aven, Musée de Pont-Aven, '1886-1986, cent ans, Gauguin à Pont-Aven'.

List of Gauguin's works

Index

Photo Credits

The publishers wish to thank all the photographers who collaborated on this book, as well as the museums, archives and other institutions which supplied additional photographic material. The numbers refer to the plates.

The photo research for this book was done by Ingrid de Kalbermatten.

Acknowledgments

I should like to thank all those who
have assisted me in my research, in particular:
Roseline Bacou and John Rewald as well as Marie-Amélie Anquetil,
Gilles Artur, Madeleine Bardet, Françoise Cachin,
Isabelle Cahn, Claire Frèches, Colette Giraudon, Konrad Oberhuber,
Patrick O'Reilly, Maxime Préaud, Catherine Puget,
Eleanor Sayre, Charles Stuckey, Arlette Sérullaz and Dominique Tailleur.
Special thanks for their advice and careful reading of the manuscript
are owed to Irene Elbaz, Paule Gillet and,
in particular, Sylvie Maignan.

This book was printed in August 1987.
Setting: TransfoTexte S.A., Lausanne (Switzerland).
Lithography, printing and binding: Dai Nippon Printing Co., Ltd., Tokyo (Japan).
Design and Production: Marcel Berger.

Printed and bound in Japan.